Graphing Calculator Resource Manual

Precalculus: A Graphing Approach

Fourth Edition

Precalculus: Functions and Graphs

Third Edition

D0207020

Graphing Calculator Resource Manual

Precalculus: A Graphing Approach

Fourth Edition

Precalculus: Functions and Graphs

Third Edition

DEMANA   WAITS   CLEMENS   FOLEY

 **ADDISON-WESLEY**

An imprint of Addison Wesley Longman, Inc.

Reading, Massachusetts • Menlo Park, California • New York • Harlow, England
Don Mills, Ontario • Sydney • Mexico City • Madrid • Amsterdam

Reproduced by Addison Wesley Longman from camera-ready copy supplied by the authors.

Copyright © 1997 Addison Wesley Longman.

ISBN   0-201-43200-5

1 2 3 4 5 6 7 8 9 10 CRW 99989796

CONTRIBUTORS

Gregory D. Foley, Editor
Sam Houston State University

Franklin Demana
The Ohio State University

David Lawrence
Southwestern Oklahoma State University

Linda Neal
San Jacinto College–South

Sharon Sledge
San Jacinto College–Central

G. T. Springer
Alamo Heights High School–San Antonio, Texas

Chuck Vonder Embse
Central Michigan University

Bert K. Waits
The Ohio State University

CONTENTS PART I

CONTENTS PART II

Part I

Chapter 1

Getting Started with Graphing Calculators

Welcome to the frontiers of calculator technology! This manual will help you use your graphing calculator to explore mathematical ideas and solve problems. Have your *grapher* (short for *graphing calculator*) out and "on" to work through the examples and activities as you read. Feel free to explore the menus and features of your grapher.

Part 1 of this manual is devoted to newer graphers. Part 2 explores the features of older models. Not all grapher models are included, nor are all features of each grapher covered in this manual. Consult your grapher owner's manual for a more complete description of your specific graphing calculator and its features.

Refer to this manual when you encounter mathematics that requires unfamiliar aspects of the grapher. The power of the grapher will be what you make it. Many students, with play, thought, and practice, have found it incredibly powerful!

1.1 _____ What Is a Graphing Calculator?

Graphing calculators are not just calculators; they are hand-held *computers*. There are several characteristics of these versatile machines that combine to make them genuine computers:

- **Large screen display.** The screen of a grapher is large enough to display both the input (command to be executed) and output (answer or response). If an answer doesn't make sense or if you've made a keying or other sort of error, you can edit and re-execute the command without rekeying the entire command. The screen can display information in tabular form so that a progression of values can be viewed and checked for patterns.

- **Interactive graphics.** You can plot a wide variety of mathematical graphs. You can overlay graphs, change views, and get a coordinate readout of specific points of interest. Graphers have built-in graphing software for statistical plots, parametric equations, polar equations, and sequences.

- **Other powerful software.** Graphers possess software to solve equations, find maximum and minimum values, generate tables, plot data, find regression models, perform statistical calculations, and manipulate matrices.

- **Programming.** The programming languages of graphers are easy to learn. Armed with a few fundamentals you can do a great deal. Programming gives you the flexibility to customize the grapher to your particular needs and interests.

1.2 _____ Why Use a Graphing Calculator?

A graphing calculator makes computation, graphing, and table-building quick and easy. The grapher helps you to visualize and solve problems. Through the speed and power of the grapher you can investigate ideas quickly and make and test conjectures based on graphical and numerical evidence.

Some specific reasons to use a grapher include:

- To study the behavior of functions and relations including conic equations, parametric equations, polar equations, and sequences.
- To accurately approximate the solutions to equations, systems of equations, and inequalities, and the relative maximum and minimum values of functions.
- To investigate and solve "real world" problems that are normally not accessible to precalculus students and build a foundation for the study of calculus, statistics, science, and higher mathematics.
- To perform complicated calculations, generate tables, plot data, find regression models, and manipulate matrices.

1.3 _____ Keys and Keying Sequences

In this manual, grapher keys appear as boxes. So, for example, the addition key is represented by $\boxed{+}$. The first few pages of your grapher owner's manual will give a brief introduction to the keys on your specific grapher. You are urged to read it.

Take a minute to study the keyboard of your grapher. The keys are grouped in "zones" according to their function: scientific calculation, graphing, editing, and various menus. Locate $\boxed{\text{ON}}$. Not only is it used to turn on your grapher, it also acts as an $\boxed{\text{OFF}}$ button as its *second function*, $\boxed{\text{2ND}}\,\boxed{\text{ON}}$.

- Practice turning your grapher on and off.

Next check your grapher owner's manual to see how to adjust the screen contrast, something you may need to do as lighting conditions change or battery power weakens.

- Adjust your screen contrast to make the screen very dark, then very light, and finally to suit your taste.

Most grapher keys have multiple functions. You can access the second function of a key by first pressing the special colored $\boxed{\text{2ND}}$ or $\boxed{\text{SHIFT}}$ and its alphabetic function by pressing $\boxed{\text{ALPHA}}$.

A **keying sequence** is always read, and entered, from left to right. For example, when we write

$$7 \;\boxed{+}\; 4,$$

you should press the three keys in exactly the order written:

$$\boxed{7} \text{ followed by } \boxed{\div} \text{ followed by } \boxed{4}.$$

Notice within keying sequences we often do not bother to use boxes around numbers.

1.4 _____ Using the "Scientific" Functions

Like any scientific calculator, graphers have many useful built-in functions. But the order in which you press the keys on a grapher differs from the order used on most traditional scientific calculators.

Graphers typically use a priority sequence similar to the standard algebraic hierarchy, called an **algebraic operating system (AOS)**, for the order of operations. So, for example, a grapher performs the operations of multiplication and division before those of addition and subtraction. Read your grapher owner's manual for the full details concerning order of operations on your specific grapher. Example 1 includes three basic calculations to get you started.

- Before working through Example 1, clear your grapher's screen. Then refer to Figure 1.1 as you proceed through the example.

EXAMPLE 1   Computing Powers and Roots

1. Compute 6^2 by keying in **6** $\boxed{x^2}$ $\boxed{\text{ENTER}}$ (see Fig. 1.1).

2. Evaluate $(-5)^4$ using $\boxed{(}$ $\boxed{(-)}$ **5** $\boxed{)}$ $\boxed{\wedge}$ **4** $\boxed{\text{ENTER}}$. Be careful not to confuse the additive inverse, or "sign change," key $\boxed{(-)}$ with the subtraction operation key $\boxed{-}$. *Note:* The exponentiation symbol $\boxed{\wedge}$ is $\boxed{x^y}$ on some graphers.

3. To evaluate $\sqrt{81}$, press $\boxed{\sqrt{}}$ **81**, *inserting parentheses as necessary to match Figure 1.1. Then press* $\boxed{\text{ENTER}}$. •

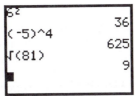

Figure 1.1 Powers and roots on a typical grapher.

Once you gain control of the power and root features, try exploring other keys on your grapher.

1.5 _____ Grapher Terms

The graphs displayed on the screen of a graphing calculator show only a selected portion of the coordinate plane. Learning how to choose and change this portion of the plane is a key grapher skill. The following definitions are given to orient you to the process of selecting and changing grapher views:

- The **viewing window** $\left[X_{\min}, X_{\max}\right]$ by $\left[Y_{\min}, Y_{\max}\right]$ is the rectangular portion of the coordinate plane determined by $X_{\min} \leq x \leq X_{\max}$ and $Y_{\min} \leq y \leq Y_{\max}$. (See Fig. 1.2.)

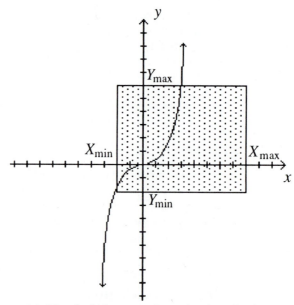

Figure 1.2 The shaded rectangular region is a viewing window.

- **Zoom in** is a process of framing a small rectangular area within a given viewing window, making it the new viewing window, and then quickly replotting the graph in this new window. This feature permits the user to create a sequence of "nested" windows that "squeeze down" on a key point of a graph. Zoom-in is useful for solving equations and inequalities and for determining maximum and minimum values of functions.
- **Zoom out** is a process of increasing the size of the viewing window. It is important to be able to zoom out in *both* the horizontal and vertical directions at the same time, in *only* the horizontal direction, or in *only* the vertical direction. The zoom-out process is useful for examining the limiting or end behavior of functions and other relations.

Chapter 2

Graphing with the HP 48G

This chapter introduces the graphing and solving capabilities of the HP 48G and HP 48GX graphing-symbolic calculators. The two models differ primarily in that the HP 48GX has more random access memory (RAM) (128K RAM vs. 32K RAM for the 48G) and has two expansion ports for additional RAM or read-only memory (ROM). In this chapter, both calculators are referred to as the HP 48G.

Like its predecessors, the HP 48S and HP 48SX, the HP 48G is a sophisticated, general purpose, mathematics calculator. Unlike its predecessors, however, the HP 48G does not require a much larger learning-time investment than other calculators on the market. This is because of its extensive use of pull-down menus and options and on-screen prompts.

Before reading the rest of this chapter, you are encouraged to read Chapters 1-3 in the *HP 48G Series User's Guide* that came with your calculator. These chapters will give you a working knowledge of stack operations and variables. If you are not familiar with reverse polish notation, then you are especially encouraged to refer to Chapter 3 in the User's Manual. The flexibility of the HP 48G and its encyclopedic capabilities make it difficult to give the reader a complete picture of its possible applications.

2.1   HP 48G Fundamentals

2.1.1   Using the Multipurpose ON Key

Press ON to turn on your calculator. This key not only turns the HP 48G on but also acts as a **general purpose interruption key** (note the word CANCEL written below the key). It halts calculator execution and returns to a previous state. For example, when you are entering a number, pressing ON clears the number and returns to the previous stack display.

Any time the calculator is in a state you want to abandon, press $\boxed{\text{ON}}$ one or more times, and it will eventually return to its default state, showing the stack. If the calculator beeps and shows an error message, press $\boxed{\text{ON}}$ to remove the message.

Press $\boxed{\rightarrow}$ $\boxed{\text{OFF}}$ to turn off the calculator. The $\boxed{\text{OFF}}$ key is a **shifted** version of the $\boxed{\text{ON}}$ key (the green $\boxed{\rightarrow}$ key).

2.1.2   Adjusting the Display contrast

With the calculator on, hold down $\boxed{\text{ON}}$ and press $\boxed{+}$ to darken or $\boxed{-}$ to lighten the display.

2.1.3   Exploring the HP 48G Keyboard

Each of the 49 keys on the HP 48G performs more than one function. A key's primary function is printed in white on the key itself. Simply pressing a key activates this function. A key's other functions are printed above the key in green and/or purple. To access these functions, press the purple $\boxed{\leftarrow}$ or the green $\boxed{\rightarrow}$ before pressing the key. For example, press

$$\boxed{\rightarrow}\quad\boxed{\text{PLOT}}$$

to activate the PLOT application. Finally, a key's alphabetic function, if any, is printed in white below and to the right of the key and is accessed using $\boxed{\alpha}$ (Alpha–Shift). For example, to type an uppercase *X* on the screen, press

$$\boxed{\alpha}\ \boxed{1/x}\ .$$

A lowercase letter can be accessed by pressing $\boxed{\alpha}$ $\boxed{\leftarrow}$ before entering the letter.

The exceptions to these rules are the menu keys, which are the blank, white keys in the top row of the keyboard. Although these keys do have fixed alphabetic functions (A–F), their other functions vary from application to application. For example, pressing $\boxed{\text{MTH}}$ displays the first six labels shown in (Fig. 2.1), while the second set of labels is made visible via $\boxed{\text{NXT}}$ (see Fig. 2.2).

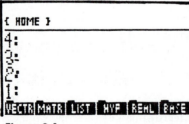

Figure 2.1

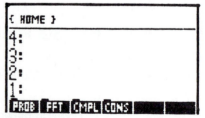

Figure 2.2

Notice that each of these labels has a small tab at the top left corner. This signifies they are file folders that contain other options and/or other file folders. To continue our current example, pressing [B:MATR] activates the MATR folder containing folders and options for matrices, as shown in Fig. 2.3 on page 7.

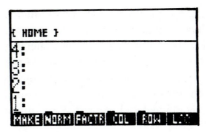

Figure 2.3

These new folders contain options such as the LSQ option as well as other file folders such as the COL folder that contains even more options (→COL, COL→, COL+, etc). Finally, note that on the keyboard the major applications, such as PLOT and SOLVE, are all grouped together and associated with the numerical keys 1–9.

2.2 _____ Learning the Graphing Essentials

The HP 48G makes extensive use of pull-down menus and on-screen prompts; so many of its operational procedures are self-explanatory. Therefore this section is devoted mainly to examples that illustrate the HP 48G's wide range of graphing capabilities.

2.2.1 The Plot Application

To demonstrate this application we will start with a simple example: graphing the function

$$Y = \sin (X).$$

Press

to activate the PLOT menu as shown in Fig. 2.4.

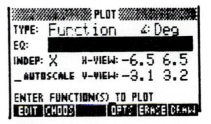

Figure 2.4

Notice the on-screen prompt that reads ′ENTER FUNCTION(S) TO PLOT′ as well as the highlight bar positioned to the right of ′EQ:′. *EQ* is a reserved variable that contains a list of the functions to be plotted. Notice also the option labels at the bottom of the screen. The

Edit option, [A:EDIT] allows you to edit the current (in this case, empty) expression; the Choos option, [B:CHOOS] allows you to choose an expression or list from among those that are currently saved in user memory. In our next example, we demonstrate how to save an expression more permanently in user memory; in this example, we will simply save our expression temporarily in the variable *EQ*. Press [A:EDIT] to place an insert cursor between two tick marks on the screen's command line (see Fig. 2.5). The tick marks, ´ ´, are used to begin and end any algebraic object. To enter our expression, press

(see Fig. 2.6) and then press ENTER . The highlight bar then moves to the next option, the independent variable (INDEP), and the on-screen prompt changes to ´ENTER INDE-PENDENT VAR(iable) NAME´ (see Fig. 2.7).

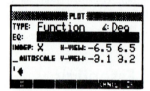

Figure 2.5

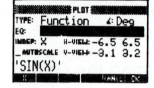

Figure 2.6

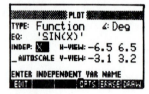

Figure 2.7

The cursor-movement keys move the highlight bar to any option on the PLOT menu. For example, to change the angle units from degrees to radians, press

◀ ◀ [B:CHOOS] ▼ ENTER.

See Figs. 2.8–2.10.

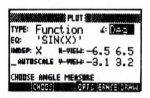

Figure 2.8

Figure 2.9

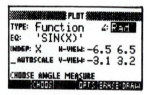

Figure 2.10

Press [E:ERASE] and [F:DRAW] to see the plot (Fig. 2.11).

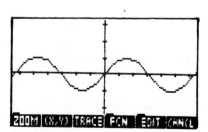

Figure 2.11

2.2.2   The Interactive Plot Mode

Once a graph is plotted, the calculator does not return to the stack; instead it enters what is called the Interactive Plot mode, which allows the user to explore and add graphical elements to the plot. While in this mode, the keyboard is redefined for graphical purposes, as follows:

1. The cursor-movement keys ◀ ▲ ▼ ▶ move the cursor in the indicated direction. Preceding a cursor key with ↦ moves the cursor to the edge of the screen in the indicated direction.

2. − removes the folder/option labels so that all of the Graph screen is visible. This is a toggle key, so pressing it again will retrieve the labels.

3. + displays the cursor coordinates. It also is a toggle key.

4. ↩ CLEAR erases the plotted graph from the screen, it does not, however, erase the cursor, which remains active. To recover the graph, press

    ON [F:DRAW].

5. ENTER places the cursor coordinates on the stack.

2.2.3   Tracing

As you can see from the labels, the HP 48G has a TRACE feature. To activate this feature, press

[C:TRACE].

Notice that a small highlighted square appears on the TRACE folder label (see Fig. 2.12). Press

[B:(X,Y)]

and use ◀ and ▶ to move the cursor along the curve (see Fig. 2.13). To retrieve the labels, press any menu key. To de-activate the TRACE feature, press [C:TRACE] again. Note that the highlighted square disappears as shown in Fig. 2.14.

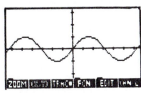

Figure 2.12

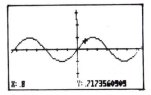

Figure 2.13

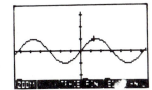

Figure 2.14

2.2.4   Zooming

To continue our example, press

[A:ZOOM]

to access the extensive zoom capabilities of the HP 48G. To change both the horizontal and vertical zoom factors to 5 press

[A:ZFACT] 5 ENTER 5 ENTER [F:OK]

(see Fig. 2.15). Press

[F:OK] [C:ZIN]

to zoom-in by a factor of 5, as shown in Fig. 2.16.

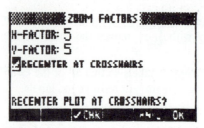

Figure 2.15

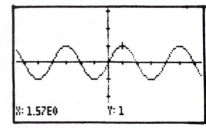

Figure 2.16

Before proceeding, zoom-out again to the default settings by pressing

[A:ZOOM] [D:ZOUT].

One option in the ZOOM folder is the ZTrig option. Press

[A:ZOOM] NXT NXT [C:ZTRIG]

(see Fig. 2.17).
With our original expression and the default plot parameters, the ZTrig option sets the horizontal step to $\pi/20$. Press

[C:TRACE] [B:(X,Y)]

and press ▶ ten times to display the value of SIN(X) when $x = \pi/2$ (see Fig. 2.18).

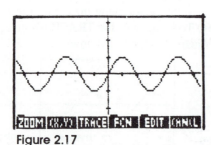

Figure 2.17

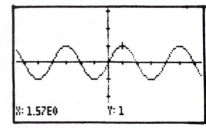

Figure 2.18

You are encouraged to take time to explore all the options in the ZOOM folder. For example, you can zoom-in or out, horizontally and/or vertically to any preset factor. In addition, you can zoom so that the Trace cursor moves through integer abscissas using the ZIntg option or by tenths, using the ZDeci option, effectively creating "friendly windows." And you can always return to the default plotting windows by using the ZDflt option.

Two of the most useful options are the ZSqr option, which changes the range so that the scale on each axis is the same, and the Boxz option, which allows the user to pick a rectangular area that then becomes the viewing window. To return to our example, press any menu key to retrieve the labels, then press

[A:ZOOM] [E:ZSQR]

(see Fig. 2.19). Press

$$[\mathtt{B:(X,Y)]}\ \boxed{\blacktriangleright}$$

to move the cursor along the *x*-axis until you reach $x = \pi/2 \approx 1.57\mathrm{E}0$. Next press $\boxed{\blacktriangle}$ to move the cursor up until it lies directly across from the first tick mark on the *y*-axis. Doing this enables you to see that the cursor, the first tick marks on each axis, and the origin are indeed the vertices of a square (see Fig. 2.20).

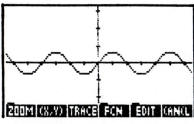

Figure 2.19

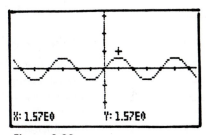

Figure 2.20

To zoom in on this square, press any menu key to retrieve the labels, then press

$$[\mathtt{A:ZOOM}]\ \ [\mathtt{B:BOXZ}]\ .$$

$(\pi/2, \pi/2)$ has already been established as one corner of the viewing window. Move the cursor down to the *x*-axis. Notice that a vertical segment follows the cursor. Next, move the cursor left towards the origin (see Fig. 2.21). Notice the zoom box is beginning to form. Continue moving the cursor until it is positioned at the origin, then press

$$[\mathtt{F:ZOOM}]$$

to obtain the display shown in Fig. 2.22. Notice that the square has been stretched horizontally to fit the rectangular viewing window.

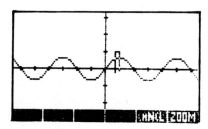

Figure 2.21

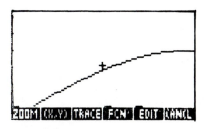

Figure 2.22

2.3 _____ Additional Graphing Capabilities

The following sections, although not an exhaustive accounting of all of the HP 48G's graphing capabilities, will give you a working familiarity with some of the many features. Before continuing, press

$$\boxed{\text{ON}} \quad \boxed{\blacktriangledown} \quad \boxed{\blacktriangledown} \quad \boxed{\blacktriangleright} \quad \boxed{\text{DEL}} \quad \boxed{\blacktriangledown} \quad [\text{F:OK}]$$

to reset the plot window to its default settings.

2.3.1   Using the Catalog

As mentioned before, you can store an expression, equation, or list in the reserved variable *EQ* on a temporary basis only. If the expression in *EQ* is changed, the old expression is overwritten and lost to the user. Often, it is useful to look at the plots of several functions at once or to store one or more functions more permanently. Suppose you want to look at the plots of both $x \cdot \sin(x)$ and $\cos(x)$. Press $\boxed{\text{ON}}$ to exit the Interactive Plot mode and use the cursor-movement keys to move the highlight bar to the current equation (*EQ*). Press

$$[\text{B:CHOOS}]$$

to see a display like that shown in Fig. 2.23. You may have other objects in memory, so your display may not match the one pictured exactly.

Figure 2.23

Press

$$[\text{D:NEW}]$$

(see Fig. 2.24). To enter the first expression 'X∗SIN(X)', press

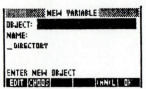

Figure 2.24

and give it the name 'F' by pressing

$$\boxed{\alpha}\quad\boxed{F}\quad\boxed{\text{ENTER}}$$

(see Fig. 2.25). Press [F:OK] to place this new function at the top of the catalog (see Fig. 2.26).

Figure 2.25

Figure 2.26

Follow the same process to place 'COS(X)' in the catalog under the name 'G'. Press

[D:NEW] $\boxed{'}$ $\boxed{\text{COS}}$ $\boxed{\alpha}$ $\boxed{X}$ $\boxed{\text{ENTER}}$ $\boxed{\alpha}$ $\boxed{G}$ $\boxed{\text{ENTER}}$ [F:OK]

(see Fig. 2.27).

Figure 2.27

To plot both of these functions, press

[C:√CHK]

to place a check mark next to the function 'G'; then press

$\boxed{\blacktriangledown}$ [C:√CHK]

to move the highlight bar down 'F' and check it (see Fig. 2.28). Press

[F:OK]

to accept your choices. Note that *EQ* is now a list containing the two functions *F* and *G*. Also, note that our original expression, 'SIN(X)', which had been in *EQ*, has been dropped. It is no longer in memory (see Fig. 2.29). On the other hand, if we were to place another function in *EQ*, *F* and *G* would still be in the catalog list, accessed by the Choose option. Press [E:ERASE] [F:DRAW] to see the plots (see Fig. 2.30).

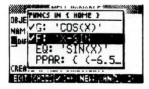

Figure 2.28

Figure 2.29

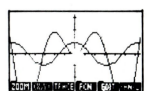

Figure 2.30

In this example, the plots were drawn sequentially. To draw the plots simultaneously, press

$$\boxed{\text{ON}} \quad [\text{D:OPTS}]$$

to reach the PLOT OPTIONS menu. Move the highlight bar to 'SIMULT' and press [C:√CHK] to activate this option (see Fig. 2.31), followed by [F:OK] to return to the main PLOT menu. Then press [E:ERASE][F:DRAW] to redraw the plots simultaneously.

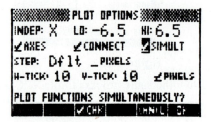

Figure 2.31

2.3.2   The Function Folder

To continue our example, press

$$[\text{D:FCN}]$$

to see the options available in the FCN (functions) folder (see Fig. 2.32). Press $\boxed{\text{NXT}}$ to see the rest of the options (see Fig. 2.33). Most of the options in this folder are concerned with characteristics of the graphs of functions.

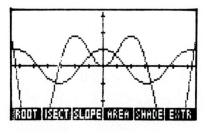

Figure 2.32

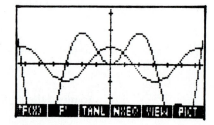

Figure 2.33

Because the first function in the list presently in *EQ* is cos(*x*), pressing

$$\boxed{\text{NXT}} \quad [\text{A:ROOT}]$$

will find a root of y = cos(*x*) that lies nearest to the cursor, which is now at its default location at (0,0). The cursor moves to the root, and the bottom line of the screen flashes the message 'SIGN REVERSAL' to indicate that the solution was estimated within the limits of the machine. The bottom line then displays the root value 1.57079632679, which is approximately equal to $\pi/2$ (see Fig. 2.34). Press any menu key to restore the option labels.

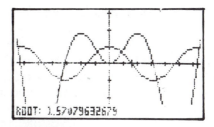

Figure 2.34

You can switch to the other function, 'X∗SIN(X)', by pressing ⌈NXT⌉ to retrieve the rest of the Fcn options as shown in Fig. 2.35, then press

[D:NXEQ].

The bottom line of the screen now displays the expression 'X∗SIN(X)' and the cursor jumps vertically to the plot of the new function (see Fig. 2.36). Press any menu key to restore the labels.

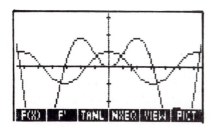

Figure 2.35

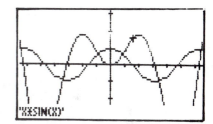

Figure 2.36

To find the root of $x{\cdot}\sin(x)$ near $x = 3$. Press ⌈+⌉ ⌈+⌉ to see the coordinates, then move the cursor near $x = 3$, and press any menu key followed by

⌈NXT⌉ [A:ROOT],

and see 'ROOT:3.14159265359', which is approximately equal to π (see Fig. 2.37).

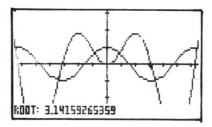

Figure 2.37

Again, press any menu key to restore the labels.

To locate the nearest intersection of the two plots at (3.42561845948, -.9599350991) press

[+]   [B:ISECT]

(see Fig 2.38).

Again, the sign reversal message flashes briefly, announcing that the solution is an approximation. The values of the roots and the intersections of the plots are all placed on the stack automatically. Press [ON] repeatedly until you return to the stack (see Fig. 2.39, your menu label may differ).

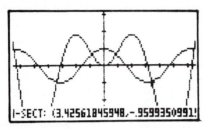

Figure 2.38

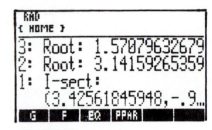

Figure 2.39

Return to the Interactive Plot mode and FCN folder by pressing

[→]   [PLOT]   [F:DRAW] [D:FCN].

Then press

[NXT]   [D:NXEQ]

to return to the cosine function, and then press any menu key to retrieve the menu labels [NXT] [F:EXTR] to find the nearest maximum or minimum of the current function, in our case the maximum of 1 for cos(x) at $x = 0$ (see Fig. 2.40).

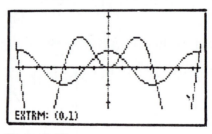

Figure 2.40

2.4 _____ Polar Graphing

Thanks to the pull-down menus, polar graphing on the HP 48G is easier than it was on the HP 48S. Press [ON] to return to the PLOT application, then press [▲] to move the highlight bar to the equation 'TYPE' and press [B:CHOOS] to see the list of options. Use the cursor-movement keys to highlight 'Polar' and press [ENTER].

EXAMPLE 1

Problem Graph the limacon $r = 1.5(1 - 2\cos\theta)$.
Solution Move the highlight bar to the current equation, by pressing [▼]. Press

to obtain 'Y = 1.5*(1–2*COS(X))' as the equation *EQ*. Because the default interval for θ is $[0, 2\pi]$, press

[E:ERASE] [F:DRAW]

to see the plot. Press [–] to remove the labels (see Fig. 2.41).

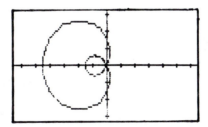

Figure 2.41

2.5 _____ Parametric Graphing

As with polar graphing, pull-down menus have simplified the plotting of parametric graphs.

EXAMPLE 2

Problem Graph the Lissajous figure $x = 3\sin(3t)$, $y = 2\sin(4t)$ for $0 \le t \le 6.5$.
Solution Press [ON] to leave the Interactive Plot mode and return to the PLOT application, then use the cursor-movement keys to move the highlight bar to 'TYPE'. Press

[B:CHOOS],

use the cursor-movement keys to move the highlight bar to 'Parametric' and press ENTER (see Fig. 2.42).

Figure 2.42

The equation must be entered in the form $(x(t), y(t))$. Move the highlight bar to 'EQ' and press

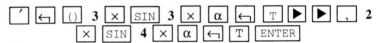

to obtain

'(3*SIN(3*t), 2*SIN(4*t)'.

Your screen will not show the entirety of this object. Change the independent variable to 't' by selecting 'INDEP' and pressing

| α | ⟵ | T | [F:OK].

Press

[E:ERASE]   [F:DRAW]

to see the plot (see Fig. 2.43).

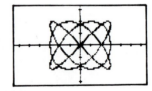

Figure 2.43

2.6 _____ Conclusion

The foregoing sections have described only a fraction of the capabilities of the HP 48G. In addition to the catalog of user-defined functions, there is an Equation Library in ROM that is accessed by pressing → EQ LIB. Equations in this library are grouped by topic name. When it is advantageous, the equations have accompanying diagrams to identify the variables. There also is an extensive UNITS application, where values can be tagged with units. The HP 48G then keeps track of the units and changes them appropriately as calculations are made. An extensive STAT (statistical) application is also available, as well as a SYMBOLIC application, which allows the user to do everything from symbolic differentiation to symbolic manipulation of an algebraic expression. Finally, the HP 48G can print graphs, etc., to a thermal printer via the infrared Input/Output port (like using your TV remote control). The I/O port also can be used to transfer programs and any other information (like matrices) from one HP 48 to another. Cables also are available that will allow you to transfer files to and from either a PC-compatible or a Macintosh computer. The owner's manual contains information on all of these topics.

Chapter 3

Graphing with the Sharp EL-9200C and EL-9300C

The Sharp EL-9200C and EL-9300C calculators are versatile, powerful tools that offer students an extremely wide range of functionality in a user-friendly format. Both utilize almost identical software that includes the following features:

- Rectangular, Polar, and Parametric graphing
- Programming
- Statistical computing
- Statistical graphing
- Matrix operations
- Complex number calculation
- Numerical calculus

Both also include a large, high-contrast screen and a hard case for protection when it's not in use. In addition the EL-9300C offers a powerful Solver mode, 32K of RAM, a communications port, and a back-up battery.

The instructions in this chapter apply to both Sharp calculators, except the discussion of the Solver mode, which applies only to the EL-9300. Section 3.1 discusses the keypad and some of the calculators' major features and functions, while Section 3.2 introduces graphing techniques. Section 3.3 addresses the Solver. There are many additional features beyond those we describe here. The best way to explore the calculator is to look inside the menus to see the available options and experiment with them. You also are urged to use the *Owner's Manual and Solutions Handbook* that came with your calculator for more information on how to use the machine.

Each calculator has a built-in self-demonstration program. To use this program, follow the steps on page 22.

To start the demonstration,

1. when the calculator is turned off, press *and hold* $\boxed{\text{ENTER}}$ and
2. press $\boxed{\text{ON}}$.

> To pause the demonstration, press $\boxed{\text{ENTER}}$.
> To restart the demonstration, press $\boxed{\text{ENTER}}$.
> To exit the demonstration, press $\boxed{\text{ON}}$.

3.1 _____ Getting Started on the EL-9200C and EL-9300C

The front of the calculator can be divided into two sections: the viewing screen in the upper third and the keys in the lower two thirds. Next, we discuss the keypad.

3.1.1 Exploring the Keypad

The major key groups occupy the top six rows. Each key has a primary function whose name or symbol is printed in white on the key. Most keys also have a second function and alphabetic function whose name or symbol is printed above the keys.

You can access the second functions printed in <u>yellow</u> by pressing $\boxed{\text{2ndF}}$ and then the desired key desired. For example, to access $\boxed{\text{sin}^{-1}}$, do the following:

1. Press $\boxed{\text{2ndF}}$.
2. Press $\boxed{\text{sin}^{-1}}$.

> To access the alphabetic functions printed in blue above the keys, do the following:

1. press $\boxed{\text{ALPHA}}$ and
2. press the desired key.

> To lock the calculator into Alpha mode, press $\boxed{\text{2ndF}}$ $\boxed{\text{A-LOCK}}$.
> To clear the Alpha lock, press $\boxed{\text{ALPHA}}$. Indicators at the top of the screen tell whether $\boxed{\text{ALPHA}}$ or $\boxed{\text{2ndF}}$ has been pressed.
> The keypad is divided into parts according to key position, as follows:

- Row 1 - the **Operation mode keys**. Used to choose the mode in which you want to work. From left to right, they are as follows:
  - Calculation mode

  - Graphing mode

  - Programming mode

  - Statistics mode

Two additional modes are available as second functions:

- Solver mode (EL-9300C only)

- Statistical graph mode

To access any mode, press the appropriate mode key or keys.

- Row 2 - the **Graph function keys**. Used to access the various operations in the Graphing mode.
- Row 3 - the **Menu keys**. Used to access menus associated with functions and operations not available directly from the key pad (see Section 3.1.2 for information on how to work with these menus).
- Row 4 - the **Control** and **Editing keys** . Used to control the operation of the calculator ($\boxed{\text{SET UP}}$)and to edit expressions and equations entered in the calculator ($\boxed{\text{DEL}}$, $\boxed{\text{2ndF}}$ $\boxed{\text{INS}}$, $\boxed{\text{BS}}$ (backspace), $\boxed{\text{CL}}$ (clear), and $\boxed{\text{2ndF}}$ $\boxed{\text{CA}}$ (clear all)).
- Rows 5—10–the **Function** and **Arithmetic keys** are similar to those on any scientific or graphing calculator. The popular $\boxed{\text{X/θ/T}}$ is located on the right-hand side, just above the $\boxed{\text{)}}$ When pressed, this key displays an X, $θ$, or T, depending on the graph coordinate system selected in the SET UP menu.

3.1.2   Operating the Menus

Many operations and functions on these calculators are accessed through a two-level menu system. All of the menus work in the same manner. The two used most often are the MATH and MENU menus. Following is a summary of what the various menus do:

- MATH menu
  Offers all the additional functions available for the current mode (see Fig. 3.1). (Functions not available will display a row of dots instead of the function.) For each available function, you can access a submenu of additional operations available for that function in the selected mode.

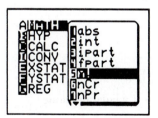

Figure 3.1

- MENU menu
  Contains all of the additional operations and submodes available for the currently selected mode.

- COMMAND menu

  Used only in the Programming mode. It contains all of the programming commands.

- OPTION menu

  Used to adjust the contrast and manage the memory. In addition, for the EL-9300C, you use it to operate the calculator's communication link to a printer, another EL-9300C, an overhead display unit or a cassette player.

  To exit from the currently displayed menu and save your current selections, press

  $\boxed{\text{QUIT}}$.

  There are two ways to make menu selections:

1. Use the cursor-movement keys. As you scroll through the menu, items on the menu are highlighted. When the menu item you want is highlighted, press $\boxed{\blacktriangleright}$ or $\boxed{\text{ENTER}}$ to move the cursor into the submenu (if there is one). Then use $\boxed{\blacktriangle}$ and $\boxed{\blacktriangledown}$ to highlight and $\boxed{\text{ENTER}}$ to select your choice from the submenu.

2. Use the letter and number keys to make quick selections.

   a. To select from the main menu, press the letter corresponding to the menu item you want.

Note: You don't have to press $\boxed{\text{ALPHA}}$ *first in this case.*

   b. To select from the submenu, press the number of your submenu selection.

3.1.3 Using the Equation Editor

The Equation Editor helps make expressions easier to see and understand by enabling you to enter and edit equations and expressions and then view them in the format in which they would appear on paper. It is the default editor on both calculators and is used in the Calculator, Graphing, and Solver modes.

A traditional "one line" editor also is available, which will make the calculator operate similar to Casio and Texas Instruments graphing calculators. To turn on this feature, press

$\boxed{\text{SET UP}}$ [F:EDIT] [2:ONE LINE].

The remainder of these instructions assume the calculator is set to the Equation Editor.

Expressions are entered as they are on any other graphing or programmable calculator, except that the expression appears in two dimensions (up/down and left/right) or (more than one line) or both. The following conventions apply:

- To exit from multi-line functions such as exponents and roots or out of a denominator, press $\boxed{\blacktriangleright}$.

- All cursor-movement keys can be used to move around an expression. However, to return quickly to the beginning or end of an expression, press $\boxed{\text{2ndF}}$ $\boxed{\blacktriangleleft}$ or $\boxed{\text{2ndF}}$ $\boxed{\blacktriangleright}$, respectively.

- To cause the calculator to compute an expression, press $\boxed{\text{ENTER}}$.

Note: It isn't necessary to be at the end of an expression when you press $\boxed{\text{ENTER}}$.

Figure 3.2 shows an example equation as it was entered in the calculator (lines one and two) and as it was edited (line 3).

$$\frac{2^6\left(1-2^6\right)}{6*6!\,\pi^6} =$$
$$-0.000970817$$
$$\frac{2^8\left(1-2^8\right)}{8*8!\,\pi} =$$

Figure 3.2

3.1.4   Entering Data in Fields

In many cases, data must be entered into a field; for example, statistical, matrix, or graph range data. Numbers, variables, and expressions can be entered in any field; however, only the final calculated values are stored. Further, calculations also can be performed on a field.

In an example using the RANGE feature, do the following:

1.   Enter this feature by pressing the Graph key and RANGE .

The x Range screen appears, as shown in Fig. 3.3.

```
X RANGE
Xmin=
      -6.283185307
Xmax=
       6.283185307
Xscl=
       1.570796327
```

Figure 3.3

To change a field value,

1. use the cursor-movement keys to move to the Range you want to change, in this case, the xMin field,
2. type the new value, for example, 3.5, and
3. press ENTER .

The new value, 3.5, replaces the old value.

To perform a calculation on a field, for example, to double the Range value of 3.5,

1. reposition the cursor on the xMin field,
2. press ✕ 2 , and
3. press ENTER .

The old value, 3.5, is replaced with the new value, 7.0 (that is, the result of 2 times 3.5).

If you make an error while entering data into a field, press CL to restore the original value.

3.1.5   Working with Memories and Variables

There are 27 global memories available: the 26 letters of the alphabet (A–Z) and θ. You can access values stored in these memories from any mode. The values entered are stored, even when the calculator is turned off, until you replace them with different values. In Programming and Solver modes, the memories operate as variables.

Lowercase variables are also available. These exist only for the specific program or equation in which they are entered, and their values are not saved after you change modes. To access lowercase variables, do the following:

1. Press $\boxed{\texttt{2ndF}}$.
2. Press the letter desired.

Lowercase variables can be strung together with numbers to form an unlimited number of possible variables. They are useful in the Programming mode to avoid accidental overwriting of the Global variables. Examples of calculator memories are A, X, and θ; examples of variables are *A, X,*θ, and area.

3.1.6   Configuring the Calculator

The general configuration of the calculator is controlled through the SET UP menu. To access this menu, press $\boxed{\texttt{SET UP}}$. Change the settings just as you make selections in other menus. For example, to select degrees, do the following:

1. Press $\boxed{\texttt{SET UP}}$

The SET UP menu is displayed (see Fig. 3.4).

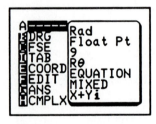

Figure 3.4

2. Press [B:DRG] and then [1:Deg] .
3. Press $\boxed{\texttt{ENTER}}$ to leave the menu.

3.1.7   Working with the Calculation Mode

Submodes.   There are four submodes of the Calculation mode, as follows:

- Real (the default)
- Nbase
  Allows hexadecimal, octal, and binary calculations and conversions.
- Matrix

- Complex

  To change modes, do the following:

1. Press MENU .

The MODE menu appears, as shown in Fig. 3.5.

Figure 3.5

2. Press the number that corresponds to the mode you want.

You are returned to the Calculation screen in the selected mode.

Playback.   In the Calculation mode, many past equations entered in the calculator can be recalled. The last 100 keystrokes are stored in playback memory.

- To recall the most recent expression, press ▲ .
- To recall expressions earlier than the most recent, press 2ndF ▲ .

  Repeat this sequence to step backward to previous expressions (up to the 100 keystroke limit).

EXAMPLE 1   Playback

Problem Evaluate $\dfrac{\sin X}{X-1}$ for values of $X = $ -1, 0, and 1.

Solution Follow these steps:

1. Press the Calculation key to enter the Calculation mode.
2. Press MENU [1:REAL] to put the calculator in Real mode (if not already there).
3. Store the value of -1 into X by entering the following key sequence:

$$\boxed{(-)}\quad 1 \quad \boxed{\text{STO}} \quad \boxed{\text{X/}\theta\text{/T}}$$

4. Press $\boxed{^a\!/_b}$ so you can enter a fraction.
5. Press ▲ BS to clear the ANS command.
6. Enter the expression by keying in the following sequence:

7. Press ENTER to calculate the equation.

The result, 0.420735492, is calculated (see Fig. 3.6).

To store 0 in *X*, do the following:

1. Enter the following key sequence:

$$\mathbf{0} \quad \boxed{\text{STO}} \quad \boxed{\text{X}/\theta/\text{T}}$$

2. Recall the equation and recalculate the expression by entering the following sequence:

$$\boxed{\blacktriangle} \quad \boxed{\text{2ndF}} \quad \boxed{\blacktriangle} \quad \boxed{\text{ENTER}}$$

The answer for 0 is calculated.

To store 1 in *X*, do the following:

1. Enter the following key sequence:

$$\mathbf{1} \quad \boxed{\text{STO}} \quad \boxed{\text{X}/\theta/\text{T}}$$

2. Recall the equation and recalculate the expression by entering the following sequence:

$$\boxed{\blacktriangle} \quad \boxed{\text{2ndF}} \quad \boxed{\blacktriangle} \quad \boxed{\text{ENTER}}$$

The calculator responds with an error message (see Fig. 3.7) because you are trying to divide by zero. There is no real-number value for $\frac{\sin X}{X-1}$ for X = 1.

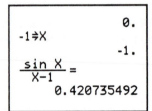

Figure 3.6

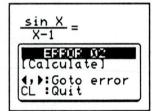

Figure 3.7

3.2 ———— Graphing with the EL-9200C and EL-9300C

3.2.1   Graphing and Tracing Multiple Functions

You can graph and trace up to four functions simultaneously. To do this, you first enter the equations for each function on the Equation screen. These four functional expressions are labeled Y1, Y2, Y3, and Y4. Example 2 explains how to enter equations.

The following conventions apply:

- To move from one expression to another, press $\boxed{\text{2ndF}}$ and either $\boxed{\blacktriangle}$ or $\boxed{\blacktriangledown}$ (depending on which expression you want to reach).

- After you enter the fourth expression, a Fill screen appears, on which you can indicate if you want to shade above or below Y1 through Y4.
- To return to the Equation screen from any other Graph screen, press $\boxed{\text{EQTN}}$.

Example 2   Using the Equation Menu

Problem Graph $\dfrac{\sin X}{X-1}$ and $\dfrac{1}{X-1}$.

Solution To graph these two equations, do the following:

1. Press the Graph key to enter the Graph mode.

The screen displays 'Y1 ='. (Press $\boxed{\text{CL}}$ if any other equation is showing).

2. Enter the first equation by keying in the following sequence:

$$\boxed{^a/_b} \quad \boxed{\text{sin}} \quad \boxed{\text{X}/\theta/\text{T}} \quad \boxed{\blacktriangleright} \quad \boxed{\text{X}/\theta/\text{T}} \quad \boxed{-} \quad 1$$

3. Press $\boxed{\text{ENTER}}$ (see Fig. 3.8).

The equation is stored; the screen clears the first equation, and displays 'Y2 ='.

4. Enter the second equation by keying in the following sequence:

$$1 \quad \boxed{^a/_b} \quad \boxed{\text{X}/\theta/\text{T}} \quad \boxed{-} \quad 1$$

5. Press $\boxed{\text{ENTER}}$.

The equation is stored; the screen clears the second equation, and displays 'Y3 ='.

If you want to graph more equations, enter them as Y3 and Y4.

Before drawing the graph, you must set the Range (also called the viewing rectangle or window). How to do this is explained in Section 3.2.2. For illustrative purposes, Example 2 continues for several sections.

3.2.2   Setting the Range and Auto Range

To set the Range values, do the following:

1. Press $\boxed{\text{RANGE}}$.

The screen displays the current values for the x Range (see Fig. 3.9). To display the y Range values, press $\boxed{\blacktriangleleft}$. To redisplay the x Range, press $\boxed{\blacktriangleright}$ again.

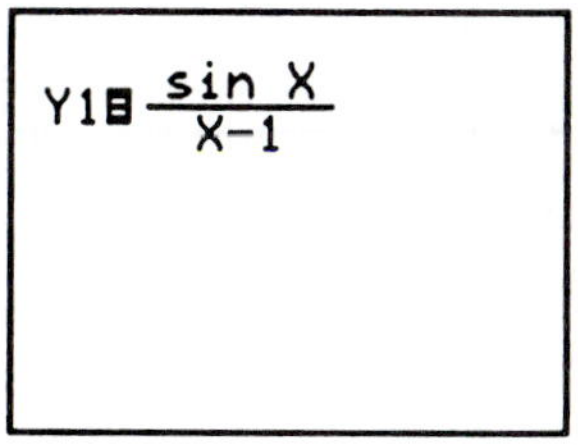

Figure 3.8

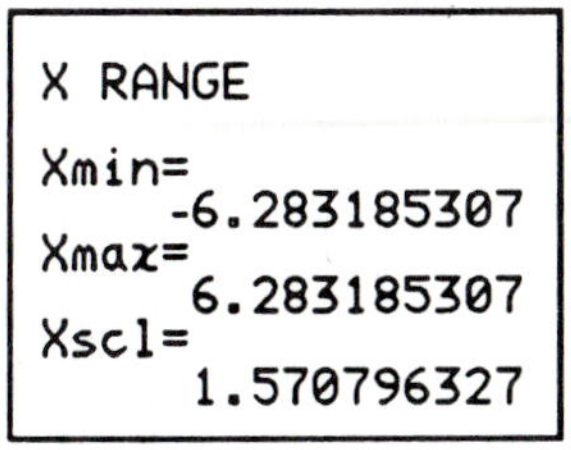

Figure 3.9

2. Either

  a. change the values for the Range, or

  b. press $\boxed{\text{MENU}}$ to select from 19 default Ranges available.

Because the equation in Example 2 works with the sine function, choose the default sine Range as follows:

3. Press $\boxed{\text{MENU}}$ [D:TRIG] [1: sin, cos].

The calculator automatically sets the x Range values from -2π to 2π and the y Range values from -1.55 to 1.55.

4. Press the Graph key to draw the graph (see Fig. 3.10).

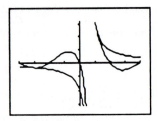

Figure 3.10

Also available is an AUTO RANGE feature that will automatically set the y Range values and then draw the graph. This feature is helpful when a function doesn't appear in the selected Range. To use the AUTO RANGE feature, press

$\boxed{\text{2ndF}}$ $\boxed{\text{AUTO}}$

3.2.3   Drawing the Graph

Several options are available for drawing graphs.

1. When viewing the graph or the equations, press $\boxed{\text{MENU}}$.

The menu shown in Fig. 3.11 is displayed.

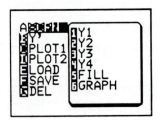

Figure 3.11

2. Select the option you want.
   The options available are as follows:

• SCRN allows you to quickly move between the Equation, Fill, and Graph screens.

- Y′enables you to turn on a derivative trace. You will learn about derivations if you continue your mathematical studies with a course in calculus.
- PLOT1 allows drawing the graphs with or without connecting the dots.
- PLOT2 allows graphs to be drawn sequentially or simultaneously.
- LOAD, SAVE, and DEL are used to store up to 99 sets of equation titles. When you choose SAVE, the four equations Y1–Y4, the Range values, selected Menu options, and the set-up configuration are stored under one name for future use.

3.2.4   Tracing a Graph

To trace the curve of the graph, do the following:

1. Press either ◄ or ► .

The blinking cross cursor appears on the screen (see Fig. 3.12).

2. Continue to press ◄ or ► to trace the graph. To move quickly to the right-hand side of the screen, press 2ndF ► ; to move quickly to the left-hand side of the screen, press 2ndF ◄ .

As the cursor traces the graph, the x-coordinate of the cursor and the corresponding functional values are given at the bottom of the screen.

3. To move the cursor between the graphs, press ▲ or ▼ .

4. To exit the TRACE feature, press CL .

   Notice that when the cursor moves off the screen, the display scrolls in the *x*-and *y*-directions as needed to keep the cursor on the screen.

   You also can obtain a Trace value for the derivative, that is, the slope of the curve at the *x*-value. This feature uses a numerical method to estimate the derivative at each *x*-value as you trace along a graph. To do this, press

$$\boxed{\text{MENU}} \quad [\text{B:Y}'] \ [1:\text{ON}]$$

See Fig. 3.13.

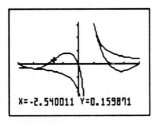

Figure 3.12

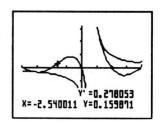

Figure 3.13

3.2.5   Zeroing in on Certain Points

It's easy to focus on certain points of interest using the JUMP feature. To view the options this feature offers, press

The cursor doesn't need to be near the selected point of interest in order for the calculator to find the desired point; the calculator will begin at the cursor position and work to the right looking for the point. If no point is found, the calculator displays the message 'NO SOLUTION IN RANGE.' Note that the TRACE feature need not be active for you to use the JUMP feature.

As an example, find the intersection of the two equations you entered in Section 3.2.1 as follows:

1. Press

    $\boxed{\text{2nd}}$ $\boxed{\text{JUMP}}$ [1:INTERSECT] ;

    where 1 is the Intersect option (see Fig. 3.14).

The calculator shows that the first intersection occurs at the point with coordinates (-4.712388, -0.175058)(see Fig. 3.15).

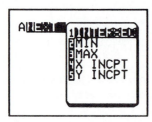

Figure 3.14

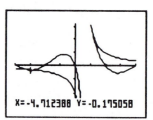

Figure 3.15

2. To find the first maximum of Y_1, press $\boxed{\blacktriangle}$ which places the cursor on Y_1.
3. Enter the following key sequence:

    $\boxed{\text{2ndF}}$ $\boxed{\text{JUMP}}$ [3:MAX]

The calculator shows that a maximum of 0.424607 occurs at X = -1.132267.

3.2.6   Using ZOOM

To get a closer look at a part of the graph, use the ZOOM feature. To use ZOOM, do the following:

1. Press $\boxed{\text{ZOOM}}$.

The screen displays the ZOOM menu, which is shown in Fig. 3.16.

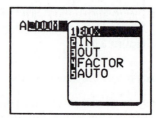

Figure 3.16

2. Press the number of the option desired.

The calculator returns you to the graph and redraws the graph according to the parameters of the option you selected.

Following are the options available:

- BOX
  enables you to draw a box on the graph that will become the new window.
- IN and OUT
  scale the graph by an amount specified by the Zoom factor.
- AUTO
  sets the *y* Range values automatically. This option is the same as $\boxed{\text{2ndF}}$ $\boxed{\text{AUTO}}$.

For example, suppose you want to zoom in on the left part of the two curves. Do the following:

1. Press $\boxed{\text{ZOOM}}$ [1:BOX], where 1 is the Box option.
2. Use the cursor-movement keys to mark the first corner of the box.
3. Press $\boxed{\text{ENTER}}$.
4. Hold down the cursor-movement keys to draw the box that will be your new viewing window (see Fig. 3.17).

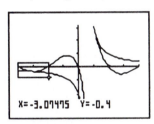

X=-3.07475   Y=-0.4

Figure 3.17

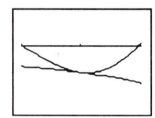

Figure 3.18

5. Press $\boxed{\text{ENTER}}$ to redraw the graph.

The graph is redrawn according to the coordinates of the box you drew (see Fig. 3.18).

3.2.7   Working with Polar Graphs

In addition to the Rectangular coordinate system, you can use other coordinate systems such as the Polar coordinate system. To change the graphing system to the Polar coordinate system, enter the following key sequence:

$$\boxed{\text{SET UP}} \quad [\text{E:COORD}] \quad [2\text{:R}\theta]$$

Then press [B:DRG] [2: Rad] to ensure your calculator is in Radian mode.

The following changes occur:

- In Graphing mode, the calculator changes the prompt from Y1 to R1.
- Pressing $\boxed{\text{X}/\theta/\text{T}}$ yields a θ (theta) instead of an *X*.

• The Range screen changes from to include θMin, θMax, and θstep. Note that θMax and θstep are linked; one automatically adjusts after you enter a value for the other.

The TRACE and ZOOM features work in the Polar coordinate system just as they do in the Rectangular coordinate system. Before continuing on to Example 3; change the graphing system to the Rectangular coordinate system.

EXAMPLE 3   Graphing with Polar Coordinates

Problem Graph an eight-petal rose (sin 4 θ with a θ Range of 0 to 2π).
Solution Follow these steps to produce the rose:

1. Enter the following key sequence:

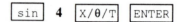

2. To set up a "square" window, press

Note: This key sequence will set up a square window in any of the graphing mode options—Rectangular, Polar, and Parametric.

3. To change θMax, to 2π, press:

| ▼ | 2 | 2ndF | π | ENTER | 2ndF | AUTO |

The result is as shown in Fig. 3.19.

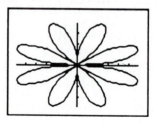

Figure 3.19

3.2.8   Working with Parametric Graphs

Parametric graphs are based on the Rectangular coordinate system, except that X and Y are individual functions that have T as an independent variable. In the Parametric graphing mode, X1T and Y1T replace Y1 as an equation prompt. tMax and $t$step are linked; one automatically adjusts after you enter a value for the other.

To change to the Parametric graphing mode, enter the following key sequence:

| SET UP | [E:COORD] [3:XYT] | QUIT |

To ensure you are in Radian mode; press

| SET UP | [B:DRG] [2:RAD] | QUIT | .

EXAMPLE 4   Parametric Graphing

Problem Graph X1T = sin 3*T*, Y1T = cos 5*T* with a *t* Range of 0 to 2π.
Solution Follow these steps to create this graph:

1. To enter the equations, press

2. To set the range, press

The result is as shown in Fig. 3.20.

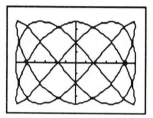

Figure 3.20

3.3 ———— Using Solver to Simplify Problem Solving (EL-9300C only)

The EL-9300 includes a powerful feature called the Solver mode. This mode allows you to solve for any variable in any equation entered. Because there is no need to rearrange the equation to solve for a particular variable, finding solutions is greatly simplified. Equations can be solved using any of three solving methods. To change to Solver mode, press

| 2ndF | | SOLVER |

3.3.1 Entering an Equation

Expressions are entered in the Solver mode just as they are in the Calculation mode, except in order to form an equation in the Solver, you must use an equals sign (=) (ALPHA =). To prevent your accidentally overwriting any Global memories, lowercase variables are used (see also Section 3.1.5 for more information on memories and variables). The following conventions apply:

- To enter a lowercase variable,
    1. press ALPHA and
    2. enter the letter.
- To enter an uppercase variable,
    1. press ALPHA   2ndF and
    2. enter the letter.

- To enter a subscript number,
   1. press [2ndF] and
   2. enter the number.

   Press [ENTER] after entering your equation.

EXAMPLE 5   Entering Equations in Solver

Problem How long does it take for a ball thrown straight up into the air to reach a height of 10 m? Assume that the person throwing the ball can do so at 20 m/sec and that that person's hand is 2 m high when the ball is released. The force of gravity is 9.88 m/sec^2. Disregard air resistance.

Solution Enter the basic equation of motion as follows:

1. Enter Solver mode by pressing [2ndF] [SOLVER]
2. Key in the following sequence:

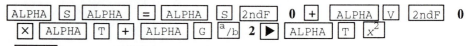

3. [ENTER]

A list of variables is displayed (see Fig. 3.21).

$$s = s_0 + v_0 * t + \frac{g}{2} t^2$$

Figure 3.21

Note: You can return to the equation by pressing [EQTN] *.*

   Observe that the multiplication sign is required between variables so that the calculator does not make 'v₀t' into one variable. For illustrative purposes, Example 5 continues in the next several sections.

3.3.2   Entering the Known Values

Enter all the values except for the single unknown one. Remember you can use the cursor-movement keys to move between the variables. Enter the variables as follows:

1. The height, *s*, we want the ball to reach is 10, therefore enter

   1 0 [ENTER]

2. The initial height, *s₀*, is 2 m when the ball is released, therefore enter

   2 [ENTER]

3. The initial velocity, v_0, is 20 m/sec, therefore enter **2 0** ENTER .
The results should be as in Fig. 3.22.

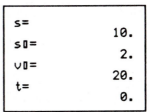

s=	10.
s0=	2.
v0=	20.
t=	0.

Figure 3.22

As time (*t*) is what we are solving for, skip it by pressing ▼ . In addition, because the acceleration due to gravity (*g*) is in the opposite direction of the initial velocity, it must be negative; therefore enter the following key sequence:

(-) 9 . 8 ENTER

3.3.3 Choosing the Solving Method

To find the unknown variable, you can select from three solving methods. To learn what those are, press

MENU [B:METHOD]

The three methods are displayed in a submenu as follows (see Fig. 3.23):

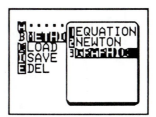

Figure 3.23

- Equation method
  Internally rearranges the variables to solve for the unknown variable. Note that it might not always be able to solve the unknown.
- Newton method
  Uses an initial guess with an iterative approach to approximate the solution.
- Graphic method
  Draws a graph of the right-hand and left-hand sides of the equation in order to find the solution.

For Example 5, we'll use the Graphic method, therefore press [3: GRAPHIC] and the calculator returns you to the previous screen, which shows the values of the variables you entered earlier.

3.3.4   Solving for the Answer

To solve for the unknown variable, do as follows:

1. Move the cursor to the variable, in this case *t*, using the cursor-movement keys.
2. Press

You must press ENTER the second time to confirm you want to solve for that variable (see Fig. 3.24).

Next, you need to enter Range values for the Graphic method. We know that the ball must be in the air for some amount of time and that the ball might remain in the air for as long as 5 sec. We use these estimates for the Range by entering the following key sequence:

See Fig. 3.25. The calculator uses the AUTO RANGE feature to draw the graph. The horizontal axis is scaled based on the variable being sought, in this case *t*, and the vertical axis is, in this case, the height of the ball. The horizontal line represents $s=10$. The curve shows the height of the ball as time passes. We can see that the ball starts a little above ground level, reaches a maximum height, and falls back to the ground.

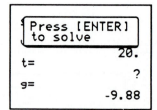

Figure 3.24

Figure 3.25

The calculator then automatically computes the solution, which occurs at the intersection of the two graphs, approximately $t = .45$ sec (see Fig. 3.26).

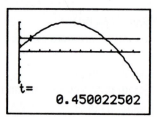

Figure 3.26

3.3.5   Solving for Additional Answers

Viewing the equation graphically, we can see that there is more than one solution. The second solution occurs when the ball falls back to the ground and is again momentarily at a height of 10 m. This solution can be found using the TRACE feature (discussed in Section 3.2.4) to move the cursor to the other solution of the ZOOM feature (discussed in section 3.2.6) to move in on the solution and then trace to measure it. You also can use the JUMP feature by pressing

| 2ndF | | JUMP |

which will cause the calculator to find the second solution, in this case, approximately $t = 3.63$ sec (see Fig. 3.27).

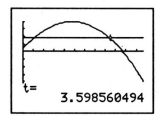

Figure 3.27

3.3.6   Storing Equations

Up to 99 equations used in the Solver mode can be named and stored for later reference. To save an equation, do the following:

1. Press MENU [D:SAVE] ENTER .
2. Enter a title for the equation.
3. Press ALPHA ENTER .

     To retrieve a function, do the following:

1. Press MENU [C:LOAD] ENTER .
2. Arrow down to highlight equation derived.
3. Press ENTER .

Chapter 4

TI-82 and TI-83 Graphing Calculators

These two graphing calculators are versatile tools for exploring mathematics. In addition to all of the features of a scientific calculator, they have large-screen computation and programming capabilities and built-in software for working with graphs, tables, lists, matrices, sequences, probability, and statistics. Hence, these calculators are actually powerful, user-friendly hand-held computers.

This chapter is designed to familiarize you with many aspects of these calculators. The two models are so similar that in most cases you can follow the same instructions, and we will refer to "your calculator," rather than the particular model number. When they do differ, specific instructions will be given for the TI-82 and the TI-83.

Have the calculator out and "on" so that you can work through the examples as you read this chapter. Feel free to explore the menus and features of your calculator. A few hours of productive play can help you reach a comfort level so that you can readily solve problems using this powerful tool.

4.1 _____ Getting Started on the TI-82 or TI-83

4.1.1 Exploring the Keyboard

Take a minute to study the keys on your calculator. There are 10 rows of keys, each with five keys, except for the four specially arranged cursor-movement keys. These keys are divided into three zones.

- **Row 1**
  Used for graphing and table building.

- **Rows 2, 3, and 4**
  Used for accessing menus and editing.

- **Rows 5–10**
  Used like those on a scientific calculator.

Thinking in terms of these three zones will help you find keys on your calculator.

4.1.2   Using the Multipurpose $\boxed{\text{ON}}$ Key

The On key $\boxed{\text{ON}}$ is in the lower left-hand corner of the keyboard. It is used to do the following:

- Turn on the calculator.
- Interrupt graphing if you want to stop before a graph is completely drawn.
- Interrupt program execution to "break out" of a program.
- Turn off the calculator. To do this, press

$$\boxed{\text{2nd}} \quad \boxed{\text{ON}}.$$

Note that the word OFF is written in colored letters just above $\boxed{\text{ON}}$ and that the color of the letters matches that of $\boxed{\text{2nd}}$. In the future, we will say, "press $\boxed{\text{2nd}}$ $\boxed{\text{OFF}}$."

To prolong the life of the batteries, your calculator automatically turns itself off after several minutes have elapsed without any activity. To turn on your calculator in these circumstances, press

$$\boxed{\text{ON}}.$$

Your calculator will turn on and will return you to the screen on which you were working when it turned itself off.

4.1.3   Adjusting the Screen Contrast

You can adjust the screen contrast as needed, choosing from 10 contrast settings that range from 0 (the lightest) to 9 (the darkest).

To darken the screen,

1. press and release $\boxed{\text{2nd}}$ and then

2. press and hold $\boxed{\Delta}$.

To lighten the screen,

1. press and release $\boxed{\text{2nd}}$ and then

2. press and hold $\boxed{\nabla}$.

If you find it necessary to set the contrast at 8 or 9, it is probably time to change your batteries. (Your calculator uses four AAA batteries.) If after you change the batteries the screen is too dark, simply adjust contrast following the steps outlined above.

4.2 _____ Calculating and Editing

4.2.1 Returning to the Home Screen

Computation is done on the Home screen. To help you remember how to get to the Home screen from other screens and menus, remember the sentence, "Quit to go Home." This means that if you get lost in a menu and want to return to the Home screen, press

$$\boxed{2nd} \quad \boxed{QUIT}.$$

($\boxed{QUIT}$ is the second function of $\boxed{MODE}$ located to the right of $\boxed{2nd}$.) If your calculator does not respond to this command, it is probably busy graphing or running a program. In this case, press

$$\boxed{ON} \text{ and then } \boxed{2nd} \quad \boxed{QUIT}.$$

4.2.2 Performing Simple Calculations

1. To compute $2 + 5 \times 8$, press:

$$\textbf{2} \boxed{+} \textbf{5} \boxed{\times} \textbf{8} \boxed{ENTER}.$$

Your screen should look like Figure 4.1.

2. Find the value of log(100) by pressing
   - on the TI-82 $\boxed{LOG}$ $\boxed{(}$ **100** $\boxed{)}$ $\boxed{ENTER}$, or
   - on the TI-83 $\boxed{LOG}$ **100** $\boxed{)}$ $\boxed{ENTER}$.

Note that on the TI-83 the left parenthesis automatically appears (see Fig. 4.2).

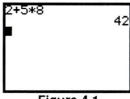

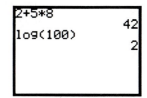

Figure 4.1   **Figure 4.2**

Note: Do not type the letters L, O, and G. The calculator would interpret this as implied multiplication of the variables L, O, and G.

4.2.3   **Working with Error Messages**

Your calculator knows the difference between the binary operation of subtraction (the blue $\boxed{-}$) and the additive inverse, or "sign change," operation (the gray $\boxed{(-)}$). To learn how the calculator handles errors related to these keys, let's purposely make a mistake. Enter the following key sequence:

$$7 \boxed{+} \boxed{-} 4 \boxed{\text{ENTER}}.$$

Your calculator should respond as show in Figure 4.3. The *error message* indicates you have made a syntax error and have two choices. This ERROR MESSAGE menu is typical of all numbered menus on your calculator. To select an item from a numbered menu, do either of the following:

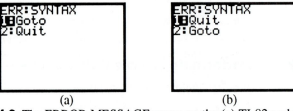

(a)   (b)

Figure 4.3 The ERROR MESSAGE menu on the (a) TI-82 and (b) TI-83.

a.   press the number to the left of the choice you want–this is the fastest way–or

b.   position the cursor next to your choice and press $\boxed{\text{ENTER}}$.

To return to the Home screen (Remember, "Quit to go Home."), press

$$\boxed{\text{2nd}} \quad \boxed{\text{QUIT}},$$

or press the number that corresponds to QUIT on your calculator.

The screen should look like Figure 4.4, with a flashing cursor below the 7.

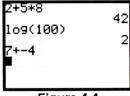

Figure 4.4

To return to the ERROR MESSAGE menu (see Fig. 4.3), press

$$\boxed{\text{ENTER}}.$$

Selecting the GO TO option at this point causes the cursor to "go to" the source of the error and clears the Home screen of all data except the expression that contains the error. Generally, the Goto option will help you find your error.

1. If you have not already done so, choose to the Goto option now.

The cursor should flash on the subtraction symbol.

2. Press [(-)] to overwrite the subtraction symbol with a negative sign.

3. Press [ENTER] to re-execute the calculation.

You should obtain the expected result: 3.

4.2.4   Editing Expressions

Using Last Entry. When you press [ENTER] on the Home screen to evaluate an expression or execute an instruction, the expression or instruction is stored with other previous entries in a storage area called the Last Entry Stack. You can recall a prior entry from the Last Entry Stack, edit it, and then execute the edited instruction, as the following example illustrates.

EXAMPLE 1 Doubling an Investment's Value

Problem You deposit $500 in a savings account earning 4.75% annual percentage rate (APR), compounded monthly. How long will it take for your investment to double in value?

Solution Because $4.75 \approx 5$ and $100 \div 5 = 20,$ you might make an initial guess of 20 yr. To check the guess, do the following:

1. Press [2nd] [QUIT] to return to the Home screen, if necessary.

2. Press [CLEAR] once or twice.

   On a line with text on the Home screen, [CLEAR] clears the text from the line.

   On a blank line on the Home screen, [CLEAR] clears the text from the entire screen.

3. Press **500** [(] **1** [+] **0.0475** [÷] **12** [)] [^] [(] **12** [×] **20** [)] [ENTER].

   (See Fig. 4.5.)

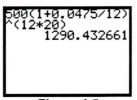

Figure 4.5

4. To display the results in a format more appropriate for calculations involving money,

   a.   Press $\boxed{\text{MODE}}$ to display the MODE screen.

   b.   Press $\boxed{\nabla}$ $\boxed{\triangleright}$ $\boxed{\triangleright}$ $\boxed{\triangleright}$ to position the cursor over the 2.

   c.   Press $\boxed{\text{ENTER}}$.

The numerical display format is changed to two fixed decimal places (see Fig. 4.6).

(a)   (b)

Figure 4.6 The Mode screen on the (a) TI-82 and (b) TI-83.

5. Press $\boxed{\text{2nd}}$ $\boxed{\text{QUIT}}$ to return to the Home screen.

6. Press $\boxed{\text{ENTER}}$ to display the result in the two-decimal-place format (see Fig. 4.7).

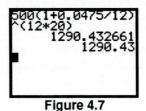

Figure 4.7

Our next guess should be quite a bit less than 20 yr, say 14 yr. In this case, do the following:

1. To edit the old expression, press $\boxed{\text{2nd}}$ $\boxed{\text{ENTRY}}$ $\boxed{\triangleleft}$ $\boxed{\triangleleft}$ $\boxed{\triangleleft}$ **14**.

2. Evaluate the edited version by pressing $\boxed{\text{ENTER}}$ (See Fig. 4.8).

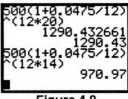

Figure 4.8

3. To change the number of years to 14.5, press

$\boxed{\text{2nd}}$ $\boxed{\text{ENTRY}}$ $\boxed{\triangleleft}$ $\boxed{.}$ 5 $\boxed{\text{ENTER}}$.

Notice that the final parenthesis can be left off and that all three results can be seen on the screen (see Fig. 4.9).

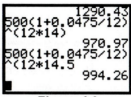

Figure 4.9

Continue this guess-and-check procedure until you obtain the accuracy you desire. Press $\boxed{\text{2nd}}$ $\boxed{\text{ENTRY}}$ several times to observe how the Last Entry Stack has stored several prior entries.

Display Cursors. There are four types of display cursors. Each of these cursors indicates what will happen when you press the next key (see Table 4.1).

TABLE 4.1 Display cursors.

Entry cursor	Solid blinking rectangle	The next keystroke is entered at the cursor; it overwrites any character.
INS (insert) cursor	Blinking underline	The next keystroke is inserted in front of the cursor location.
2nd cursor	Blinking ↑	The next keystroke is a 2nd operation.
ALPHA cursor	Blinking A	The next keystroke is an alphabetic character.

Using the Edit Keys.   The Edit keys help you make effective use of your calculator. Study Table 4.2 on the next page.

TABLE 4.2   Edit keys.

Key	Comments
◁ or ▷	Moves the cursor within a line. These keys repeat.
Δ or ∇	Moves the cursor between the lines. These keys repeat.
2nd ◁	Moves the cursor to the beginning of expression. Can be used for fast-tracing on the Graph screen.
2nd ▷	Moves the cursor to end of expression. Can be used for fast-tracing on the Graph screen.
ENTER	Evaluates an expression or executes an instruction. This key acts as a Pause key when graphing, press it a second time to resume graphing.
CLEAR	• On a line with text on the Home screen, this key clears (blanks) the current command line. • On a blank line on the Home screen, it clears the screen. • In an editor, it clears (blanks) the expression or value on which the cursor is located. It does not store zero as the value.
DEL	Deletes the character at the cursor. This key repeats.
2nd INS	Inserts characters at the underline cursor. To end the insertion, press 2nd INS or a cursor-movement key.
2nd	Means the next key pressed is a 2nd operation (the color-coded operation to the left above a key). The cursor changes to an ↑. To cancel 2nd, press 2nd again.
ALPHA	Means the next key pressed is an ALPHA character (the color-coded character to the right above a key). The cursor changes to an A. To cancel ALPHA, press ALPHA or a cursor-movement key.
2nd A-LOCK	Sets ALPHA-LOCK Each subsequent key press is an ALPHA character. The cursor changes to an A. To cancel ALPHA-LOCK, press ALPHA Note that prompts for names automatically set the keyboard in ALPHA-LOCK.
X,T,θ	Allows you to enter an x in Function (Func) mode, a t in Parametric (Par) mode, or a θ in Polar (Pol) mode without pressing ALPHA first. Additionally on the TI-83, the key X,T,θ,n allows you to enter an n in Sequence (Seq) mode.

4.2.5   Scientific Notation and the Answer Key

Example 2 illustrates a geometric progression—a sequence of numbers that grows by a constant factor—while demonstrating some important features of your calculator.

EXAMPLE 2   Generating a Geometric Sequence

Problem   Display the sequence that begins with 1.7×10^3 and grows by a factor of 100.

Solution   To generate the sequence, do the following:

1. Return your calculator to Floating Point Numerical Display (Float) mode by pressing

    $\boxed{\text{MODE}}$ $\boxed{\nabla}$ $\boxed{\text{ENTER}}$.

2. Press $\boxed{\text{2nd}}$ $\boxed{\text{QUIT}}$ to return to the Home screen.

3. Clear the Home screen by pressing $\boxed{\text{CLEAR}}$ $\boxed{\text{CLEAR}}$.

4. To enter 1.7×10^3 onto the Home screen, press **1.7** $\boxed{\text{2nd}}$ $\boxed{\text{EE}}$ **3** $\boxed{\text{ENTER}}$.

Notice that entering the number in scientific notation did not cause the result to be displayed in scientific notation (see Fig. 4.10).

5. Press $\boxed{\times}$ **100**.

As soon as you press $\boxed{\times}$, 'Ans *' is displayed on the screen. **Ans** is a variable that contains the last calculated result (see Fig 4.11).

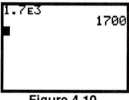

Figure 4.10

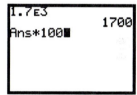

Figure 4.11

6. Press $\boxed{\text{ENTER}}$ four times.

Each time you press $\boxed{\text{ENTER}}$, the previous answer is multiplied by 100 and Ans is updated. Notice the display automatically becomes scientific notation (see Fig. 4.12).

7. Press $\boxed{\text{ENTER}}$ twice to see the geometric progression continue (see Fig. 4.13).

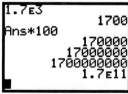

Figure 4.12

Figure 4.13

4.2.6   Other Computation Features and Menus

Clear the Home screen and then try the following calculations.

1. **Integer arithmetic**

    To calculate $^-2 - ^-3 + ^-4 \times 5$, press

    $\boxed{(-)}$ **2** $\boxed{-}$ $\boxed{(-)}$ **3** $\boxed{+}$ $\boxed{(-)}$ **4** $\boxed{\times}$ **5** $\boxed{\text{ENTER}}$.

2. **Rational-number arithmetic**

    To add the fractions $\dfrac{1}{3}$ and $\dfrac{4}{7}$, press

    1 $\boxed{\div}$ **3** $\boxed{+}$ **4** $\boxed{\div}$ **7** $\boxed{\text{MATH}}$ [1 : Frac] $\boxed{\text{ENTER}}$.

3. **Real-number arithmetic**

    To approximate the principal square root of 10, press

    • on the TI-82 $\boxed{\text{2nd}}$ [√] $\boxed{(}$ **10** $\boxed{)}$ $\boxed{\text{ENTER}}$.

    • on the TI-83 $\boxed{\text{2nd}}$ [√] **10** $\boxed{)}$ $\boxed{\text{ENTER}}$.

(See Fig. 4.14.)

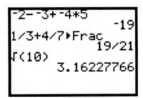

Figure 4.14

4. **Order of operations**

    To show that exponents take precedence over negation, and thus $(-6)^4 \neq -6^4$, press

    $\boxed{\text{CLEAR}}$ $\boxed{(}$ $\boxed{(-)}$ **6** $\boxed{)}$ $\boxed{\wedge}$ **4** $\boxed{\text{ENTER}}$.

Then press

    $\boxed{(-)}$ **6** $\boxed{\wedge}$ **4** $\boxed{\text{ENTER}}$.

and compare the results (see Fig. 4.15).

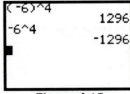

Figure 4.15

5. **Trig and angle computation**

   To calculate tan 60° without switching to Degree mode, press

   $\boxed{\text{CLEAR}}$ $\boxed{\text{TAN}}$ **60** $\boxed{\text{2nd}}$ $\boxed{\text{ANGLE}}$ [1 : °] $\boxed{\text{ENTER}}$.

   Then press

   $\boxed{\text{2nd}}$ $\boxed{\sqrt{}}$ **3** $\boxed{\text{ENTER}}$.

   and compare the results. Re-enter these expressions adding parentheses as needed to match Figure 4.16.

6. **Roots**

   To evaluate $\sqrt[5]{-16807}$, press either

   $\boxed{\text{CLEAR}}$ **5** $\boxed{\text{MATH}}$ [5 : $\sqrt[x]{}$] $\boxed{\text{(-)}}$ **16807** $\boxed{\text{ENTER}}$

   or

   $\boxed{(}$ $\boxed{\text{(-)}}$ **16807** $\boxed{)}$ $\boxed{\wedge}$ $\boxed{(}$ **1** $\boxed{\div}$ **5** $\boxed{)}$ $\boxed{\text{ENTER}}$.

   (See Fig. 4.17).

7. **Greatest integer function**

   To determine the greatest integer less than or equal to –4.916, press

   - on the TI-82 $\boxed{\text{MATH}}$ $\boxed{\triangleright}$ [4 : int] $\boxed{\text{(-)}}$ **4.916** $\boxed{\text{ENTER}}$, or
   - on the TI-83 $\boxed{\text{MATH}}$ $\boxed{\triangleright}$ [5 : int] $\boxed{\text{(-)}}$**4.916** $\boxed{\text{ENTER}}$.

   Add parentheses if you wish to match Figure 4.18.

8. **Factorial**

   To evaluate $10! = 10 \cdot 9 \cdot 8 \cdot 7 \cdot 6 \cdot 5 \cdot 4 \cdot 3 \cdot 2 \cdot 1,$ press

   10 $\boxed{\text{MATH}}$ $\boxed{\triangleleft}$ [4 : !] $\boxed{\text{ENTER}}$.

   (See Fig. 4.18.)

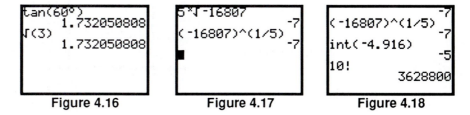

Figure 4.16   Figure 4.17   Figure 4.18

4.2.7   Computing with Lists

Next, set the display format to five fixed decimal places as follows:

1. Press MODE .

2. Press ∇ and then ▷ six times.

3. Press ENTER .

4. Return to the Home screen by pressing 2nd   QUIT .

5. Clear the Home Screen by pressing CLEAR .

Patterns in logarithmic outputs

Then refer to Figure 4.19 as you proceed through these steps:

1. To enter $\log(2^1)$, press

LOG   († 2 ∧ 1) ENTER .

†*This first parenthesis automatically appears on the TI-83.*

2. To enter $\log(2^2)$, press

2nd ENTRY ◁ ◁ 2 ENTER .

3. To enter $\log(2^3)$, press

2nd ENTRY ◁ ◁ 3 ENTER .

See Figure 4.19. Do you see the pattern? A rule of logarithms states that for positive numbers x, $\log(x^n) = n\log(x)$. To see the pattern in a different way,

1. Press LOG   2nd   { 2 , 4 , 8 2nd   } ENTER , *adding parentheses if needed.*

2. Press and hold ▷ to see the third item in the "list." (See Fig. 4.20.)

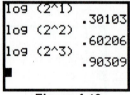
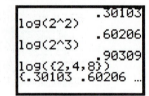

Figure 4.19   **Figure 4.20**

The curly braces { } are used to enclose an ordered set of numbers, or **list.** List notation looks just like set notation, but you can add, subtract, multiply, and divide lists, whereas you operate on sets differently, using operations such as union and intersection. Your calculator manual has a chapter on lists. You also can learn about lists through experimentation; try using them in various ways and observe the results.

4.2.8   Using Variables

EXAMPLE 3   Finding the Height of a Triangle

Problem   A triangle encloses an area of 75 cm² and has a base of 11 cm. What is its height?

Solution   Recall that the area is given by one half the base times the height: $A = (1/2)bh$.

Therefore to find the height, do the following:

1. To put your calculator in Floating Point mode,

    a.   press MODE and

    b.   select the Float option.

2. Return to and clear the Home screen.

3. To store the value 11 as the variable B, press

    11 STO▷ ALPHA B ENTER .

4. Because one-half the base is about 5, the height should be about 15. Therefore press

    • on the TI-82,

    15 STO▷ ALPHA H 2nd : (1 ÷ 2) 2nd A-LOCK B H ENTER .

    • on the TI-83,

    15 STO▷ ALPHA H ALPHA : (1 ÷ 2) 2nd A-LOCK B H ENTER .

    (See Fig. 4.21.)

5. Our guess was too big, so enter

    2nd ENTRY Δ 14 ENTER .

(See Fig. 4.22.)

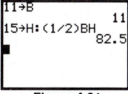
Figure 4.21

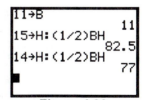
Figure 4.22

The next guess would be between 13 and 14 and would require inserting extra digits for the number being stored in H (press 2nd INS at the appropriate location). Continue the guess-and-check process to practice using the editing features of your calculator and to find the height with an error of no more than 0.01.

4.3 _____ Function Graphing and Table Building

Graphing and table building on your calculator involve the top row of keys. There are four graphing modes on your calculator: Function, Parametric, Polar, and Sequence. Each has a corresponding table-building mode. Thus changing the setting on the fourth line of the Mode screen affects both graphing and table building (see Fig. 4.23).

(a)   (b)

Figure 4.23 The Mode screen on the (a) TI-82 and (b) TI-83.

For this section, be sure your calculator is in Function mode (Func). In Section 4.4 we explore the Parametric and Polar modes. The remainder of this section is built around various calculator methods for solving equations, using the example

$$\cos x = \tan x \ \text{ for } 0 \le x \le 1.$$

4.3.1   Method A: Graphing Each Side and Zooming In

1. Enter each side of the equation as a function on the Y= screen by pressing

   $\boxed{\text{Y=}}$ $\boxed{\text{COS}}$ $\boxed{\text{X,T,}\theta}$ $\boxed{\text{ENTER}}$ $\boxed{\text{TAN}}$ $\boxed{\text{X,T,}\theta}$ $\boxed{\text{ENTER}}$.

Insert parentheses if you wish to match Figure 4.24.

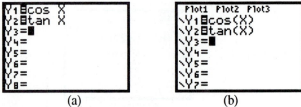

(a)   (b)

Figure 4.24 The Y= screen on the (a) TI-82 and (b) TI-83.

2. Press $\boxed{\text{ZOOM}}$ [4 : ZDecimal].

   Watch as the curves are graphed in sequence. The vertical lines are pseudo-asymptotes of $y = \tan x$. The calculator is actually connecting points that are off the screen (see Fig. 4.25).

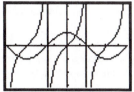

Figure 4.25

3. Press $\boxed{\text{WINDOW}}$ to see what portion of the plane is being used for graphing. The viewing rectangle, or window, being used is $\left[X_{\min}, X_{\max}\right]$ by $\left[Y_{\min}, Y_{\max}\right]$, in this case [–4.7, 4.7] by [–3.1, 3.1]. Because Xscl = 1 and Yscl = 1, the tick marks on each axis are one unit apart (see Fig. 4.26). The TI-83 has an extra line on the Window screen to set the resolution. For our purposes, keep Xres = 1.

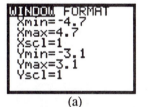
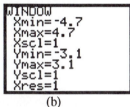

(a)   (b)

Figure 4.26 The Window editor screen on the (a) TI-82 and (b) TI-83.

4. Press $\boxed{\text{TRACE}}$.

    Observe the coordinate readout at the bottom of the screen as you press and release $\boxed{\triangleright}$ *repeatedly. Stop when x = 0.7. The graphs appear to intersect at x = 0.7; actually this is a rough approximation of the solution we seek for cos x = tan x for 0 ≤ x ≤ 1 (see Fig. 4.27).*

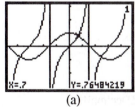
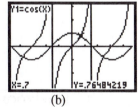

(a)   (b)

Figure 4.27 Tracing on the (a) TI-82 and (b) TI-83.

Now you can probably see why the fourth ZOOM feature is called Zoom Decimal (ZDecimal). It adjusted the viewing window to give a nice *decimal* readout. Notice the 1 in the upper right-hand corner of the TI-82 screen. It lets you know that you are tracing on Y_1, which in this case is $\cos x$. The TI-83 shows the equation.

5.   Press $\boxed{\nabla}$ to move the Trace cursor to Y_2.

The x value does not change, but the y value does, because you are now tracing on $Y_2 = \tan x$. Notice the screen indicator has changed to show you are racing on Y_2 (see Fig. 4.28).

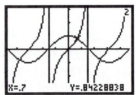

Figure 4.28 TI-82 version.

6.   Press $\boxed{\text{GRAPH}}$.

The Trace cursor, the coordinate readout, and the number in the upper right-hand corner of the screen all disappear and only the graph itself is displayed (see Fig. 4.29).

7.   Press any of the cursor-movement keys. You now are using a free-moving cursor that is not confined to either of the graphs. Notice that this cursor looks different from the Trace cursor.

8.   Experiment with all four cursor-movement keys.

Watch the coordinate readout change. Move to the point (0.7, 0.8). Notice $y = 0.8$ is not the value of either function at $x = 0.7$, it is just the y-coordinate of a dot (pixel) on the graphing screen (see Fig. 4.30). The coordinates (0.7, 0.8) are the *screen coordinates* of the pixel. Notice that the free-moving cursor yields a nice decimal readout for both x and y. This is because we used Zoom Decimal to set the viewing window.

Figure 4.29

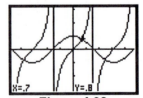

Figure 4.30

Using ZOOM Box. This option lets you use the cursor to select opposite corners of a "box" to define a new viewing window. Continuing the example from above, do the following:

1. Press $\boxed{\text{ZOOM}}$ [1 : Box]. Then move the cursor to $(0, 0)$. (See Fig. 4.31.)

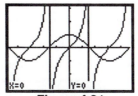
Figure 4.31

2. To select a new viewing window of [0, 1] by [0, 1.2], which will limit x so that
    $$0 \leq x \leq 1,$$

    a. press $\boxed{\text{ENTER}}$ to select the point $(0, 0)$ as one corner of the new viewing window and

    b. use the cursor-movement keys to move to the opposite corner $(1, 1.2)$. (See Fig. 4.32.)

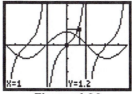
Figure 4.32

3. To select $(1, 1.2)$ as the opposite corner of the new viewing window, press $\boxed{\text{ENTER}}$.

The graphs of the two functions will be drawn in the new viewing window (see Fig. 4.33).

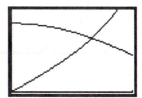
Figure 4.33

4.   To remove the cursor and coordinates from the screen, press $\boxed{\text{GRAPH}}$.

5.   To verify that the new viewing rectangle is [0, 1] by [0, 1.2], press $\boxed{\text{WINDOW}}$.

Notice that Xscl and Yscl are still both equal to one. The Zoom Box option does change the scale settings (see Fig. 4.34).

6.   To approximate the solution as $x \approx 0.6702$,

   a.   press $\boxed{\text{TRACE}}$ and

   b.   use the cursor-movement keys to move to the point of intersection (see Fig. 4.35).

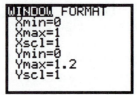

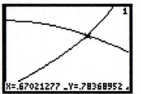

Figure 4.34 TI-82 version.   **Figure 4.35** TI-82 version.

Finding an error bound. Next, using the approximate solution we found in number 6 above, we want to find the error bound for *x*, as follows:

1.   To return to and clear the Home screen, press $\boxed{\text{2nd}}$ $\boxed{\text{QUIT}}$ $\boxed{\text{CLEAR}}$.

2.   To see the approximate solution, press x(X,T,θ) $\boxed{\text{ENTER}}$.

3.   Press

   • on the TI-82 $\boxed{\text{VARS}}$ [1 : Window] [7 : Δx] $\boxed{\text{ENTER}}$ or

   • on the TI-83 $\boxed{\text{VARS}}$ [1 : Window] [8 : Δx] $\boxed{\text{ENTER}}$.

The value of Δx is the horizontal distance between consecutive pixels in the current viewing window, which in this case is about 0.011. This is an error bound for x. Our approximate solution 0.6702, has an error of at most 0.011.

We need to pick X_{min} and X_{max} so that they are closer together to decrease this error bound (see Fig. 4.36).

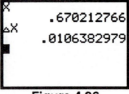

Figure 4.36

Do the following:

1. To enter the smaller window of [0.5, 0.8] by [0.6, 1.0], press WINDOW , followed
    on the TI-82 by ▽ ; then press

    0.5 ENTER **0.8** ENTER **0.1** ENTER **0.6** ENTER **1** ENTER **0.1** ENTER .
    (See Fig. 4.37.)

2. To move to the point of intersection —approximately (0.666, 0.786), press

    TRACE

    and then after the graph is drawn use the cursor-movement keys (see Fig. 4.38).

Figure 4.37 TI-82 version

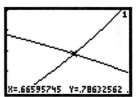

Figure 4.38 TI-82 version.

3. To display the previous approximation and error bound along with the new and
    improved approximation and error bound (see Fig. 4.39), press

    2nd QUIT X,T,θ ENTER VARS [1 : Window] [7 : Δx] ENTER .

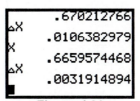

Figure 4.39

4. Evaluate $\cos x$ and $\tan x$ on your calculator. You should see that $\cos x$ and $\tan x$
    are nearly, but not exactly, equal when $x = 0.6659...$(see Fig. 4.40).

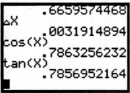

Figure 4.40

4.3.2   Method B: Table Building

The Y= screen is used to enter functions for both graphing and table building. To build a table, do as follows:

1. Press $\boxed{\text{Y=}}$ to check that $Y_1 = \cos x$ and $Y_2 = \tan x$ (see Fig. 4.41).

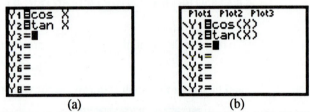

(a)   (b)

Figure 4.41 The Y= screen on the (a) TI-82 and (b) TI-83.

2. To reveal the Table Setup screen, press $\boxed{\text{2nd}}$ $\boxed{\text{TblSet}}$.

3. Press $\boxed{0}$ $\boxed{\text{ENTER}}$ $\boxed{0.1}$ $\boxed{\text{ENTER}}$ and ensure the Auto option is selected for both the independent variable (x) and the dependent variable (y) (see Fig. 4.42).

Figure 4.42

4. Press $\boxed{\text{2nd}}$ $\boxed{\text{Table}}$ and notice that the first x-value is the TblMin (=0) and that the increment from one row to the next in the x column is Δ Tbl (=0.1) (see Fig. 4.43).

5. Press $\boxed{\nabla}$ repeatedly to move down the x column of the table 0.7. Notice that the solution lies between $x = 0.6$ and $x = 0.7$ (see Fig. 4.44).

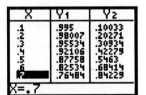

Figure 4.43   Figure 4.44

Use the cursor-movement keys to move around the table and explore. Pay attention to the readout at the bottom of the screen as you move to different "cells" in the table.

6. Press

$$\boxed{\text{2nd}} \quad \boxed{\text{TblSet}} \quad \textbf{0.6} \quad \boxed{\text{ENTER}} \quad \textbf{0.1} \quad \boxed{\text{ENTER}}.$$

The value of Δ Tbl will serve as the error bound for table building, just as Δx did for graphing (see Fig. 4.45).

7. Press $\boxed{\text{2nd}}$ $\boxed{\text{Table}}$ and then press $\boxed{\nabla}$ repeatedly until you reach $x = 0.67$. This is a solution with an error of at most 0.01 (see Fig. 4.46).

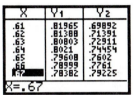

Figure 4.45   **Figure 4.46**

4.3.3   Method C: Solving an Equivalent Equation

To solve $\cos x = \tan x$ for $0 \le x \le 1$, you can solve the equivalent equation

$$\cos x - \tan x = 0$$

for the same interval. To do this, follow these steps:

1. Press

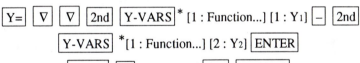

$$\boxed{\text{Y=}} \quad \boxed{\nabla} \quad \boxed{\nabla} \quad \boxed{\text{2nd}} \quad \boxed{\text{Y-VARS}}^* \, [1 : \text{Function...}] \, [1 : \text{Y}_1] \quad \boxed{-} \quad \boxed{\text{2nd}}$$
$$\boxed{\text{Y-VARS}} \, ^*[1 : \text{Function...}] \, [2 : \text{Y}_2] \quad \boxed{\text{ENTER}}$$

*On the TI-83, use $\boxed{\text{VARS}}$ $\boxed{\triangleright}$ in place of $\boxed{\text{2nd}}$ $\boxed{\text{Y-VARS}}$.

(See Fig. 4.47).

2. To deselect Y_1 and Y_2, press

$$\boxed{\Delta} \quad \boxed{\Delta} \quad \boxed{\triangleleft} \quad \boxed{\text{ENTER}} \quad \boxed{\Delta} \quad \boxed{\text{ENTER}}.$$

Now only Y_3 should have its equals sign highlighted (see Fig. 4.48).

Figure 4.47 TI-82 version.   **Figure 4.48** TI-82 version.

3.   To see the graph of $y = \cos x - \tan x$ in a "friendly" viewing window, press

$\boxed{\text{ZOOM}}$ [4 : ZDecimal]; and after the graph is drawn, press

$\boxed{\text{TRACE}}$ $\boxed{\text{2nd}}$ $\boxed{\triangleright}$ $\boxed{\triangleright}$ $\boxed{\triangleright}$.

Notice $\boxed{\text{2nd}}$ $\boxed{\triangleright}$ *moves the cursor five pixels to the right for fast tracing (see Fig. 4.49).*

4.   To enter the Zoom Factors screen, press

$\boxed{\text{ZOOM}}$ $\boxed{\triangleright}$ [4 : SetFactors. . .]

and enter 10 as both the horizontal and the vertical magnification factor by pressing

10 $\boxed{\text{ENTER}}$ **10** $\boxed{\text{ENTER}}$.

(See Fig. 4.50.)

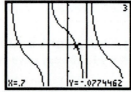
Figure 4.49 TI-82 version.

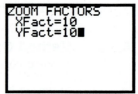
Figure 4.50

5.   To center your zoom-in at the point $(x, y) = (0.7, 0)$, press

$\boxed{\text{ZOOM}}$ [2 : ZoomIn]

and move the cursor to $(0.7, 0)$. (See Fig. 4.51.)

Then press $\boxed{\text{ENTER}}$ to zoom in.

6.   After the graph is redrawn, you can obtain the same approximation that was found by Method B by pressing

$\boxed{\text{TRACE}}$ $\boxed{\triangleleft}$ $\boxed{\triangleleft}$ $\boxed{\triangleleft}$.

Check the value of Δx; it is the same as the Δ Tbl in Method B! (See Fig. 4.52).

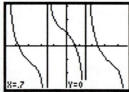
Figure 4.51 TI-82 version.

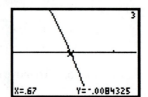
Figure 4.52

4.3.4   Other Equation-Solving Methods

Traditional algebra and trigonometry can be used to determine the exact solution is

$$x = \sin^{-1} \frac{-1 + \sqrt{5}}{2}$$

Do the following:

1.   To evaluate this expression on your calculator, enter it as shown in Figure 4.53. *You obtain an approximation that is accurate to 10 decimal places. It should be consistent with those found by Methods A, B, and C, and it is (see Fig. 4.53).*

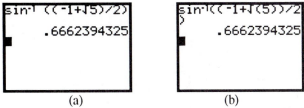

(a)   (b)

Figure 4.53 An arcsin computation on the (a) TI-82 and (b) TI-83.

2.   Set up your Y= screen as you did for Method C. Then, to obtain a graph, press

ZOOM [4 : ZDecimal].

3.   Press 2nd CALC [2 : root]. (On the TI-83, the word "zero" appears rather than "root.")

This should yield a prompt requesting a Lower Bound or Left Bound (see Fig. 4.54).

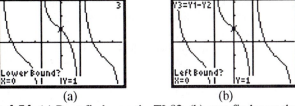

(a)   (b)

Figure 4.54 (a) Root finder on the TI-82, (b) zero finder on the TI-83.

4.   Because we are seeking a solution for $0 \le x \le 1$, the lower bound should be $x = 0$; so press ENTER.

5.   To move the cursor to $x = 1$, press

2nd ▷ 2nd ▷

followed by ENTER to enter it as the upper bound.

6.   Move the Trace cursor to $x = 0.7$ and enter it as your guess by pressing

$\boxed{\triangleleft}$ $\boxed{\triangleleft}$ $\boxed{\triangleleft}$ $\boxed{\text{ENTER}}$.

The calculator should yield a root value of $x = 0.66623943$ (see Fig. 4.55).

7.   To compare the value found using the root finder and the value found in Part 1 above, press

$\boxed{\text{X,T,}\theta}$ $\boxed{\text{ENTER}}$.

They match perfectly to 10 decimal places! (See Fig. 4.56.)

Figure 4.55 TI-82 version.

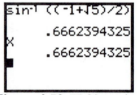

Figure 4.56 TI-82 version.

There are many other ways to solve equations on your calculator. Feel free to explore them.

4.4 _____ Other Graphing and Table Building

4.4.1   Parametric Graphing and Table Building

Parametric equations are ideal tools for representing and solving problems in geometry and the physics of motion. Your calculator has a built-in parametric graphing utility. This utility is similar to the function graphing utility and is almost as easy to use. To graph a parametric curve, you

- select the Parametric (Par) mode on the Mode screen,
- type the desired equations in the Y= screen,
- set the intervals for t, x, and y using the Window screen, and
- press $\boxed{\text{GRAPH}}$.

Parametric equations are written in the form:

$$x = f(t) \quad \text{and} \quad y = g(t).$$

In this setting t is called a parameter; however, t actually is an independent variable, not a parameter in the sense that m and b are parameters in the equation $y = mx + b$. Unlike the independent variable x we are used to in Function-graphing mode, the parameter t is not a plotted, visible coordinate; it is hidden from view when we look at a parametric curve. When we use the TRACE feature, we see a readout of the parameter t and the coordinates x and y, which are the dependent variables of the parametric representation.

EXAMPLE 4   Graphing a Parametric Curve

Problem   Graph the curve represented by the following parametric equations:

$$x = t^2 \quad \text{and} \quad y = t - 1 \quad \text{for} \quad -2 \le t \le 2.$$

Solution   To solve this problem, follow these steps:

1.   Press $\boxed{\text{MODE}}$ to enter the Mode screen and

   a.   select Parametric Graphing (Par) and

   b.   choose the default (leftmost) settings for the other mode settings.

2.   Because we are in Parametric mode, pressing $\boxed{\text{X,T,}\theta}$ will yield the letter t. To enter the given parametric equations, press

$$\boxed{\text{Y=}} \quad \boxed{\text{X,T,}\theta} \quad \boxed{\text{x}^2} \quad \boxed{\text{ENTER}} \quad \boxed{\text{X,T,}\theta} \quad \boxed{-} \quad 1 \quad \boxed{\text{ENTER}}.$$

The screen should look like Figure 4.57.

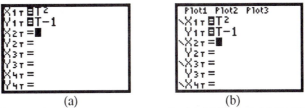

(a)   (b)

Figure 4.57 The Y= screen on the (a) TI-82 and (b) TI-83.

3.   Press $\boxed{\text{WINDOW}}$ and then set the Window screen as shown in Figure 4.58. (Note that you won't be able to see the entire screen at once because it has too many lines.)

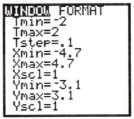

Figure 4.58 Facsimile of the Window screen.

   The t step on the Parametric Window screen is the change between the successive t-values that the calculator uses to compute and plot (x, y) pairs. In this case, the t step of 0.1 will yield 40 steps from the t Min of -2 to the t Max of 2. Thus 41 points will be calculated and plotted, with the points corresponding to

$$t = -2.0, -1.9, -1.8, -1.7, \dots, 1.9, 2.0.$$

Table 4.3 shows the numerical relationship between the parameter t and the coordinates x and y for some of the points to be plotted.

The last two columns of Table 4.3 determine the (x, y) coordinate pairs to be plotted. The values of the parameter t will not appear on the graph.

You can create a table like Table 4.3 on your calculator as follows:

1. Press 2nd TblSet (–) **2** ENTER **0.1** ENTER . (See Fig. 4.59.)

2. Then press 2nd TABLE .   (See Fig. 4.60.)

TABLE 4.3
Table of Parameter and Coordinate Values

t	$x = t^2$	$y = t - 1$
−2.0	4.00	−3.0
−1.9	3.61	−2.9
−1.8	3.24	−2.8
−1.7	2.89	−2.7
.	.	.
.	.	.
.	.	.
1.9	3.61	0.9
2.0	4.00	1.0

Figure 4.59

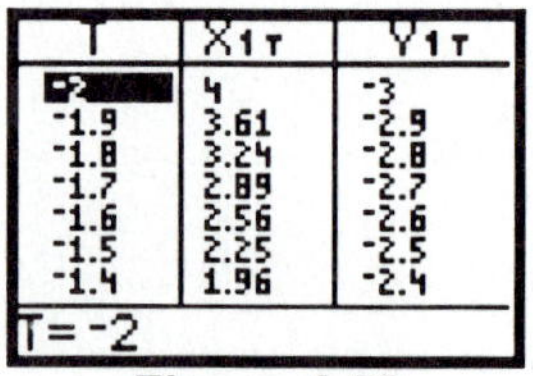

Figure 4.60

To obtain the graph corresponding to Table 4.3 and Figure 4.60, do the following:

1. Press GRAPH to yield the plot shown in Figure 4.61.

Because the calculator is in Connected mode, the plotted points in Figure 4.61 are connected by line segments.

2. To display only the 41 plotted points, choose the Dot mode from the Mode screen and press GRAPH again (see Fig. 4.62).

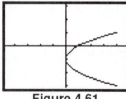

Figure 4.61

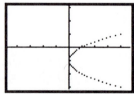

Figure 4.62

Return to Connected mode and use the TRACE feature and the left and right cursor-movement keys to explore the graph numerically. Notice that the values of the parameter t and the x- and y-coordinates are all shown on the screen (see Fig. 4.63 and 4.64). Can you find the six points that correspond to the completed rows of the table shown in Figure 4.62?

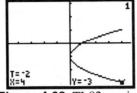

Figure 4.63 TI-82 version.

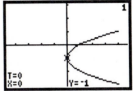

Figure 4.64 TI-82 version.

4.4.2   Polar Equation Graphing

The Polar Equation graphing mode is similar to the other graphing modes.

EXAMPLE 5   Graphing Two Equations Simultaneously

Problem   Graph $r = 9\sin 5\theta$ and $r = 9$.

Solution

1. Press ⎍MODE⎍ (see Fig. 4.65) and

    a.   select Polar (Pol) mode and Simultaneous (Simul) mode and

    b.   choose the defaults for the other modes.

2. Press ⎍Y=⎍ to display the Polar Equation screen.

3. To define the two desired equations, press

    9 ⎍sin⎍ 5 ⎍X,T,θ⎍ ⎍ENTER⎍ 9 ⎍ENTER⎍ .

(See Fig. 4.66.)

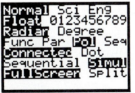

Figure 4.65 TI-82 version.

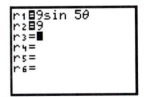

Figure 4.66 TI-82 version.

4.   Press ZOOM [6 : ZStandard].

The graph of r = 9 is supposed to be a circle of radius 9 centered at the pole. The circle circumscribes the five-petaled rose curve r = 9sin 5θ (see Fig. 4.67).

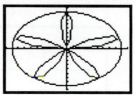

Figure 4.67

5.   Set θmax = π.

6.   To "square up" the window, press

ZOOM [5 : ZSquare].

The entire rose curve is plotted using the interval 0 ≤ θ ≤ π. Press TRACE and explore the two curves (see Fig. 4.68).

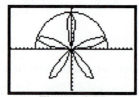

Figure 4.68

Chapter 5

The HP 38G Graphing Calculator

The Hewlett-Packard HP 38G is a flexible tool for exploring mathematical topics from algebra through calculus. Algebraic entry and total recall of previous computations make this machine easy to use, while built-in applications for everything from graphing to table-building make the HP 38G a complete mathematical laboratory. This chapter will introduce you to the basic structure and functionality of the calculator. Have your calculator handy as you read through the following pages. It is not necessary to read the sections in order; feel free to browse.

5.1 — Getting Started With The HP 38G

5.1.1 The Keyboard

The HP 38G keyboard basically contains nine rows of keys with up to six keys in each row. The top row of keys are blank. These are called menu label keys because their function changes as you change menus on the display. The first three keys in the second row reflect an emphasis on exploring mathematics graphically (PLOT), symbolically or algebraically (SYMB), and numerically (NUM). The first three keys in the third row open the doors to the calculator's advanced capabilities. The next six rows contain the traditional functionality found on scientific calculators. Under the ENTER key, there is a column of keys that require some mention. This column contains the alpha-shift and blue-shift keys. The alpha shift, A...Z, allows you to make alphabetical entries, while the blue shift allows you to access the commands or menus printed in blue above the various keys. Below these are the DEL key for deleting characters and the ON key. Notice that the blue shift of the DEL key is CLEAR, for cleaning up entire screens at once instead of just deleting one character in the command line or one field in a menu. Also notice that the blue shift of the ON key will turn the calculator off. Of course, the calculator will also shut itself off after a few minutes if no keys are pressed.

5.1.2   Display Basics

The ON key turns the calculator on, but it has other purposes as well. Pressing the ON key while typing in the command line will clear what has been typed. Holding down the ON key while pressing the − or + keys will decrease or increase the contrast of the display, respectively. Finally, the HOME key will take you back to the computational screen.

5.2 ____   Computations and Editing

5.2.1   The Home Screen

The home screen is divided into four areas. At the top is the annunciator bar, with the home screen title as well as an annunciator that tells you whether angle measures are in degrees or radians. Below this is the computational window, where your computations are displayed. A line at the bottom of the computations window separates it from the command line, wherein all computations are originally entered. Finally, at the very bottom of the screen, there is a row of up to six menu labels. These labels tell you what the functions, if any, the top row of blank keys will perform at any given moment.

5.2.2   Working in the Home Screen

The HP 38G is a straightforward, algebraic entry calculator. In most cases, you just enter expressions as you see them in your text. For instance, to calculate $3 + 4\sin(20°)$, simply press 3 + 4 SIN 20 ENTER. Of course you must be in degree mode (see page 79). It is not necessary to enter the multiplication symbol. In most cases, juxtaposition implies multiplication. Also, it is not necessary to supply the final right parenthesis. While the expression is being entered in the command line, it contains a blank where the multiplication should be (Figure 5.1). After the ENTER key is pressed, the expression is changed so that it not only contains that multiplication symbol explicitly, but also has the final right parenthesis (Figure 5.2).

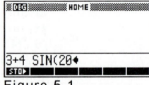

Figure 5.1

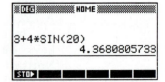

Figure 5.2

The numerical approximation, 4.368..., is displayed below the expression. The first label in the menu at the bottom of the display is now the STORE key, in case you wish to save this result in a variable. Suppose that you wish to edit the original expression so that it reads $3 + 4\sin(35°)$ instead. It is not necessary to type in the entire expression. All computations are available to you at any time. Simply use the up cursor movement key to highlight the original expression, as in Figure 5.3. Then press the COPY menu label key (the fourth key in the top row of blank keys) to see the expression redisplayed in the command line (Figure 5.4). To change the angle from 20° to 35°, use the left cursor movement key to highlight the 2 in 20 (Figure 5.5), press the DEL key twice to delete that figure, and type in 35. Press the ENTER key to display the new expression and its approximate value (Figures 5.6 and 5.7).

As has been mentioned before, all computations are recorded in the Home Screen. The computations window will scroll upward to reveal previous calculations that are no longer visible. When you wish to clear all of these calculations from the Home screen, press the blue shift of the DEL key; CLEAR will erase them all. Even after a CLEAR, the result of the last operation performed is still available to you in the reserved variable Ans. The ANSWER key, which is the blue shift of the ENTER key, allows you access to the contents of this variable. For example, to find the square root of $3 + 4\sin(35°)$, press the $\sqrt{x}$ key, then the blue shift of the ENTER key. The calculator pastes in **Ans**, as in Figure 5.8. Press the ENTER key to see the result. In addition, the calculator automatically pastes Ans into any expression that begins

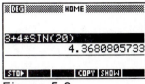
Figure 5.3

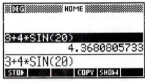
Figure 5.4

Figure 5.5

Figure 5.6

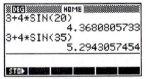
Figure 5.7

Figure 5.8

with an operation that requires some antecedent. For example, to now multiply the result by 17, press * 17. The calculator display pastes Ans, which in this case is $\sqrt{3+4\sin(35)}$, into the command line first, and then follows with the rest (Figure 5.9). Press the ENTER key to see the new result, which now, in turn, replaces the old result in the Ans register.

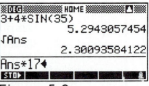

Figure 5.9

Finally, there is one more editing feature of note. Suppose that you are entering an expression with several parenthetical layers, such as $e^{\pi/2^3}$ and you are unsure about where you do and don't need parentheses. Press the blue shift of the + key (e^), and then (π / (2 X^y 3)), even though the parentheses around 2^3 are not necessary (see Figure 5.10). To paste in the symbol π, press the blue shift of the 3 key. When you press the ENTER key, the result is displayed, but the editor has cleaned up the expression by removing the superfluous parentheses (Figure 5.11). To see the expression displayed as it would be found in a standard textbook, highlight the expression by pressing the up cursor movement key twice (Figure 5.12) and press the SHOW menu label key. The expression is typeset, as in Figure 5.13. This gives you an easy means of proofreading your expressions for accuracy. Press the OK menu label key to return to the Home screen. Notice that the highlight bar is still on the expression and that there is an arrow in the rightmost quarter of the annunciator bar at the top of the display that is pointing upward. The purpose of this arrow is to remind you that there are more expressions above the computation window that are not presently visible. Depending on where your window is in relation to the entire scrolling screen, you may see a downward pointing window instead, or both. Press the up cursor movement key three times to see Figure 5.14.

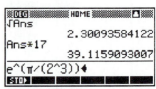

Figure 5.10

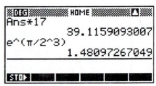

Figure 5.11

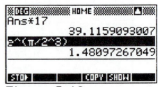

Figure 5.12

Figure 5.13

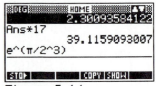

Figure 5.14

Here, we have scrolled to where there are calculations or expressions both above and below the current window onto the Home screen and both arrows are visible in the annunciator bar.

5.3 — Introduction to Aplets

The HP 38G has built-in applications designed to simplify many mathematical processes. These applications are called **Aplets**. Each aplet has graphic, symbolic, and numerical views. The following table lists the title and major uses of each of the native aplets. You may also design and save your own custom aplet, based on a particular set of tasks or some experiment or other.

Aplet Name	Major Purposes
Function	This aplet will plot a graph or build a table based on a function, $y = f(x)$.
Parametric	This aplet plots graphs and builds tables for parametric equations, $x = f_1(t)$ and $y = f_2(t)$.
Polar	This aplet handles polar equations, $r = f(\theta)$.
Sequence	This aplet will plot the staircase graph of a sequence or the cobweb graph of an iterative function. It will also build tables based on a sequence defined by the user.
Solve	This aplet allows you to evaluate expressions and solve equations, including systems of equations.
Statistics	This aplet contains the tools for calculating both one-variable and two-variable statistics. It will also graph scatter plots of data as well as finding and plotting regression equations.

Whether custom or built-in, aplets may be transferred from one calculator to another via the infrared port located at the top of the calculator. Refer to your owner's manual for information regarding the exchange of aplets. Here, it suffices simply to point out that sending someone an aplet is easy and quick. For example, you might send your Statistics aplet to a colleague, complete with all the data, any regresion equation, the plot window settings, and even notes and diagrams. You amy even save aplets to a diskette or your computer's hard drive using the connectivity software. In each of the following sections, you will be given a brief tour of one of the built-in aplets.

5.3.1   The Aplet Library Commands

Press LIB, the Aplet Library key, to see the catalog of available aplets (Figure 5.15). Notice the arrow in the bottom right hand corner, indicating that there are more aplets below the viewing window. Also notice the six menu labels. The SAVE command allows you to save any of the built-in aplets in their present state, with whatever equations, window settings, variable values, and notes that are presently set. The RESET command does exactly that, restoring a built-in aplet to its factory settings, clearing out the various equation registers and setting default viewing windows. This command has no effect on custom aplets. The SORT command allows you to sort the aplets, in either alphabetical or chronological order. The SEND and RECV commands control transfer of aplets between calculators or between a calculator and a computer. Finally, the START command allows you to enter an aplet environment.

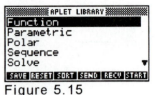

Figure 5.15

Figure 5.16

Figure 5.17

5.3.2   The Solve Aplet

The Solve aplet allows you to work with equations, substituting known values for variables and evaluating the result or solving for a remaining unknown variable. Use the down cursor movement key to highlight the Solve aplet, as in Figure 5.16. Then press the START menu label key to see Figure 5.17. The Solve aplet automatically starts in the Symbolic View which, as you remember, is one of the three views available in each of the aplets. Here, you enter up to ten equations in symbolic form. To return to this view at any time while you are in the solve aplet, press the SYMB key.

Suppose that you wish to find the volume of a cylinder that is 4 meters in height, with a base whose radius is 2 meters. For a right cylinder, $V = \pi r^2 h$. Enter this equation in the E1 register. Remember to use the A...Z shift key to access variable names. Also, notice that the third menu label shows the equal sign. Finally, the π character is the blue shift of the 3 key. Your equation should appear in the command line as in Figure 5.18. Notice that the calculator makes the multiplication explicit when you press ENTER, as in Figure 5.19. Also, a check mark is placed to the left of the equation to show that it is the active equation. You may use the CHK menu label key to activate or deactivate any of the ten equations, but only one equation may be active at any given time.

Figure 5.18

Figure 5.19

Press the NUM key to enter the Solve Numeric View (Figure 5.20). In the numeric view, you enter values for known variables and solve for an unknown variable. Use the down cursor movement key to highlight the field for R, the radius, and enter 2, as in Figure 5.21. The highlight bar moves on down to the next variable field in the menu, which is H, the height. Enter 4, as in Figure 5.22. Again, the highlight bar moves on to the next variable in the menu, which is V. This time, since we wish to know the value of V when r = 2 and h = 4, press the SOLVE menu label key to see the solution, $V = 16\pi \approx 50.625$, as in Figure 5.23.

Figure 5.20

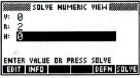

Figure 5.21

It is just as easy to solve this equation for r or h as it is to solve it for V. Suppose that you wish to find the radius of a cylinder whose volume is the same as the cylinder above, but whose height is 8 meters. Use the up cusor movement key to highlight the H field and enter 8 (see Figure 5.24). Notice that you do not have to clear out the old value. Just type the replacement value in the command line and press the ENTER key or the OK menu label key. Then press the down cursor movement key to bypass the V field, since we want to keep the volume constant. With the highlight bar on the R field, press the

Figure 5.22

Figure 5.23

Figure 5.24

SOLVE menu label key. R = $\sqrt{2}$ ≈ 1.414, appears as the solution as in Figure 5.25.

Figure 5.25

To the left of the SOLVE menu label key is the DEFN key, which typesets the symbolic definition of the active equation, in case you are working with several equations and have forgotten which one is currently active. Press the DEFN key now to see our volume formula in Figure 5.26. Press the OK menu label key to return to the numeric view of the Solve aplet.

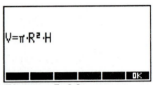

Figure 5.26

We now wish to enter the Plot View of the Solve aplet. Here you may examine the graph of either the radius or height plotted against the volume of the cylinder. With the R field highlighted in the Solve Numeric View menu, press the blue shift of the PLOT key to see the Plot Setup menu. Here we shall set a window for viewing the graph of radius vs. volume for cylinders whose heights are all 8 meters.

Figure 5.27

Set the options in the Plot Setup menu as they appear in Figure 5.27. This is the first of two pages in this menu. Notice the double-width menu label key that allows you to move from page to page in this menu. Press this key to see Figure 5.28. Check marks have been placed to activate certain options. You may change these settings as you see fit using the CHK menu label key.

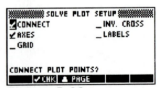

Figure 5.28

Press PLOT to see the graph, as in Figure 5.29. The horizontal line represents the current value of V, about 50.3 m^3. The curve is the plot of radius vs. volume, with h held constant at its present value: 8. In other words, the curve is the parabola V = $8\pi r^2$. In the Plot View, you are automatically tracing. In this case, you are tracing on the line. To move to the curve, press the up- or down- cursor movement

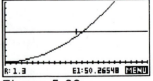

Figure 5.29

key to move the tracing cursor to the curve (Figure 5.30). Use the left- and right-cursor movement keys to trace along the curve. Figure 5.31 shows the cursor near our previous solution for V.

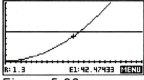

Figure 5.30

You may also view the plot of height against volume, with the radius held constant at some value. To plot height against volume for cylinders whose radii are all 2 meters, press the NUM key to return to the numeric view. Change the value of R to 2, as in Figure 5.32. Notice that the calculator carried over the last value of r to which we had traced: r=1.4. With the highlight bar on the H field, return to the Plot Setup Menu by pressing the blue shift of the PLOT key. We are now plotting height against volume, with the radius held constant at r=2. In other words, we are graphing $V = 4\pi h$. Since this graph is linear, you will need to change the window settings. Figure 5.33 shows one acceptable window. Press PLOT to see the graph, as in Figure 5.34. Tracing as before to H=4 shows our first numeric solution of 16π for the volume when r=2 and h=4 (Figure 5.35).

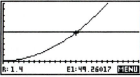

Figure 5.31

Figure 5.32

Figure 5.33

In this way, you may examine any two-variable relationship expressed within any of your equations. The calculator will make the left member of the equation the dependent variable and will use whatever variable is highlighted in the Numeric View menu as the independent variable.

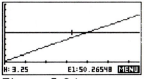

Figure 5.34

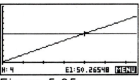

Figure 5.35

Suppose you wish to save these three views with the current equation, window settings, and the values of V, h, and r, for later use. Press the LIB key to see the highlight bar still on the SOLVE aplet. Press the SAVE menu label key to see Figure 5.36. At the prompt, type a new name for this version of the Solve aplet. In this case, we have chosen the name V OF

Figure 5.36

CYLINDER, as in Figure 5.37. Pressing the ENTER key pastes the new name into the field and returns you to the Aplet Library, where you can see your new custom aplet (Figure 5.38). Now you may use the Solve aplet for other purposes and still return to the volume formula by starting the V OF CYLINDER aplet. This aplet will remain available to you until you delete it. To delete an aplet, simply highlight its name in the aplet library and press the DEL key. The calculator prompts you for reassurance that you wish this aplet deleted (Figure 5.39) and then proceeds.

Figure 5.37

Figure 5.38

Figure 5.39

Each of the aplets we shall tour in this section has a symbolic view, a numeric view, and a plot view; however, not all the views behave exactly the same as in the Solve aplet.

5.3.3   The Function Aplet

The function aplet contains tools for graphing and table-building with functions. This section will introduce you to the three views of the Function aplet.

Press the LIB key to enter the Aplet Library, highlight the Function aplet, and press the START menu label key. Like the Solve aplet, the Function aplet starts in the Symbolic view, where you can see there are ten function registers (Figure 5.40). Unlike the Solve aplet, as many of these functions as you like may be activated at one time, so that you may plot the graphs of up to ten functions on one screen. Again, the CHK menu label key allows you to activate and deactivate a selection.

Suppose that you wish to plot the graphs of $y = \sin(x)$ and $y = x^2 - 4x + 2$ simultaneously on the same set of axes. With the highlight bar on F1(X), press the SIN key and the X,T,θ key to enter the sine function in register F1. You do not need to enter the closing parenthesis; the HP 38G supplies that for you when you

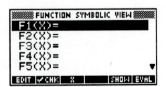
Figure 5.40

press ENTER (or the OK menu label key). Also notice that you could have used the X menu label key to supply the variable. In general, the menu labels try to provide typing aides of this sort, so watch for them. After you have entered the first function, the highlight bar moves down to F2(X). Here, enter the quadratic function, $x^2 - 4x + 2$ (Figure 5.41).

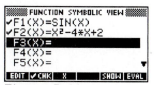

Figure 5.41

When both functions have been entered, press the SHIFT of the SYMB key to enter the Function Symbolic Setup menu. Check here to make sure that angles are being measured in radians. If not, press the CHOOS menu label key and highlight the Radians option, as in Figure 5.42. Press the OK menu label key to accept your selection.

Figure 5.42

Press the SHIFT of the PLOT key to enter the Function Plot Setup Menu. This menu has two pages, both of which are identical to the corresponding pages in the Solve aplet of the previous section. The first page sets the position of the plotting window and the spacing of ticks along the axes. Pressing the SHIFT of the DEL key (Clear) will reset all the options to their standard defaults (Figure 5.43). The Page menu label key gives access to the second page of the menu, as in Figure 5.44. Here, the CHK menu label key allows you to choose SIMULT for simultaneous graphing of both functions. By default, it is already active. Press the PLOT key to see Figure 5.45.

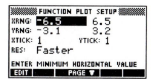

Figure 5.43

Figure 5.44

The plot window automatically places you in trace mode, with the cursor in the middle of the domain. If more than one function is active, the tracer defaults to the first active function. In this case, F(X) = sin(X) is the function being traced, as you can see from the labels at the bottom of the screen. Pressing either the up- or

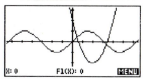

Figure 5.45

down cursor movement keys will move the cursor through the cycle of active functions. Press the MENU menu label key to see Figure 5.46. Press the first menu label key, ZOOM, to see the options in the Zoom menu (Figure 5.47). CENTER will change the plot window's center to the current cursor position and redraw the graphs. BOX zooms in on a user-drawn rectangle. In (4×4) and Out (4×4) zoom in and out by the scaling factors indicated. As you can see in Figure 5.48, you can also zoom in or out along just one or the other of the axes by the indicated scale factor. By default, all of these commands change the center of the plotting window to the current cursor position. To zoom in or out on a particular feature of the graph(s), simply place the cursor on the desired feature and choose the desired zoom option to redraw the graph centered on the desired feature. All subsequent zooms will take this point as their center as long as the cursor has not been moved. Again, this obviously does not apply to the Box zoom option. The last two options are SQUARE and SET FACTORS (Figure 5.49). SQUARE keeps the current domain, but rescales the range so that the units along both axes are equal in length. SET FACTORS opens a dialogue box in which you may change the horizontal and vertical zoom factors (Figure 5.50). Notice that this box also contains the RECENTER option. Deactivating this option forces you to manually recenter the plot window on a given feature, using the Center command, before you can zoom in on that feature.

Suppose that you wish to zoom in on the second intersection of the curves shown in Figure 5.45 on the previous page. Use the cursor movement keys to move to the Box option of the zoom menu and press the OK menu label key (Figure 5.51). The calculator prompts you to move the cursor

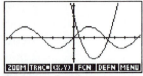

Figure 5.46

Figure 5.47

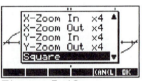

Figure 5.48

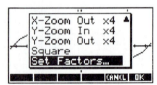

Figure 5.49

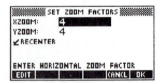

Figure 5.50

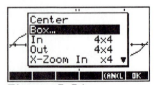

Figure 5.51

to one of the corners of the zoom box, as in Figure 5.52. Press the OK menu label key and the calculator will prompt you to move the cursor to the diagonally opposite corner of the zoom box. The box is drawn as you move the cursor (Figure 5.53). Pressing the OK menu label key completes the operation. Figure 5.54 shows the plot window after the box zoom. Your graph window may be slightly different.

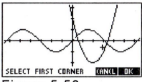

Figure 5.52

There are other options available for controlling the characteristics of the plotting window that are similar to zooms, but are actually preset windows. For example, suppose you wish to establish a window, centered at the origin, that allows each pixel width to represent one unit or one tenth of one unit. These and other so-called friendly windows are contained in the Views Menu. But there are more options here than just preset friendly windows. The HP 38G is able to split the screen vertically to show a graph and a zoom or a graph and a table. Before we look at the Views menu and split the screen, we need to reconsider our window settings. In the full screen, there are 130 plotting pixels, so a domain that starts at $X = -6.5$ and ends at $X = 6.5$ makes each pixel 0.1 unit wide. In the split screen, there are 64 plotting pixels on either side of a vertical split that is 3 pixels wide. Since the height of the screen remains 63 pixels, the result is a pair of windows that are almost square. With this in mind, return to the Plot Setup menu (SHIFT-PLOT) and change the window settings to agree with Figure 5.55, where each pixel is a 0.1×0.1 square.

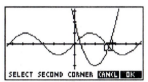

Figure 5.53

Figure 5.54

Figure 5.55

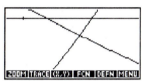

Figure 5.56

Press VIEWS (SHIFT-LIB) to see the options shown in Figure 5.56. Now press the OK menu label key to see Figure 5.57. Press the MENU menu label key to restore the menu bar and choose ZOOM again.

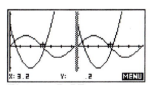

Figure 5.57

This time, place the cursor as near to the second point of intersection as possible and choose the Zoom In 4×4 option. The result is shown in Figure 5.58. Notice the rightmost menu label key: ←. Pressing this key will replace the graph on the left with the zoom on the right, effectively preparing for another zoom. Also note that trace mode is no longer automatically activated. You may activate the tracer by pressing the TRACE menu label key. Activating trace mode does not automatically display the cursor coordinates; to activate cursor coordinate dislay, whether or not the tracer is enabled, press the (X,Y) menu label key. The cursor moves simultaneously in both halves of the screen. If the tracer is active, then the DEFN menu label key will display the symbolic form of the function being traced.

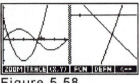

Figure 5.58

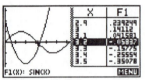

Figure 5.59

Figure 5.60

Return to the VIEWS menu (SHIFT-PLOT) and choose the Plot-Table option to see Figure 5.59. Here, the previous plot on the left is complemented with a table of values on the right. The tracer has been automatically activated and the table of values reflects the fact that the tracer has chosen the first function in the list of active functions, F1(X). In Figure 5.59, the DEFN menu label key has also been pressed, so that one can see a symbolic as well as a graphic and numeric view of this function. As the tracing cursor is moved on the graph of the function, the highlight bar also moves in the table of values to highlight the current cursor position. In this view, the tracer is always on. As you can see in Figure 5.60, the other options in the Views menu are self-explanatory. **Overlay Plot** allows you to plot one function or set of functions over another. **Auto Scale** keeps the current domain, but chooses a range that will show at least one pixel lit in each pixel column. **Decimal** is the default graphing window, in which each pixel width represents 0.1 units. **Integer** makes each pixel width 1 unit, while **Trig** makes each pixel $\pi/24$ units wide.

For example, choose the Trig option and move the cursor to the right 12 times ($12\pi/24=\pi/2$ units) to see Figure 5.61, in which the cursor sits at ($\pi/2$,1) on the sin(x) function.

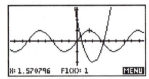

Figure 5.61

With the calculator screen as shown in Figure 5.61, move the cursor a few spaces to the right, press the MENU menu label key, and then press the FCN menu label key to see the Functions Menu, as in Figure 5.62. **Root** finds x-intercepts of the function last traced. It does not always find the root nearest the cursor position, especially if the cursor is near a relative maximum or minimum. On the other hand, moving the cursor to one of the pixels adjoining the desired root will suffice for most functions. In this case, since the cursor is somewhere between $\pi/2$ and π, the calculator will find the root at $x = \pi$, as shown in Figure 5.63. To find a root of our quadratic function in F2(X), simply press the down-cursor movement key and repeat the steps outlined above.

Return to the FCN menu by pressing the MENU menu label key and then the FCN menu label key. Move the highlight bar to the **Intersection** command, as in Figure 5.64. This option finds the intersection of the active function and either another function or the x-axis. Press the OK menu label key to see Figure 5.65. Here the message at the top of the choose box indicates that $F1(x) = \sin(x)$ is the active function. The choose box itself prompts you to decide whether you would like the intersection of $F1(x)$ with $F2(x)$ or the x-axis. Choosing the x-axis would amount to the same thing as choosing the **Root** command. Press OK to find the intersection of $F1(x)$ and $F2(x)$ that is closest to the current cursor position at $x=\pi$. The display briefly flashes the message SIGN REVERSAL, as in Figure 5.66, to indicate that the upcoming intersection has been estimated within the limits of the machine's prcision. The cursor then moves to the intersection and the estimate is displayed as in Figure 5.67.

Figure 5.62

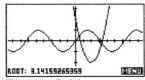

Figure 5.63

Figure 5.64

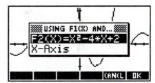

Figure 5.65

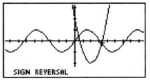

Figure 5.66

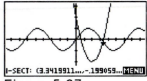

Figure 5.67

Again, return to the FCN menu. There are still three more commands in this menu: **Slope**, **Area**, and **Extremum**. The slope command calculates the numerical derivative of the active function at the value of x indicated by the current cursor position. Choosing the slope option now (Figure 5.68) will give the slope of the sin(x) function at the intersection of the two graphs. Since the cursor is close to π and the slope of the sin(x) function at $x=\pi$ is -1, one would expect a slope value near -1 and such is the case in Figure 5.69.

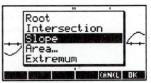
Figure 5.68

Figure 5.69

Like the Intersection command, the **Area** command starts with the last chosen function and allows the user to choose to estimate the area between that function and the x-axis or between that function and another function. In this way, one may estimate the area under a curve or between two curves. As you will see in the next example, the Area command is sensitive to the order in which the endpoints are chosen. Basically, the Area command estimates the numerical integral.

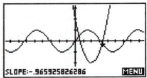
Figure 5.70

Suppose that we wish to estimate the area between the two curves from their second positive intersection back to their first positive intersection. Since the direction of integration is from greater to lesser x-values, the area will be negative. With the cursor still at the second positive intersection of the two curves, return to the FCN menu and choose the Area option, as in Figure 5.70. Press the OK menu label key to see Figure 5.71. Since the cursor is already at the desired location, simply press the OK menu label key. The display shows Figure 5.72, where one has the option to choose the area under the sin(x) function or the area between F1(x) and F2(x). Press OK to choose the area between the curves and move the cursor left until the cursor rests as close as

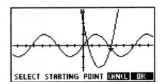
Figure 5.71

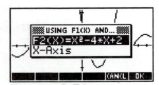
Figure 5.72

possible to the other chosen intersection (Figure 5.73). Notice that the area is shaded as the cursor moves. Press the OK menu label key to see the area calculated, as in Figure 5.74. Note again that the area is negative, as indicated. Since the cursor coordinates are not displayed, this is only an estimate of the desired area. A more accurate numerical method is available with the integral command (see Section 7.4).

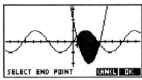
Figure 5.73

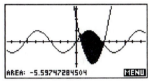
Figure 5.74

Return to the FCN menu one last time and move the highlight bar to the **Extremum** option (Figure 5.75). This command finds both the location and value of the maximum or minimum of the chosen function that is nearest the current cursor location. The cursor is moved to the critical point and the coordinates are displayed at the bottom of the screen, as in Figure 5.76. Since the cursor rests near x=0.5 and the chosen function is still sin(x), the Extremum command in this case found the maximum of sin(x) at x=π/2. To find the minimum of our quadratic function, simply press the down-cursor movement key and repeat the above steps.

Figure 5.75

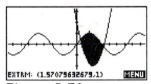
Figure 5.76

Table-building with the HP 38G is as easy as pressing the NUM numerical view key. With the current equations, press the NUM key to see Figure 5.77, which shows columns for x, F1(x), and F2(x). You may use the up- or down-cursor movement keys to move anywhere in a chosen column. Use the left- and right-cursor movement keys to change columns. If you wish to move quite a ways up or down the column of x-values, there is a nice shortcut. Suppose that you wish to see F1(200) and F2(200). With the cursor anywhere in the x-column, type 200 and press ENTER. The table reconfigures itself very quickly, as in Figure 5.78. Notice that the step between

Figure 5.77

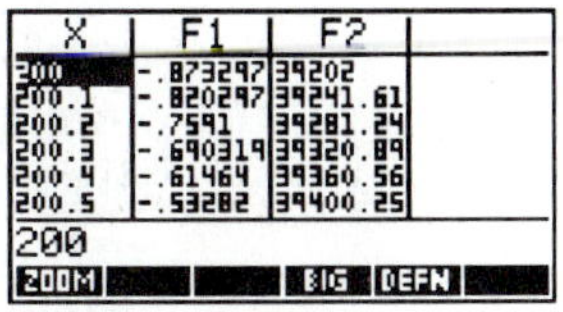

Figure 5.78

the x-values remains 0.1. If you wish to change the step, go to the Numerical Setup menu (Shift-Num) to see Figure 5.79. **Numstart** controls the first value displayed in the table, although you can always scroll up the table with the up-cursor movement key. **Numstep** dictates the change between successive x-values. Set the step to 1 by moving the highlight bar down to highlight the Numstep field, typing 1 and then pressing ENTER (Figure 5.80). Press NUM now to return to the table and see that the table starts at x=200 and shows only integer values for x (Figure 5.81). Notice that there is a ZOOM menu label key to allow you to zoom in numerically on a chosen value. As you can see from Figure 5.80, the zoom factor is set by default at 4, although you can change it at any time. If you wish to zoom in on the behavior of our function at x=202, for example, move the highlight bar down to that value in the x-column and press the ZOOM menu label key to see Figure 5.82. Here you may choose to zoom IN so that the step between x-values is 0.25 or OUT so that the step is 4. You may also select one of the preset zooms, as in the Views menu. Press the OK menu label key to zoom in so that the x-values step by 0.25, as in Figure 5.83.

Return to the Numerical Setup menu and move the highlight bar to the **Numtype** field. Press the CHOOS menu label key to see the options available for the types of tables you can build. There are two types of tables: **Automatic**, the default choice, supplies all the values for all the active functions, as well as the column of x-values. **Build Your Own** leaves the entire table blank to allow you to type in any values for x that you wish. The machine then calculates the function values. Choose this last option and press the NUM key to see Figure 5.84. With the

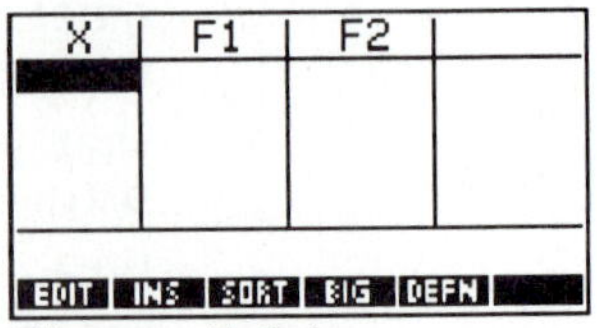

Figure 5.79

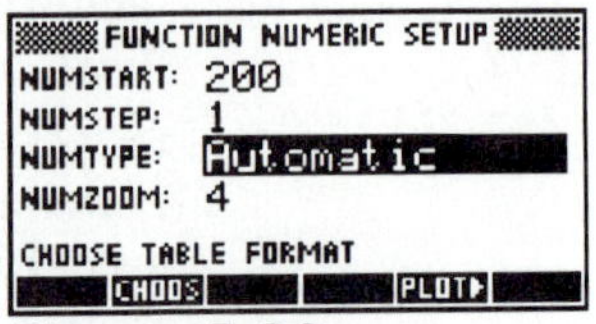

Figure 5.80

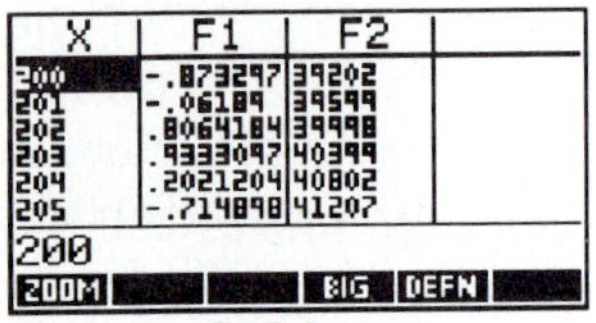

Figure 5.81

Figure 5.82

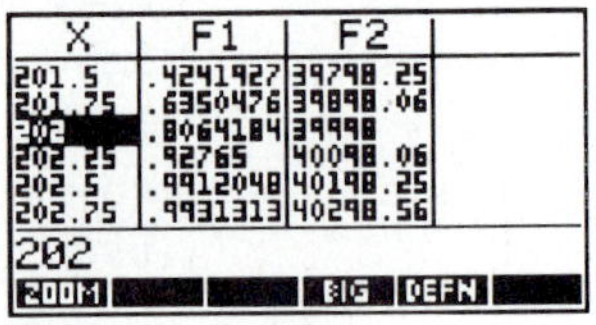

Figure 5.83

Figure 5.84

highlight bar anywhere in the x-column, type in any value you please, say 3.85, and press ENTER. The calculator displays F1(3.85) and F2(3.85), as in Figure 5.85. Notice that the menu label keys have changed once again. The **Edit** command allows you to edit any of the x-values. The **Ins** command allows you to insert a new row between any two successive rows. Suppose that you have entered a variety of x-values, as in Figure 5.86. The **Sort** command will place these x-values in either increasing or decreasing order. In Figure 5.87, the Sort menu label key has been pressed, while in Figure 5.88, the **Ascending** option from the Sort choose box has been chosen. The **Big** command increases the display font size and the **DEFN** command displays the definition of the currently chosen column, much like its counterpart in the Plot menu.

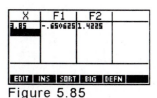

Figure 5.85

Figure 5.86

Figure 5.87

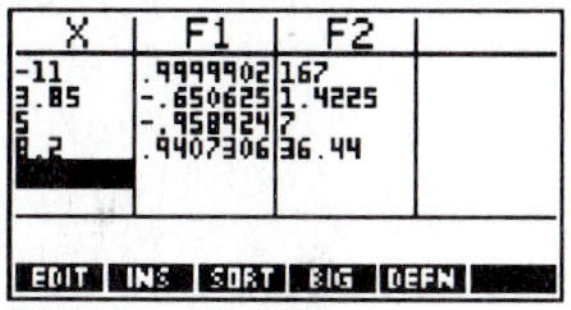

As with the Solve aplet, you may save the current equations, windows, and other plotting options by pressing the aplet library key (LIB), choosing the Save option from the menu labels, and typing a new name for your custom function aplet.

Figure 5.88

5.3.4   The Parametric Aplet

The Parametric aplet does for parametrically defined relations what the Function aplet does for functions defined in Cartesian terms. As in the Function aplet, there are three separate views: symbolic, graphic, and numeric. Another similarity is that both aplets start in the symbolic view, where there are ten equation registers. Go to the Aplet Library menu by pressing the LIB key and move the highlight bar down to the Parametric option. Press the Start menu label key to enter the Parametric Symbolic View menu, where you can see the ten empty equation registers.

Suppose that we wish to examine the ellipse defined by the parametric equations $X = 4 \cdot \cos(T) - 1$ and $Y = 2 \cdot \sin(T) + 1$. With the highlight bar on the X1(T) register, type in the above definition of X and press the ENTER key. To insert the variable T, either press the X,T,θ key or the T menu label key. The function of the X,T,θ key changes with your choice of aplet. In the parametric aplet, it will always insert T. After pressing ENTER, the highlight bar moves down to the Y1(T) register. Enter our definition of Y and press ENTER to see Figure 5.89. Note that the relation is automatically activated after both definitions have been entered, signaled by the check marks placed to the left of the definitions. As in the Function aplet, you may activate or deactivate a relation with the CHK menu label key and as many of the ten possible relations as you wish may be active at one time.

Go to the Symbolic Setup menu (Shift-Symb) and choose the Degree option for measuring angles in the Angle Measure choose box (Figure 5.90). Then go to the Plot Setup menu (Shift-Plot) and set the options on the first page to agree with Figure 5.91. Finally, press PLOT to see the graph, as in Figure 5.92. As in the Function aplet, Trace mode is automatically enabled and the screen displays both the current value of T as well as the ordered pair that marks the current cursor location. Press the MENU menu label key to see the Zoom, Trace, (X,Y), and DEFN menu label keys that operate just as they do in the Function aplet. Notice the absence of the FCN menu, since we are now dealing with relations that may or may not represent functions.

Go to the Numeric Setup menu (Shift-Num) and set the T-step to 1, as in Figure 5.93. Then press the NUM key to visit the Numeric View, where you can see the table of T-, X-, and Y-values, as shown in Figure 5.94. Again, note that you may zoom in or out on any t-value numerically.

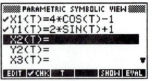

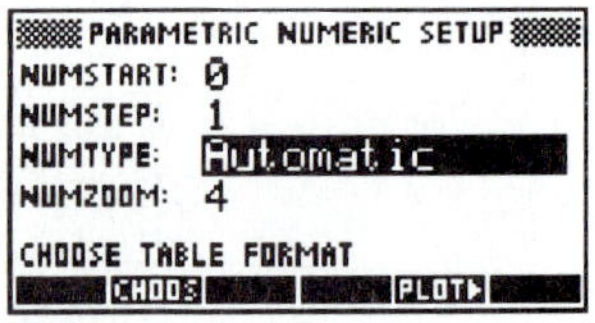

Figure 5.89

Figure 5.90

Figure 5.91

Figure 5.92

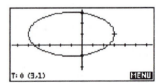

Figure 5.93

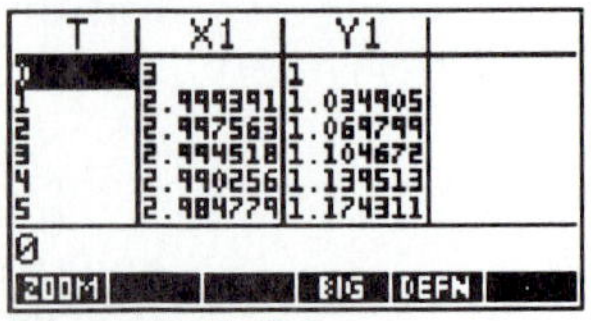

Figure 5.94

5.3.5   The Polar Aplet

The Polar aplet contains the same symbolic, graphic, and numeric views that distinguish the other aplets. This aplet also starts in the symbolic view, where there are (again!) ten equation registers.

Go to the Aplet Library menu and move the highlight bar down to the Polar aplet, as in Figure 5.94. Press the Start menu label key to see Figure 5.95, which shows the Polar Symbolic View menu. Suppose that we wish to plot the graph of the five-petaled rose R=3sin(5θ) and then circumscribe the circle R=3 around the rose. Enter these equations into the R1(θ) and R2(θ) registers, respectively, as shown in Figure 5.96. Go to the Plot Setup menu (Shift-Plot) and set the options on the first page to agree with Figure 5.97. To set θSTEP as shown, go to the Symbolic Setup menu and set the Angle Measure field to radians (see Figure 5.90); then highlight the θSTEP field and press the DEL key. Go to the Views menu (Shift-Lib) and choose the Plot-Table option to see Figure 5.98. Here, trace mode is automatically enabled and the highlight bar in the table shows the current cursor position on the active function. By default, R1(θ) has been chosen as the active function for tracing. To switch both the cursor and the table to R2(θ), simply press the down cursor movement key. To see the table alone, with both relations showing, enter the Numeric View by pressing the NUM key. To see the graph alone, enter the Graphic View by pressing the PLOT key.

As in the other aplets, you may save the present equations and plot settings of this polar aplet by returning to the Aplet Library menu, pressing the Save menu label key, and typing a new name for your custom aplet.

Figure 5.94

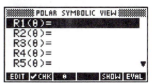

Figure 5.95

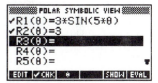

Figure 5.96

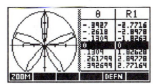

Figure 5.97

Figure 5.98

5.4 ——— The Math Commands Menu

In addition to the built-in aplets, the HP 38G makes a wide range of tools available to the mathematician. All of the math functions may be viewed in the Math Functions menu. While there are too many functions available to list and describe them all here, some of the more common ones are shown in Figures 5.99 - 5.102 below. Press the MATH key to see Figure 5.99 below. Move the highlight bar down through the topics listed in the left column to see the commands that are available. Move the highlight bar to the right to highlight a command and then press the OK menu label key to choose a particular function.

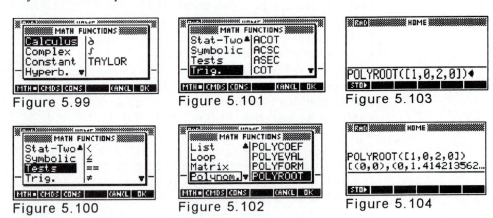

Figure 5.99

Figure 5.101

Figure 5.103

Figure 5.100

Figure 5.102

Figure 5.104

For example, suppose we wish to find all roots, real and complex, of the polynomial x^3 - 2x. This polynomial has one real root at x=0 and two complex roots, at $x = \pm\sqrt{2}i$. Figure 5.102 shows the **POLYROOT** command being selected, while Figure 5.103 shows the coefficients of the ploynomial entered in a matrix as the argument for this command. Finally, Figure 5.104 shows the first and second solutions, with the ellipsis indicating that there is a further solution that is not being displayed.

5.5 ——— Conclusion

The reader is urged to browse through the owner's manual to see all of the commands available. The reader is also encouraged to explore the other aplets, especially the Sequence and Statistics aplets.

Chapter 6

The Casio CFX-9850 Graphing Calculator

6.1 _____ Preliminaries

The Casio CFX-9850G is a graphing calculator with the added capability of using color. In this chapter many of its features will be introduced. Some will incorporate color and others will not, as color is only one of its assets. In order to ease the process of reading the material, a boxed notation will be used. When referring to the primary function of a key, the single function name written on the key will be in the box; when referring to a secondary (or alpha) function of a key, the box will have the function name of the key followed by a colon and the name function needed. For example, "to insert" the instructions would be "press $\boxed{\text{SHIFT}}$ $\boxed{\text{DEL : INS}}$". Bold italics will be used to indicate a Menu such as press $\boxed{\text{MENU}}$ to activate the *Main Menu* screen.

6.1.1 Keyboard

The keys on the calculator are color coded to allow each key to be used for three different commands. Primary key functions are printed on the key in white, secondary key functions are printed in yellow, and alpha key functions are in orange red. For example, if e^x is needed, press $\boxed{\text{SHIFT}}$ $\boxed{\text{ln} : e^x}$ or, if the symbol for theta is needed, press $\boxed{\text{ALPHA}}$ $\boxed{\wedge : \theta}$.

The six keys labeled F1 through F6 at the top of the keyboard will be referred to as "soft menu keys". The soft menu keys control user-activated commands located on the calculator screen just above the keys. The cluster of four arrow keys located at the upper right of the keyboard will be referred to as cursor keys or **replay keys.**

6.1.2   Menus

The Casio CFX-9850G is menu-driven with fourteen menu choices. The *MAIN MENU* screen, shown below, is activated when the calculator is turned on. Any

Figure 6.1
Main Menu

of the fourteen sub-menus can be activated by either pressing the number on the calculator corresponding to the number displayed in the lower right corner of the menu block or by using the cursor arrows to highlight the needed menu followed by pressing EXE .

Each of the fourteen menus on the *Main Menu* screen has its own set-up screen which is activated by pressing SHIFT followed by MENU : SET UP after getting into the desired menu. As a reference, an example of two of the fourteen set-up screens is illustrated. An arrow above the soft menu key F6 indicates that there are more items on the set-up screen to be seen.

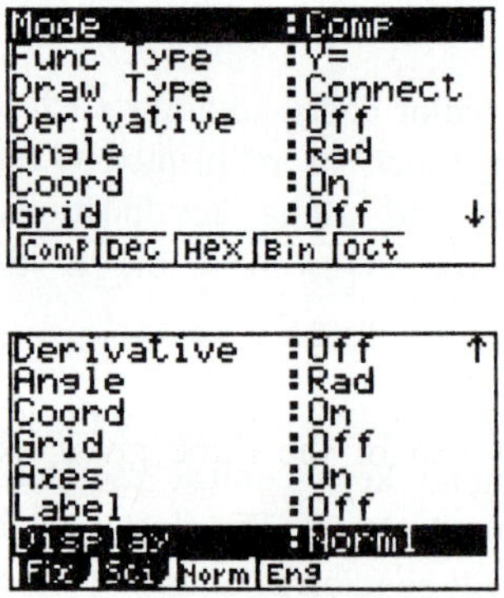

Figure 6.2
Run Menu

Figure 6.3
Graph Menu

6.1.3   Color Feature

Color is the new feature of the Casio series of calculators. It is an excellent feature to clarify a graph's position in relation to another graph as well as providing a shading tool. As a default, inequality graphs are shaded in orange, integral graphs (for calculus students) are shaded in blue. Since color is used with the *Graph* and *Stat Modes*, those are the sections in which color will be addressed more thoroughly.

6.2_____   Basic Operations

6.2.1   Exiting a Screen

It is always frustrating to get into a menu screen and find that it seems impossible to get out of the operation. To get out of a screen, **always** remember to press $\boxed{\text{EXIT}}$ until the calculator no longer changes screens; then press $\boxed{\text{MENU}}$.

6.2.2   Calculating Numerical Expressions

In order to enter numerical expressions, activate the *Run Menu* by highlighting it and pressing the execute key or by pressing the number 1 when the *Main Menu*   is displayed. Begin by evaluating the following expressions. Enter each expression followed by $\boxed{\text{EXE}}$.

$$(1) \quad 2(3+5)$$

$$(2) \quad \sqrt{4}$$

$$(3) \quad (3+5)2$$

•Receiving Error Messages

In evlauating the first two of the three given expressions, notice that the answer for the first was found to be   16   and the answer to   the second was found to be   2.   However, when attempting to evaluate   the third expression, observe that "Syn ERROR"   appears at the bottom of the screen. To locate the error, press either the **right** or the **left replay arrows**. By pressing the replay arrow a cursor will blink at the point at which the calculator does not recognize the syntax. In this particular problem the cursor is blinking on the number 2 indicating that the calculator does not know what to do with this number. The Casio does not recognize the number on the right of a parentheses without an operational symbol.

•Editing

To edit the expression (3 + 5)2 with the blinking cursor on the number 2, press SHIFT DEL : INS   Observe that the blinking cursor over the 2 has changed from solid to open in the middle. This form of the cursor is used to indicate insert mode. Press x followed by EXE to get the correct result of 16.

Enter the number 235652701, EXE . To change the 3 in the number to a 4, press the **right replay arrow**. The **right replay arrow** will place the cursor at the far left of the number to indicate it will move to the right for correction. Arrow to the number 3 to be changed and put a 4 in its place; EXE .

Suppose the number 7 should have been another 2. Press the **left replay arrow** to place the cursor at the far right of the last entry, indicating the cursor will move left to make corrections. Arrow to the left until the 7 is blinking and change it to a 2, EXE .

6.2.3   Using the Deep Stack

A useful feature of the Casio 9850 is the deep stack. Assuming that the calculator has not been turned off since the first calculations were entered in section 6.2, press AC/ON one time followed by the **up replay key**. The last changed entry, 245652201, will appear on the screen.

Continue to press the up **replay key** until the first entry 2(3+5) is reached. Any of the previous computational entries may be accessed and edited by using the deep stack feature as long as the *Run Menu* was never exited. When at the top of the stack, the **down replay arrow** may be used to return to another entry.

6.2.4   Working with Fractions

Fraction operations are easy to work with by using the $\boxed{\text{a b/c}}$ key. Enter 2/3 by pressing 2 $\boxed{\text{a b/c}}$ 3 $\boxed{\text{EXE}}$. The result will appear on the screen as 2⌐3. See Figure 4.

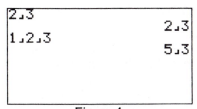

Figure 4
Fractions Operations

To change this result to a decimal press $\boxed{\text{F}\leftrightarrow\text{D}}$. This key acts as a toggle between the fraction and its decimal equivalent. To see this , press $\boxed{\text{F}\leftrightarrow\text{D}}$ again to return to 2⌐3. The second function of this key acts as a toggle between a mixed number and its improper equivalent. Press 1 $\boxed{\text{a b/c}}$ 2 $\boxed{\text{a b/c}}$ 3 $\boxed{\text{EXE}}$. This will be shown as 1⌐2⌐3 on the screen. Press $\boxed{\text{SHIFT}}$ $\boxed{\text{a b/c : c/d}}$ to get a result of 5⌐3.

Suppose the fractions 1/5 and 7/8 are to be added. Enter 1 $\boxed{\text{a b/c}}$ 5 $\boxed{+}$ 7 $\boxed{\text{a b/c}}$ 8 $\boxed{\text{EXE}}$. The result is given as 1⌐3⌐40. If $\boxed{\text{SHIFT}}$ $\boxed{\text{a b/c : d/c}}$ is pressed, the improper fractional equivalent 43⌐40 is given. Now press $\boxed{\text{F}\leftrightarrow\text{D}}$ to see that the decimal equivalent is 1.075. At this point, if $\boxed{\text{F}\leftrightarrow\text{D}}$ is pressed again, 1⌐3⌐40 will be returned; however, if $\boxed{\text{SHIFT}}$ $\boxed{\text{a b/c : d/c}}$ is pressed, the result will be the improper form 43⌐40 once again.

6.2.5   Using Complex Numbers

Although the Casio 9850 is not a calculator based on the complex number system, it has the capability to calculate using complex numbers. To perform complex number operations in the *Run Menu* press the options key $\boxed{\text{OPTN}}$ on the keyboard.

Soft menus are now found at the bottom of the viewing screen. Observe that each of the menu names is solid with the bottom right corner cut off. This indicates that there is another function under the menu.

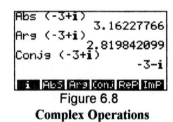

LIST	MAT	CPLX	CALC	STAT	▷

Figure 6.5
Cut Off Corners

| i | Abs | Arg | Conj | ReP | ImP |

Figure 6.6
Solid Menu Commands

Press ⎡F3 : CPLX⎤ . Observe that the soft menu commands are now solid (no corners are cut off). This indicates that the menu commands are a function in and of themselves and there is no other command to be found after pressing the key.

To enter the complex number $(3 - 2i)$ and add it to $(2 + 7i)$, press ⎡(⎤ ⎡3⎤ ⎡−⎤ ⎡2⎤ ⎡F1 : i⎤ ⎡)⎤ ⎡+⎤ ⎡(⎤ ⎡2⎤ ⎡+⎤ ⎡7⎤ ⎡F1 : i⎤ ⎡)⎤ ⎡EXE⎤ . (Note that it is not necessary to put parentheses in this expression, but the same two numbers will be edited to perform other complex operations which will need the parentheses.) The answer to this addition problem should be $5 + 9\,i$. To subtract the same two complex numbers, press the **right (or left) replay arrow**, and cursor to the '+' symbol in the problem; change this plus to minus, and press ⎡EXE⎤ . Now the result should be $1 - 9\,i$. Continue the edit process to multiply (Ans:$20 + 17\,i$) and divide the two numbers (Ans:$-0.1509433962 - 0.4716981132\,i$) by pressing the replay arrow and moving the cursor until it is over the operation symbol to change. Replace the operation with the multiplication ($\times$) or division ($\div$) symbol.

```
(3-2i)+(2+7i)
                    5+5i
(3-2i)-(2+7i)
                    1-9i
(3-2i)×(2+7i)
                   20+17i
 i  Abs Arg Conj ReP ImP
```

Figure 6.7
Complex Operations

```
Abs (-3+i)
                3.16227766
Arg (-3+i)
               2.819842099
Conj (-3+i)
                     -3-i
 i  Abs Arg Conj ReP ImP
```

Figure 6.8
Complex Operations

To see other features of the calculator's complex operations , press ⎡F2 : Abs⎤ ⎡(⎤ ⎡(-)⎤ ⎡3⎤ ⎡+⎤ ⎡F1 : i⎤ ⎡)⎤ ⎡EXE⎤. This series of key strokes find the absolute value (or maginitude) of the complex number $(-3 + i)$ which is seen to be 3.16227766.

The other menu keys, in order from left to right, will display the Argument ⎡Arg⎤ of the complex number, its Conjugate ⎡Conj⎤ , its Real Part ⎡ReP⎤ and its Imaginary Part ⎡ImP⎤ . The function command and complex number should be entered in the same way it was entered to find the complex number's absolute value.

6.2.6   Computing with Variables

Suppose that the polynomial $x^2 + x - 5$ is to be evaluated for multiple values of x without using a table. This can be accomplished by storing an initial value for x in its variable location followed by a colon and the polynomial. After pressing $\boxed{\text{EXE}}$ for the first answer, the **right or left replay arrows** may be used to change the stored value of x and the expression evaluated again upon pressing $\boxed{\text{EXE}}$.

For example, enter the following keystrokes and observe the results obtained in the first illustration. Press 1 $\boxed{\rightarrow}$ $\boxed{\text{x,}\theta\text{,}\tau}$ $\boxed{\text{SHIFT}}$ $\boxed{\text{VARS : PRGM}}$ $\boxed{\text{F6 : }\triangleright}$ $\boxed{\text{F5 : :}}$ $\boxed{\text{x,}\theta\text{,}\tau}$ $\boxed{x^2}$ $\boxed{+}$ $\boxed{\text{x,}\theta\text{,}\tau}$ $\boxed{-}$ 5 $\boxed{\text{EXE}}$.   The answer of -3 is displayed. Press the **right arrow replay** key and change the value stored in x to 5, then press $\boxed{\text{EXE}}$.   This time 25 is the result. If a two or more digit number is required, then remember to press $\boxed{\text{DEL : INS}}$ first before inserting the additional digit.

This procedure can be used to change more than one varible in an expression. Evalute $A^3 + 2 B^2 - 7C$ for various values of A, B, and C. As initial values, store 3 in A, 1 in B, and 2 in C following each entry by the colon; then enter the expression to be evaluated and press the execute key. Press either the **right** or the **left replay** to change any of the values for A, B, or C, and after the desired change has been made, press $\boxed{\text{EXE}}$.

Figure 6.9
Polynomial Evaluation

Figure 6.10
Multiple Variables

6.2.7   Computing with Lists

Be sure to create a List under the *List Menu* before operating with lists in the *Run Menu.*   If a list is not available for computation, proceed to to the *List Menu* section of this chapter where the topics of entering, editing and comptuing with lists are explained.

If lists are entered, press $\boxed{\text{OPTN}}$ and $\boxed{\text{F1 : LIST}}$ to activate the *LIST* commands.   Basic arithmetic operations may be performed using lists. For example, to add **List 1** to **List 2** simply press $\boxed{\text{F1 : LIST}}$ 1 $\boxed{+}$ $\boxed{\text{F1 : LIST}}$ 2 $\boxed{\text{EXE}}$ If the lists being added have a different number of entries, a dim error will appear, since in order to perform arithmetic operations on lists, the dimensions must be the same.

Figure 6.11
List Menu

Figure 6.12
List More

Functional operations may be performed on lists while in the **Run Menu** . Press OPTN F1 : LIST . To take the natural log of the elements in **List 1,** press ln F1 : LIST 1 EXE . If values appear in the list which are not in the domain of the natural log function, "ma ERROR" is displayed.

Other List operations are performed in the **Run Menu** such as determining the dimension of a stored list, its minimum value, its maximum value, its mean and its median.

6.2.8   Computing with Matrices

To add, subtract and multiply matrices, the **Run Menu** must be used. After entering the **Run Menu,** press OPTN on the keyboard followed by F2 : MAT . If matrices have been entered into the locations A and B using the **Matrix Menu**, press F1 : Mat ALPHA x,θ,τ : A + F1 : Mat ALPHA log : B EXE to add the matrices. To find any other matrix property, always remember to insert the word

Figure 6.13
Matrix Menu

Figure 6.14
Matrix More

matrix first. For example to find the determinant of matrix while in the **Run Menu** under OPTN F2 : MAT , press F3 : Det F1 : Mat ALPHA x,θ,τ : A EXE .

6.2.9   Discovering Other Number Functions

Other number functions which are found in the ***Run Menu*** include absolute value, integer part of a number, fractional part of a number, random number and greatest integer.

To access the number features listed, press $\boxed{\text{OPTN}}$ on the keyboard, $\boxed{\text{F6} : \triangleright}$ and $\boxed{\text{F4} : \text{NUM}}$. The number concepts are shown as a soft menu. While arrowing through the soft menus for $\boxed{\text{OPTN}}$, other menu items observed which have not been addressed at this time include CALC, STAT, COLR, HYP, PROB, ANGL, ESYM, PICT, FMEM, and LOGIC. Menus which have not been adddressed, but which relate to topics in this manual, will be presented in later sections.

6.3_____   Graphs

6.3.1   Graphing in the Run Menu

Graphs can be sketched in the ***Run Menu*** in the same way graphs were sketched on the first Casio Graphing Calculator produced. It is not as an efficient way to draw graphs, but it can allow the user to stay in the same menu when working with computation.

To draw the graph of $y = x^2$ while in the ***Run Menu,*** press $\boxed{\text{SHIFT}}$ $\boxed{\text{F4} : \text{Sketch}}$ $\boxed{\text{F5} : \text{GRPH}}$ $\boxed{\text{F1} : \text{Y} =}$ $\boxed{\text{x}, \theta, \tau}$ $\boxed{\text{x}^2}$. To set the Viewing Window before drawing the graph, $\boxed{\text{SHIFT}}$ $\boxed{\text{F3} : \text{V-Window}}$ $\boxed{\text{F3} : \text{STD}}$ $\boxed{\text{EXE}}$ $\boxed{\text{EXE}}$. (Note: The first execute returns to the screen where the function was entered, the second execute draws the graph .)

It is important to remember that when graphing in the ***Run Menu***, $\boxed{\text{F1} : \text{Cl s}}$ must be pressed each time a graph is sketched unless the previous graph is also needed. Otherwise, all previous graphs will appear on the same graph screen as the one presently being sketched. The previous graphs can also be erased by changing the viewing window.

6.3.2   Using the Graph Stack

The graph stack is activated by pressing the number 5 on the *Main Menu* screen or by highlighting the fifth square of the menu and pressing $\boxed{\text{EXE}}$. There are twenty possible entries of graphs on the stack. When using the graph stack, the "function mode" of the highlighted graph is given at the top of the screen.

A graph in any mode, (rectangular, polar or parametric) and inequality graphs may be entered on the same stack. After entering the functions on the stack, the different modes may be sketched on the same screen or they may be chosen to be sketched alone.

Remember, when changing to a new function mode, the change must be made on a blank line. The mode of the function to be entered on a line cannot be changed when the line is not empty.

●**Entering Equations and Inequalities on the Stack**
To illustrate the versitility of the Casio 9850 graph stack, the following functions will be entered and sketched in various combinations:

(1) $y = x(x - 1)(x + 1)$ (2) $y = \sin 2x$

(3) $r = \sin 2\theta$ (4) $\begin{cases} xt = t^2 \\ yt = t \end{cases}$

(5) $y \geq |x + 1| - 3$ (6) $y \leq -|x + 1| + 3$

(7) $y = [x]$ (8) $y = \text{intg}(x)$

Before entering the given equations, delete any previous functions from the stack by highlighting the function to be deleted, and press $\boxed{\text{F2 : DEL}}$ and $\boxed{\text{F1: YES}}$.

The first equation to be entered is **rectangular**. Therefore, press $\boxed{\text{F3 : TYPE}}$ $\boxed{\text{F1 : Y =}}$. Then, to enter the first equation press $\boxed{\text{x, 0,τ}}$ $\boxed{(}$ $\boxed{\text{x,0,τ}}$ $\boxed{-}$ 1 $\boxed{)}$ $\boxed{(}$ $\boxed{\text{x,θ,τ}}$ $\boxed{+}$ 1 $\boxed{)}$ $\boxed{\text{EXE}}$. (The execute command, at the end of the key strokes, places the equation on the stack and highlights the next position on the stack.) If an error is made while entering a function, press the **right replay arrow** with the position to be corrected highlighted. The equation line will be reactivated to allow the correction to be made.

In the second position, enter the next rectangular equation with the key strokes $\boxed{\text{sin}}$ 2 $\boxed{\text{x, θ, τ}}$ $\boxed{\text{EXE}}$.

• Changing Graph Types on the Stack
The next equation to be entered is a **polar equation**. Since it is not the same as the rectangular equations entered in Y1 and Y2, the **Graph Type** must be changed before entering it on the stack. While the highlight is on the empty position, Y3, press $\boxed{\text{F3 : TYPE}}$ $\boxed{\text{F2 : r =}}$ $\boxed{\text{s i n}}$ 2 $\boxed{\text{x,θ,τ}}$ $\boxed{\text{EXE}}$.

Equation four is given in the form of **parametric equations**. To enter the set of parametric equations, the **Graph Type** must be changed again. Highlight $\boxed{\text{F3 : TYPE}}$ $\boxed{\text{F3 : Parm}}$.

Observe that all locations from position four and higher have both xt and yt; i.e., on entry 4, both xt4 and yt4 are found. Next to xt4 enter $\boxed{\text{x,θ,τ}}$ $\boxed{x^2}$ $\boxed{\text{EXE}}$ and next to yt4 enter $\boxed{\text{x,θ,τ}}$ $\boxed{\text{EXE}}$.

Figure 6.15
Graph Stack

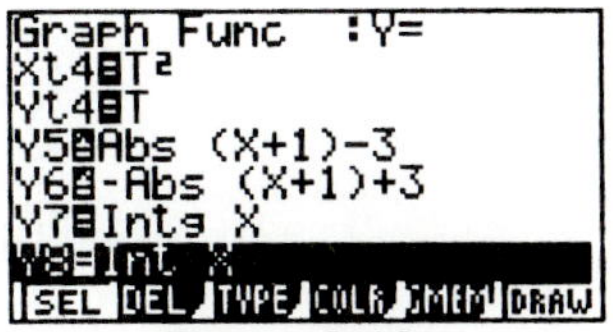

Figure 6.16
Multiple Graph Types

An **inequality** expression is to be entered next, requiring once again that the **Graph Type** must be changed. Highlight the next empty position represented at this point by xt5. Press $\boxed{\text{F3 : TYPE}}$ $\boxed{\text{F6 : } \triangleright}$ $\boxed{\text{F3 : } \geq}$. To access absolute value, press $\boxed{\text{OPTN}}$ $\boxed{\text{F5 : NUM}}$ $\boxed{\text{F1 : Abs}}$. Continue to enter the expression by pressing $\boxed{(}$ $\boxed{\text{x,}\theta,\tau}$ $\boxed{+}$ 1 $\boxed{)}$ $\boxed{-}$ 3 $\boxed{\text{EXE}}$. The inequality expression number (6) may now be entered without changing the type, and by following essentially the same instructions for the number (5) inequality. Be careful, however, to put the minus (-) sign in front of the absolute value symbol and use F4 for $\leq$ instead of F3.

To enter the last two equations the **Graph Type** must be returned to **rectangular.** Once again, this is accomplished by highlighting the first empty position, Y7, and pressing $\boxed{\text{F3 : TYPE}}$ $\boxed{\text{F1 : Y=}}$. The following key strokes will enter graphs (7) and (8). Press $\boxed{\text{OPTN}}$ $\boxed{\text{F5 : NUM}}$ $\boxed{\text{F2 : Int}}$ $\boxed{\text{x,}\theta,\tau}$ $\boxed{\text{EXE}}$; $\boxed{\text{OPTN}}$ $\boxed{\text{F5 : NUM}}$ $\boxed{\text{F5 : Intg}}$ $\boxed{\text{x,}\theta,\tau}$ $\boxed{\text{EXE}}$.

•Selecting a Function's Color

Suppose the graphs of y = sin 2x and   r = sin 2θ are to be drawn on the same viewing screen window. In order to visualize the difference between the two graphs, it is decided that the rectangular graph will be sketched in blue, but the polar graph will be sketched in orange.

Use the **replay arrows** to highlight Y2. To select a color for the highlighted graph, press $\boxed{\text{F4 : COLR}}$ and choose $\boxed{\text{F1 : Blue}}$. Move the highlight down to r3 and press $\boxed{\text{F2 : Orng}}$. While changing colors, highlight Y7 and change it to green $\boxed{\text{F3 : Grn}}$, then highlight Y8 and choose orange $\boxed{\text{F2 : Orng}}$.

•Selecting a Function to be Sketched

Now that all of the functions have been entered on the stack, and colors selected, the equations and inequalities may be chosen to be sketched when needed. Observe that when a function is entered on the stack, there is a colored square over the equals sign opposite the highlight; i.e., if the equation is highlighed, the square over the equations is clear; if the equation is not highlighted, the square over the equals **is** highlighted. If the square over the equals is the opposite of the highlighted equation then that equation has been selected to be sketched. If the square over the equals is the same shading as the highlighted graph's shading then the function will not be drawn. Press EXIT until no change is being made on the screen. The stack should be on the screen and the soft menu above F1 should be SEL . This key acts as a toggle to turn the graphs on and off.

Use the **replay arrows** and highlight Y1. Turn this function off by pressing F1 : SEL . Repeat for all functions except Y5 and Y6. If all lines on the stack are turned off except the two inequalities, press F6 : DRAW .

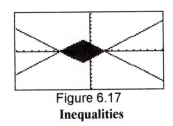

Figure 6.17
Inequalities

6.3.3 Using the Soft Menu Keys

The graph just drawn should look similar to the illustration. If this is not the case the graph's viewing window may be set differently.

•V-Window

To set the viewing window, press SHIFT F3 : V-Window if the graph is not visible. If the graph is visible, the same result will occur by simply pressing the function key F3 . The window can now be put to any desired setting. The soft menu keys provide three pre-set screens. The INIT or initialized window is based on the spacing of the pixels on the Casio calculator, TRIG provides a standard window for most trigonometry functions, and STD provides a standard viewing window used on most calculators for algebraic functions. If another window is needed, a custom viewing window can be entered by the user.

To enter a user defined viewing window, enter each number followed by EXE . The minus used is not significant in the viewing window format. It should also be noted that the only function of scale is to put "tick" marks on the graph screen to indicate divisions.

The V-window screen is activited with the rectangular graph's settings. To observe the settings for polar and additional settings needed for parametric equations, arrow down to the next screen. On this extension of the V-window screen, "min" and "max" refer to the values of θ and T, pitch indicates the point change. For example, if 0.5 was entered for pitch in the radian mode, the calculator would plot one point (or pixel) every 0.5 radian.

Set the V-Window to $\boxed{\text{STD}}$, $\boxed{\text{EXIT}}$ and press $\boxed{\text{F6 : DRAW}}$. $\boxed{\text{EXIT}}$ and use $\boxed{\text{F1 : SEL}}$ to unselect Y5 and Y6. Select Y1 and press $\boxed{\text{F6 : DRAW}}$.

•Trace

With the Y1 function drawn on the screen, activate the trace feature by pressing $\boxed{\text{F1}}$. The shift key only needs to be used when the graph screen is not showing.

On the graph screen, the equation of the drawn function is displayed at the top of the screen, and the x and y coordinates of the cursor location are shown at the bottom of the screen while the trace feature is on. Use the **right replay arrow** to move the cursor into view and observe the location indicated. Remember, the trace only addresses the pixels on the screen; therefore, false information could be obtained if looking for particular features of the graph.

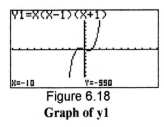

Figure 6.18
Graph of y1

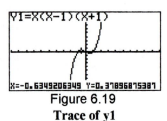

Figure 6.19
Trace of y1

•Zoom

Activate the **Zoom** feature by pressing $\boxed{\text{F2}}$. Five soft menus appear at the bottom of the screen with an arrow over $\boxed{\text{F6}}$ indicating there is more to the menu. Press $\boxed{\text{F6}}$ and press it again. It is seen that there are two complete soft menu lists for **Zoom** .

Observe, in particular $\boxed{\text{F1 : BOX}}$ and $\boxed{\text{F5 : AUTO}}$ on the first menu set and $\boxed{\text{F1 : ORG}}$, $\boxed{\text{F2 : SQR}}$, and $\boxed{\text{F5 : PRE}}$ on the second menu set. $\boxed{\text{F5 : AUTO}}$ sets the V-window to a zoom screen determined by the calculator $\boxed{\text{F1 : ORG}}$ puts the

V-window to the orginal screen settings used to sketch the graph, and $\boxed{\text{F5 : PRE}}$
returns the V-window to the setting most recently used (that is, its previous setting).
$\boxed{\text{F2 : SQR}}$ is useful to make graphs such as circles, look like circles. This command
allows the "squaring" of the V-Window. Finally $\boxed{\text{F1 : BOX}}$ allows the user to define
exactly the region to be enlarged.

     To isolate a region using the box command, press $\boxed{\text{F1 : BOX}}$ with the graph
of Y1 on the screen. When this command is activated, the cursor is initially placed at
the origin (0,0). Using the **replay arrows,** move the cursor approximately to the point
(2,3). Press $\boxed{\text{EXE}}$ to fix one corner of the box. Observe that the cursor has changed to
a fixed "+". Arrow down and left to approximately (-2,-3). Notice that as the cursor
moves, a box is formed. Press $\boxed{\text{EXE}}$ to zoom in on this region.

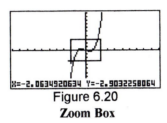

Figure 6.20
Zoom Box

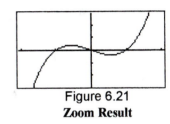

Figure 6.21
Zoom Result

•Sketch
     While in the *Graph Menu*, the soft menu key $\boxed{\text{F4 : Sketch}}$ can be used to draw
the inverse of a function as well vertical and horizontal lines. The commands are also
found in this soft menu for drawing a circle, the tanget line to a curve and the normal
line to a curve.

•G-Solv
     The graph of Y1 should be on the screen with a V-Window of approximately
x-min = -2 to x-max = 2 and a scale of 1 due to using the Zoom Feature. Enter the
function "y = x" on the stack in the Y9 location and press $\boxed{\text{F6 : DRAW}}$ to overlay its
graph over Y1.

     Press $\boxed{\text{F5 : G-Solv}}$. To illustrate the features of Graph Solve, press
$\boxed{\text{F1 : ROOT}}$. The cursor will appear at the far left corner of the screen, and the
equation of the function which the cursor is on will be displayed at the top of the
screen. Press $\boxed{\text{EXE}}$ to activate the cursor; it will stop on the first root x = -1.

Now press the **right replay arrow** and the cursor will move to the   next   root x = 0;
press the **right replay arrow** again to get to the last root x = 1.

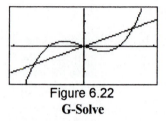
Figure 6.22
G-Solve

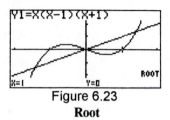
Figure 6.23
Root

Press $\boxed{\text{F5 : G-Solv}}$ for the soft menu choices to return to the screen. $\boxed{\text{F2 : MAX}}$ places
the cursor on the maximum value of the function and $\boxed{\text{F3 : MIN}}$ places it on the
minimum value of the function. $\boxed{\text{F3 : Y-ICPT}}$ moves the cursor to the functions
y-intercept.

Press $\boxed{\text{F5 : ISCT}}$. The cursor automatically advances to the first point of
intersection of the two graphs and the equations of the two graphs being used are once
again displayed at the top of the screen. To move to the next intersection point, the
right relay arrow must be pressed. Continue to press the **replay arrows** to see the
value of each intersection. Press $\boxed{\text{F5 : G-Solv}}$ to return to the G-Solve menu screen.

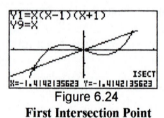
Figure 6.24
First Intersection Point

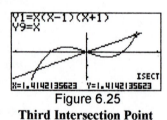
Figure 6.25
Third Intersection Point

Press $\boxed{\text{F6 : }\triangleright}$ followed by $\boxed{\text{F1 : Y-CAL}}$ $\boxed{\text{EXE}}$. The equation of the function
being used is displayed at the top and before pressing $\boxed{\text{EXE}}$, "x=" is   displayed   on
the lower left corner of the screen after pressing $\boxed{\text{EXE}}$.   Enter any value for x, say
3, and press $\boxed{\text{EXE}}$. The displayed words, "Not Found", mean that the the value of x
chosen is not on the viewing screen. Return to the soft menu screen by pressing
$\boxed{\text{F5 : G-Solv}}$ $\boxed{\text{F6 : }\triangleright}$ $\boxed{\text{F1 : Y-CAL}}$ $\boxed{\text{EXE}}$. Now enter 1.5 for x.   The answer of
1.875 is displayed. $\boxed{\text{F2 : X-CAL}}$ evaluates the value for x when y is the input.

•G ↔T

$\boxed{\text{F6 : G} \leftrightarrow \text{T}}$ allows the user to toggle between the text (graph stack) and the graph screen.

6.3.4   Using Color to Distinguish Graphs

The greatest integer function and the function obtained by using the integer part of the number can not be easily separated if both are drawn on the same screen in the same color. Select Y7 and y8 and unselect y1 and y9. In the section on changing a graph's color, Y7 was given the color of green, and y8 was given the color of orange. Since both Y7 and Y8 are piecewise functions, change the Graph Set Up to Plot. To do this press $\boxed{\text{SHIFT}}$ $\boxed{\text{MENU : SET UP}}$ while in the *Graph Menu*. With **Draw Type** highlighted, press $\boxed{\text{F2 : P l o t}}$ $\boxed{\text{EXIT}}$. Change the V-Window to $\boxed{\text{F3 : STD}}$ and draw the graphs.

Now select Y2 and Y3, unselect Y7 and Y8, change the V-Window to $\boxed{\text{F2 : TRIG}}$, and the **Graph Set Up** back to connected. Y2 should be drawn in blue and Y3 in orange. Draw the graphs. Now draw the same graph by pressing and using $\boxed{\text{F2 : Z o o m}}$ on the $\boxed{\text{F2 : SQR}}$ set of soft menu commands. It can be seen in both cases that color allows the two graphs to be visually separated from one another on the screen, but different view screens also allow for a better graph.

6.3.5   Using the Dual Screen with Graphs

The Sketch command accessed by the soft menu key $\boxed{\text{F4}}$ is one way to sketch the inverse of a function. Another way is to use parametric equations. Unselect all functions previously sketched. Replace the function in Y1 with $y = x^2$. To do this, activiate the graph stack and highlight Y1. Press $\boxed{\text{x,θ,τ}}$ $\boxed{x^2}$ $\boxed{\text{EXE}}$. The new function will replace the previous. Draw this function on $\boxed{\text{F1: INIT}}$ under the V-Window menu.

Press $\boxed{\text{SHIFT}}$ $\boxed{\text{MENU : SET UP}}$. Highlight Dual Screen on the Set Up menu. Press $\boxed{\text{F1 : G r p h}}$. The dual screen has been activated to be used with graphs. Another choice is to use a table with the graph. $\boxed{\text{EXIT}}$ and $\boxed{\text{F6 : DRAW}}$. Press $\boxed{\text{OPTN}}$ to see the options available. When graphing, the left screen is active while the right screen is passive. At any time the viewing scale can be changed by selecting $\boxed{\text{F3 : V-W i n d o w}}$ and selecting either right or left.

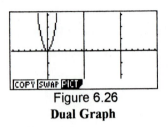
Figure 6.26
Dual Graph

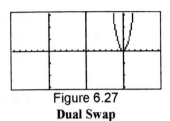
Figure 6.27
Dual Swap

Press $\boxed{\text{F2 : SWAP}}$ to move the drawn function to the passive screen. $\boxed{\text{EXIT}}$ to return to the graph stack and select the parametric equation in position 4.   Press $\boxed{\text{F3 : V-W I n d o w}}$ and press $\boxed{\text{F3 : STD}}$. Press $\boxed{\text{EXIT}}$ $\boxed{\text{F6 : DRAW}}$. Note that only a part of graph 4 was drawn. To correct this, return to $\boxed{\text{F3 : V-W I n d o w}}$. The range data is given for the left screen. Arrow down to the second screen of the range.

Observe that 'T' is starting at zero which does not allow for negative values. Enter the number -5 for the min of T and 5 for the max of T, then return to draw. by pressing $\boxed{\text{EXIT}}$ $\boxed{\text{F6 : DRAW}}$.

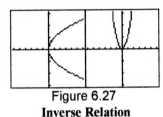
Figure 6.27
Inverse Relation

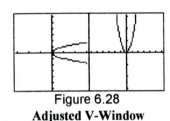
Figure 6.28
Adjusted V-Window

To get the left side to look more like the inverse relation of the right   side, switch the x and y min and x and y max on the left side V-Window.

Try using one of the zoom commands while in split window. The original function will stay on the left, the zoomed part of the function will appear on the right. All functions available to the calculator are also available on the active side of the screen. The G $\leftrightarrow$ T key, however, in split screen acts as a 3-way toggle. It will enlarge the left side to full screen, the right side to full screen and will return to the screen to the graph stack

Before leaving this section, return to SET UP and turn off Dual Screen.

6.3.6   Exploring the Dynamic Graphing Mode

Return to the menu by pressing $\boxed{\text{EXIT}}$ until the calculator no longer responds, then press $\boxed{\text{MENU}}$.   Activate menu number 6, ***Dyna Menu***. This is the menu known as the dynamic graphing menu. Observe that all the graphs entered on the graph stack are available in this menu. Unselect any graphs that may have been selected. Arrow to function line Y10.   If the type is not rectangular, make this change.   Enter $Y10 = A(x + B)^2 + C$ using the alpha keys to enter A, B, and C and using the $\boxed{x, \theta, \tau}$ key for x. Press $\boxed{\text{EXE}}$ to put this equation on the stack.

The purpose of the dynamic grapher is to observe the change a function makes when the value of a variable changes. Press $\boxed{\text{F4 : VAR}}$ and select the variable B by highlighting the B and pressing $\boxed{\text{F1 : SEL}}$. By selecting B the horizontal movement of the graph will be observed. Enter constant values for A and C on this screen. Let A = 1 and C = 2. Enter one number followed by the execute key then arrow down to the next value to be entered. Enter the number and press $\boxed{\text{EXE}}$. [Note: It is not necessary to enter a value for the variable which is varying.]

Figure 6.29
Dynamic Equation

Figure 6.30
Dynamic Variable

Press $\boxed{\text{F2 : RANG}}$ to set the range of movement. Enter -5 for the start and 5 for the end. Set the pitch at 1. (This means that the graph will move from -5 to 5 every integer unit.) $\boxed{\text{EXIT}}$ and press $\boxed{\text{F3 : SPEED}}$. Stop and Go allows the user to look at the position and press the execute key to move the graph to each new position. Select normal speed by highlighting normal and pressing $\boxed{\text{EXE}}$.

Finally, press $\boxed{\text{F6 : DYNA}}$ to see the movement of the graph. The calculator dispays a "time line" while it is preparing the graph.

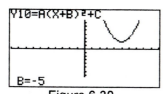

Figure 6.30
Position when B = -5

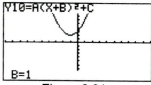

Figure 6.31
Position when B = -1

To stop the graph, press $\boxed{\text{AC/}^{\text{ON}}}$. This command will return the view screen to a menu where the speed can be changed. To return to the original screen, press $\boxed{\text{EXIT}}$. Be careful, however, the variable to be changed has reverted back to A and must be selected again. $\boxed{\text{EXIT}}$ to return to the graph stack. $\boxed{\text{F5 : B-IN}}$ activates

6.4_____   Tables and Lists

In the previous section on exploring graphs, the Split Screen Feature was introduced to be used with graphs. In this section the use of the Split Screen with tables will be explored.

6.4.1   Creating Tables

Tables may be created by using *Table Menu* or created from the pixels on a graph while in the **Dual Screen** feature of the *Graph Menu.*

•Using the Table Menu

Return the calculator's screen to show the *Main Menu.* Activate menu item number 7, **Table,** on the *Main Menu*. The graph stack is once again displayed with all equations present from previous use. This allows the user to work in several modes and do many operations with the same functions. Since the graph stack is getting cluttered with previous operations, delete all functions.   This will allow this section to be presented with a "clean slate."

Enter the following rectanglar functions on the stack:

$$Y1 = x\,(x + 1)\,(x - 1) \qquad Y2 = x^2 - 3x + 4 \qquad Y3 = x$$

Press $\boxed{\text{F5 : RANG}}$ to set the parameters of the table. Enter the starting value of x at -5 and the ending value at 5. The pitch indcates how often a value in the table is needed; change this value to 0.5. $\boxed{\text{EXIT}}$ to return to the soft menu screen and press $\boxed{\text{F6 : TABL}}$ to obtain a table of values for each of the selected functions.

Arrow up and down the x-values of the functions and compare the three. Are there any values where all y-values are the same? Are there any values where one of the functions becomes zero?   Where do the values change from positive to negative? Observe that Y2 never crosses the x-axis. (Function values are always positive.)   Are there any other significant similarities or differences among the three functions?

Tables allow a visual study of a function without sketching its graph. However, if the graph of the function is also required, simply press either $\boxed{\text{F5 : G-CON}}$ or $\boxed{\text{F6 : G-PLT}}$ for graph connected or graph plot respectively.

•Using the Dual Screen

Return to *Graph Menu* and press $\boxed{\text{SHIFT}}$ $\boxed{\text{MENU : SET UP}}$. Highlight **Dual Screen** and press $\boxed{\text{F2 : G to T}}$. This activates the Dual Screen Mode to be used to create tables from graphs.

$\boxed{\text{EXIT}}$ and press $\boxed{\text{F6 : DRAW}}$. Press $\boxed{\text{F1 : Trace}}$. Arrow until a desired x-value is reached. Press $\boxed{\text{EXE}}$. This will record the y-value for every function on the screen to the table even though only Y1 is visible on the Dual Screen.

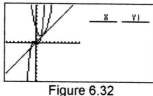

Figure 6.32
G↔T Dual Screen

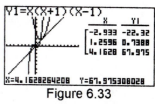

Figure 6.33
Graph to Table

The G-Solve features can be used in Dual Screen; therefore an intersection can be found and recorded in the table. To see the table of values for all three functions, press $\boxed{\text{OPTN}}$ $\boxed{\text{F1 : CHG}}$ $\boxed{\text{F6 : G↔T}}$ $\boxed{\text{F6 : G↔T}}$ allowing the entire table to be seen.

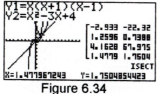

Figure 6.34
Intersection to Table

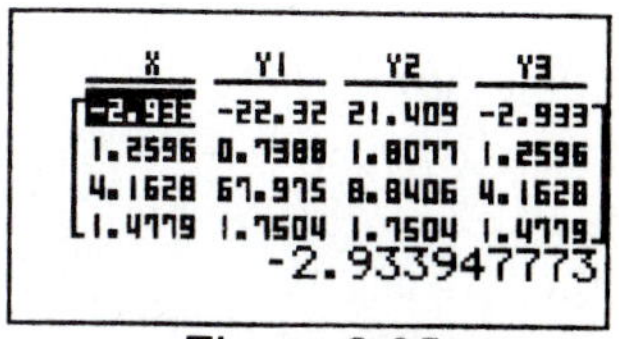

Figure 6.35
Table of All Functions

6.4.2   Creating Lists

To create a list, return to the *Main Menu* and activate menu item number 4, *List Menu*. Lists may be created in several ways. For example, a list may be created from a stored function, from a sequence or by simply entering the data. There are 6 columns in which to enter lists.   Before a list may be stored from another function of the calculator, the List column must be empty.   Delete any lists previously in the calculator by pressing   F4 : DEL~ A   F1 : YES .

To enter a list from a stored function, press MENU and the number 7 to enter the *Table Menu.* The three functions previously used should still be on the stack. Press F6 : TABL to activate the table generated by the functions.   Restructure the table for integer values of x from 1 to 10 by pressing EXIT   F5 : RANG .   Change the start value to 1, end value to 10, and pitch to 1.   EXIT   F6: TABL .   The table is now in integer increments from 1 to 10. Highlight any number under Y1 and press   OPTN . Press   F1 : LIST   F2 : LMEM   F1 : LIst1 . The function values for Y1 are now stored in List 1.   Repeat the procedure for Y2 and Y3 to store them in List 2 and List 3, respectively.   That is, highlight a value under Y2, press   F2 : LMEM   F2 : List2   ; highlight a value under Y3, press   F2 : LMEM   F3 : List3   .   To verify that the functions are stored in the required lists, return to the *Main Menu* and activate the *List Menu.*

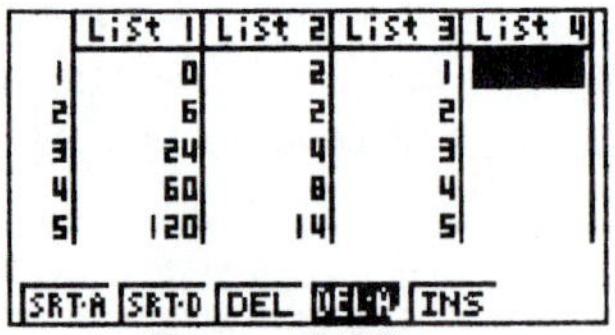

Figure 6.36
Stored Lists

Figure 6.37
Operations with Lists

Lists can also be created from sequence functions. Return to the *Main Menu* and activate the *Recurrsion Menu* (number 8).   To store the arithmetic sequence with $a_1 = 2$ and a common difference of 3 in List 4, press   F3 : TYPE   F1 : a$_n$ and enter 2   +   3   (F4 : n   –   1   )   EXE .   Press F5 : RANG and set the start at 1 and the end at 10.   EXE   F6: TABL .   To store the result in List 4, press   OPTN   F1 : LIST . Highlight a number under a$_n$ and press F2 : LMEM   F4 : LIst4 .

Experiment by putting other sequences into Lists and by just entering the elements of a desired list.   Then return to the *Run Menu* and work with the lists as described in section 1 of this chapter.

6.5_____ Equations and Systems of Equations

Equations were solved when the soft menu keys were introduced under the *Graph Menu.* For example, the function y = x (x + 1) (x − 1) was entered on the graph stack and its roots were found using $\boxed{\text{F5 : G-S o l v}}$. The equation was further studied using the trace function and zoom features.

6.5.1   Using the Equation Menu

The equation y = x (x + 1)(x − 1) can also be solved by using the *Equa Menu.* Activate this menu by pressing highlighting menu A on the *Main Menu* screen and pressing $\boxed{\text{EXE}}$. Press $\boxed{\text{F2 : POLY}}$ for the polynomial choice, followed by $\boxed{\text{F2}}$ for a third degree equation. The equation needs to be rewritten as y = x ^{3} − x in order to enter the cooefficients into the data form. On the data matrix enter 1 $\boxed{\text{EXE}}$ 0 $\boxed{\text{EXE}}$ $\boxed{\text{(-)}}$ 1 $\boxed{\text{EXE}}$ 0 $\boxed{\text{EXE}}$. Press $\boxed{\text{F1 : SOLV}}$. The answer immediately appears on the screen.

To solve a system of equations using this menu, $\boxed{\text{EXIT}}$ until the choice screen is reached. This time press $\boxed{\text{F1 : SIML}}$. Press $\boxed{\text{F2}}$ to indicate that there will be three equations. The following system will be used to demonstrate this menu.

$$\begin{cases} x + y + 2z = 1 \\ x + y + z = 2 \\ 2x - y + z = 5 \end{cases}$$

Enter the coefficients and constants of the first equation across the top, then the same values for the second and finally the third equation. Thus, enter 1 $\boxed{\text{EXE}}$ 1 $\boxed{\text{EXE}}$ 2 $\boxed{\text{EXE}}$ 1 $\boxed{\text{EXE}}$; 1 $\boxed{\text{EXE}}$ 1 $\boxed{\text{EXE}}$ 1 $\boxed{\text{EXE}}$ 2 $\boxed{\text{EXE}}$; 2 $\boxed{\text{EXE}}$ $\boxed{\text{(-)}}$ 1 $\boxed{\text{EXE}}$ 1 $\boxed{\text{EXE}}$ 5 $\boxed{\text{EXE}}$. Press $\boxed{\text{F1 : SOLV}}$ to see the result of (3,0,1). $\boxed{\text{EXIT}}$ three times and press $\boxed{\text{MENU}}$.

6.5.2   Using Matrices to Solve Systems

•Using the Inverse of a Matrix

Systems of two equations in two unknowns can be solved using G-Solv and ISECT . However, the three equation system previously solved can not be solved on this calculator by graphs. With the *Main Menu* on the screen, activate **MAT**, item number 3.

A list of matrix locations appear. With location A highlighted type 3 EXE 3 EXE to enter a dimension of 3 x 3 for matrix A. Enter the coefficients of the variables as in the previous example, without entering the constants. That is, 1 EXE 1 EXE 2 EXE ; 1 EXE 1 EXE 1 EXE ; 2 EXE (-) 1 EXE 1 EXE 1 EXE . EXIT to return to the matrix list. Highlight location B and type 3 EXE 1 EXE , then enter the constants in the column matrix displayed. 1 EXE 2 EXE 5 EXE .

Activate the *Run Menu* and press OPTN . Press F2 : MAT F1 : Mat ALPHA x,θ,τ : A SHIFT) : x⁻¹ EXE . This result is the inverse of matrix A. Store this matrix in location C by pressing F1 : Mat SHIFT (-) : Ans → F1 : Mat ALPHA In : C EXE .

To find the solution, simply multipliy the inverse of A (Matrix C) times the Constant Matrix. That is press F1 : Mat ALPHA In :C × F1 : Mat ALPHA log : B EXE . The same result of (3,0,1) is displayed.

•Using Elementary Row Operations

Activate the *Matrix Menu.* Display the matrix stored in location A by pressing EXE when it is highlighted. Highlight any number in column 3 and press F3 : COL F3 : ADD . This will add a 4th column to the columns of matrix A. Enter the constants of the system in this new column. Matrix A should now look like the first matrix displayed in the Figure 6.38 on the next page.

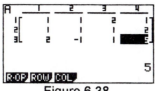

Figure 6.38
Matrix Entries

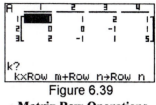

Figure 6.39
Matrix Row Operations

Press EXIT F1 : R-OP to activate the row operations commands. Press F3 : XR w + . The command is to multiply a row by a real number and add the result to another row. The object is to get 1's in the a_{ii} positions and 0's everywhere else. Enter (-) 1 EXE 1 EXE 2 EXE . (That is, multiply 1 times row 1 and add it to row 2). The result is immediate. Press F3 again and enter (-) 2 EXE 1 EXE 3 EXE . (Multiply -2 times row 1 and add the result to row 3). Press F1 : S w a p . Press 2 EXE 3 EXE to swap rows 2 and 3. Press F2 : XR o w . Enter (-) 1 a b / c 3 EXE 2 EXE to multiply row 2 by -1/3. Press F3 : XR w + . Enter (-) 1 EXE 2 EXE 1 EXE .

Moving to the third column, press F4 : R w + . Enter 3 EXE 1 EXE . (This adds row three to row 1). Press F4 again and enter 3 EXE 2 EXE . Finally press F2 one more time and enter (-) 1 EXE 3 EXE . The same answer is present once again this time in column four of the matrix.

Part II

Chapter 1

Overview of Part 2

1.1 Introduction

This part of the manual gives step-by-step instructions to acquaint you with early generations of graphing calculators. Some of the earliest graphing calculators are not covered in this manual. Consult your *Owner's Manual* for a more complete description of your specific graphing calculator and its features.

Refer to this manual when you encounter mathematics that requires unfamiliar aspects of your calculator. The power of the graphing calculator will be what you make it. Many students, with play, thought, and practice, have found it extremely powerful!

1.2 Objectives of Calculator Based Graphing

A calculator drawn graph is accurate and easy to obtain. Calculator drawn graphs can be used as tools to solve equations and enhance the teaching, learning, and understanding of mathematics. Listed below are several important objectives for a graphing calculator approach to learning mathematics.

> THROUGH THE SPEED AND POWER OF CALCULATORS,
> YOU CAN INVESTIGATE MANY EXAMPLES QUICKLY
> AND MAKE AND TEST GENERALIZATIONS
> BASED ON STRONG GRAPHICAL EVIDENCE

(1) To study the behavior of functions and relations including conic equations, parametric equations, and polar equations.

(2) To deepen understanding and intuition about a wide variety of functions and relations and to provide a foundation for the study of calculus, statistics, and higher mathematics.

(3) To graphically determine the number of solutions to equations and systems of equations. To solve equations, systems of equations, and inequalities graphically with accuracy equal to any numerical approximation method.

(4) To determine relative maximum and minimum values of functions graphically with accuracy equal to any numerical approximation method.

(5) To graphically investigate and determine the solution to "real world" problem situations that are normally not accessible to precalculus students.

(6) To provide geometric representations for problem situations and to analyze their connections with algebraic representations for the problem situations.

> COMPUTER GRAPHING IS A FAST AND EFFECTIVE TOOL THAT
> YOU CAN USE TO EXPLORE MATHEMATICS AND SOLVE PROBLEMS

1.3 Definitions

(1) Two other names for a graphing calculator are **graphing utility** and **grapher**. The three terms are used interchangeably in this manual.

(2) The **viewing rectangle** [L, R] by [B, T] (see Figure 1.1) is the rectangular portion of the coordinate plane determined by $L \leq x \leq R$ and $B \leq y \leq T$. The $[-10, 10]$ by $[-10, 10]$ viewing rectangle is called the **standard viewing rectangle**. We also use Xmin for L, Xmax for R, Ymin for B, and Ymax for T.

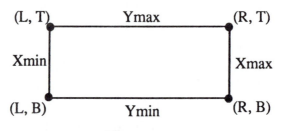

Figure 1.1

(3) **Zoom in** is a process of framing a small rectangular area within a given viewing rectangle, making it the new viewing rectangle, and then quickly replotting the graph in this new viewing rectangle. This feature permits the user to create a decreasing sequence of nested rectangles that "squeeze down" on a key point on a graph. Zoom-in is very useful for solving equations, inequalities, systems of equations and inequalities, and for determining maximum and minimum values of functions.

(4) **Zoom out** is a process of increasing the absolute value of the viewing rectangle parameters. It is important to be able to zoom out in *both* the horizontal and vertical directions at the same time, in *only* the horizontal direction, or in *only* the vertical direction. The zoom-out process is useful for examining limiting, end behavior of relations, and for determining "complete" graphs of relations.

(5) **A complete graph** is either the entire graph or a portion of a graph that shows all of the important behavior and features of the graph. For example, the graph of the relation $x^2 + y^2 = 16$ in $[-10, 10]$ by $[-10, 10]$ is complete because it is the entire graph of $x^2 + y^2 = 16$. The graph of $f(x) = x^3 - x + 15$ in $[-10, 10]$ by $[-10, 30]$ is a complete graph because we can see all of its local extremum values and real zeros. Of course, it is possible to create a function for which you cannot determine *one* viewing rectangle that gives a complete graph. Thus, several viewing rectangles may be needed to describe a complete graph.

(6) The **error** in using a particular point (x, y) in the viewing rectangle $[L, R]$ by $[B, T]$ to approximate any other point (a, b) in the viewing rectangle is *at most* $R - L$ for x and $T - B$ for y. There are also better error bounds possible by using scale marks appearing in a viewing rectangle.

Chapter 2

Getting Started with Graphing Calculators

2.1 Introduction

Welcome to the frontiers of calculator technology! The purpose of Chapters 3–6 of this part of the manual is to acquaint you with features of older models of graphing calculators that are useful in a graphical approach to precalculus mathematics. There are many important features of each graphing calculator that are not covered at all. Consult the *Owner's Manual* for a more complete description of your specific graphing calculator and its features.

Graphing calculators are not just calculators; they are hand-held *computers*. There are three characteristics of these versatile machines that combine to make them worthy of the name computer:

(1) **Large screen display.** The screen of a graphing calculator is large enough to display both the input (problem to be done) and output (answer). If an answer doesn't make sense or if you've made a keying or other type of error, you can go back and change (edit) any part of the input and reexecute the problem. The screen can display information in tabular form so that a progression of values can be viewed and checked for patterns.

(2) **Interactive graphics.** You can create virtually any mathematical graph: functions, relations, and geometric figures. You can overlay graphs, change views, and get a coordinate readout of specific points of interest.

(3) **On-screen programming.** The programming language of graphing calculators is simple and easy to learn. Armed with a few fundamentals you can do a great deal. Programming is ideal for repeated calculations (table building, sequences, etc.) and repeated graphs (family of curves). The programs provided in this manual are designed to turn your graphing calculator into a powerful tool for exploring and solving a wide variety of mathematical problems.

The next five chapters provide some general information about using graphing calculators, explain how to do basic computation, discuss the basics of graphing, and offer some programming ideas to enhance your calculator's graphing capability. So get ready to explore the exciting new world of the hand-held graphics computer. The quickest way to learn about your graphing calculator is to *experiment*. Explore! Be curious! And always have your graphing calculator handy while reading the appropriate chapter of this manual.

2.2 Keys and Keying Sequences

In this manual, graphing calculator keys appear as boxes. So, for example, the addition key is represented by $\boxed{+}$. The first few pages of your calculator *Owner's Manual* will give a brief introduction to the keys on your specific calculator. You are urged to read it.

A **keying sequence** is always read from left to right. For example, when we write $\boxed{7}$ $\boxed{\div}$ $\boxed{4}$, you should press the three keys in exactly the order written: $\boxed{7}$ followed by $\boxed{\div}$ followed by $\boxed{4}$. Keying sequences for numbers are abbreviated. For instance, 9.31 is represented by $\boxed{9.31}$ rather than $\boxed{9}$ $\boxed{\bullet}$ $\boxed{3}$ $\boxed{1}$.

2.3 How a Graphing Calculator Draws the Graph of a Function

A graphing calculator draws the graph of a function in much the same manner that paper-and-pencil graphs are produced. It plots points of the form $(x, f(x))$. To plot a graph, a graphing calculator needs a function $y = f(x)$, a minimum input value (Xmin), and a maximum input value (Xmax). It uses the Xmin and Xmax values to obtain a large but finite set of input values (x) to substitute into the given function f to determine the output values ($f(x)$).

A graphing calculator typically tries to plot as many points as there are columns of pixels in its graphics window. Assume your graphing calculator has 96 columns of pixels (as is the case with the TI-81). We will denote the 96 x-values that the graphing calculator tries to substitute into f as $x_0, x_1, x_2, x_3, \ldots, x_i, \ldots, x_{95}$. The first x-value, x_0, always equals Xmin, and the last x-value, x_{95}, always equals Xmax. To determine the other 94 x-values, the graphing calculator first computes the difference between consecutive x's, that is, the change in x required to go from one x-value to the next. We denote this change in x by Δx, read "delta x" or "the change in x." The change in x is computed using the following formula:

$$\Delta x = \frac{\text{Xmax} - \text{Xmin}}{95} \qquad (1)$$

The set of x-values to be substituted into the function f is the following:

$$x_0 = \text{Xmin}, \quad x_1 = \text{Xmin} + \Delta x, \quad x_2 = \text{Xmin} + 2\Delta x, \quad x_3 = \text{Xmin} + 3\Delta x, \ldots,$$

$$x_i = \text{Xmin} + i\Delta x, \ldots, \quad x_{95} = \text{Xmin} + 95\Delta x = \text{Xmax}.$$

A graphing calculator computes a functional value $y_i = f(x_i)$ for each of these x_i beginning with x_0, and immediately plots the point (x_i, y_i) in the graphics window and may (depending on the calculator and mode) connect it to the preceding point, if any, by a line segment. If any one of these x-values causes the function f to be undefined *or yields a y-value that is off the screen*, the graphing calculator moves on to the next x-value and repeats the process.

2.4 The Discrete Nature of Graphing Calculators

Graphing calculators use a *finite* number of points to represent the graph of a function that usually consists of an *infinite* collection of points. When we look at a calculator generated graph, we see a representation that is only suggestive of the actual graph. It is impossible to plot *all* of the points belonging to the graph of most functions. Sometimes important behavior of a function is "hidden" from view unless the graph is magnified many times. There are many examples of hidden behavior in the Demana, Waits, and Clemens textbooks.

2.5 Error

Determining the size of Δx defined by (1) in Section 2.3 provides a mathematically sound and accurate **estimate** of the error in using a calculator-displayed x-value as a graphic solution to an equation. To determine the size of Δx, you can use a formula like (1), or simply pay close attention to which digits change in the x-coordinate readout, and by how much, as you *Trace* from point to point.

If you need to estimate the error in both the x- *and* y-coordinates of a point on the screen as a solution, then you need to know the number of y-values used by the calculator. Assume your graphing calculator has 64 rows of pixels (as in the case with the TI-81). The 64 y-values can be denoted by y_0, y_1, ..., y_{63}, where $y_0 = Y\min$ and $y_{63} = Y\max$. To determine the other 62 y-values, the graphing calculator first computes the difference between consecutive y's, that is, the change in y required to go from one y-value to the next. We denote this change by Δy, read "delta y" or "the change in y," and its value is given by the formula:

$$\Delta y = \frac{Y\max - Y\min}{63} \qquad (2)$$

Thus, we have the following representation for the y-values:

$y_0 = Y\min,\ y_1 = Y\min + \Delta y,\ y_2 = Y\min + 2\Delta y, \ldots, y_j = Y\min + j\Delta y, \ldots,$
$y_{63} = Y\min + 63\Delta y = Y\max.$

An accurate **estimate** of the error in using a given y-coordinate in a solution is Δy. The set of coordinates (x_i, y_j), where $x_i = X\min + i\Delta x$ and $y_j = Y\min + j\Delta y$, are the "screen coordinates" of points on the display of a graphing calculator.

If you use the *Trace* feature, the y-values displayed are actual functional values, not the "screen y-coordinates" y_j as defined in the previous paragraph. Their successive differences give approximations to the error in y, the function values. In actual examples, you will see that these successive differences can vary quite a bit as you trace across the screen. The differences also depend on the value of x as well as the error in the x-value.

2.6 Order of Operations

Most graphing calculators use a priority sequence similar to a standard algebraic hierarchy called AOS to determine the order of operations when performing computations. So, for example, it performs the operations of multiplication and division before those of addition and subtraction. Read your calculator *Owner's Manual* for the full details concerning order of operations on your specific calculator.

2.7 Using the "Scientific" Functions

Like any scientific calculator, graphing calculators have many useful built-in functions. But the order in which you press the keys on some graphing calculators differs from most traditional scientific calculators. Here are some examples to get you started using the scientific functions. Once you gain control of these functions, try exploring other keys on your own.

Powers and Roots. Clear your calculator's screen. Perform the following three computational examples. Figure 2.1 shows how these computations should appear on typical AOS graphing calculator screens. Refer to the figure as you proceed through the computations.

(1) Evaluate $\sqrt{81}$ by pressing $\boxed{\sqrt{}}$ $\boxed{81}$ $\boxed{\text{ENT}}$.

(2) Compute 5^2 by keying in $\boxed{5}$ $\boxed{x^2}$ $\boxed{\text{ENT}}$.

(3) Evaluate $(-5)^4$ using $\boxed{(}$ $\boxed{(-)}$ $\boxed{5}$ $\boxed{)}$ $\boxed{\wedge}$ $\boxed{4}$ $\boxed{\text{ENT}}$. Remember not to confuse the additive inverse, or "sign change," key $\boxed{(-)}$ with the subtraction operation key $\boxed{-}$. Also the exponentiation symbol $\boxed{\wedge}$ is $\boxed{x^y}$ on some calculators.

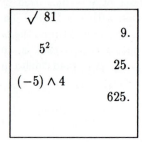

Figure 2.1. Powers and roots on the TI-81.

Chapter 3

The TI-81 Graphing Calculator

The TI-81 is a second generation graphing calculator. It is unique in its user friendly yet powerful functionality. The keys of the TI-81 are grouped by color and physical layout to allow easy location of the key you need. The keys are divided into four zones: graphing keys, editing keys, advanced function keys, and scientific calculator keys (see Figure 3.1). We will describe the keys by rows.

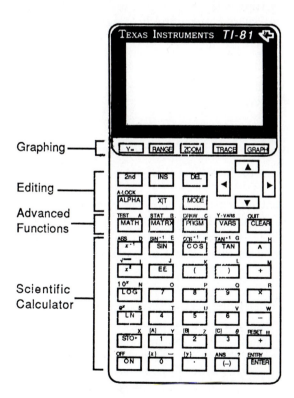

Figure 3.1

(1)   The **Graphing Keys** (first row) are most frequently used to access the interactive graphing features of the TI-81.

(2)   The **Editing Keys** (second and third row) are mostly used for editing expressions and values.

(3)   The **Advanced Function Keys** (fourth row) are used to access the advanced functions of the TI-81 through full-screen menus.

(4)   The **Scientific Calculator Keys** (the fifth and remaining rows) are used to access the capabilities of a standard scientific calculator.

3.1   Getting Started on the TI-81

3.1.1   Setting the Display Contrast: Turn the TI-81 on by pressing $\boxed{\text{ON}}$. The brightness and contrast of the display depend on room lighting, battery freshness, viewing angle, and adjustment of the display contrast. The contrast setting is retained in memory when the TI-81 is turned off. You can adjust the display contrast to suit your viewing angle and lighting conditions at any time. As you change the contrast setting, the display contrast changes, and a number in the upper right corner between 0(lightest) and 9(darkest) indicates the current contrast setting.

   To adjust the contrast:

(1)   Press and release the $\boxed{\text{2nd}}$ key.

(2)   Use one of two keys:

   •   To increase the contrast to the setting that you want, press *and hold* $\boxed{\triangle}$.

   •   To decrease the contrast to the setting that you want, press *and hold* $\boxed{\triangledown}$.

Caution   If you adjust the contrast setting to zero, the display may become completely blank. If this happens, press $\boxed{\text{2nd}}$ and then press and hold $\boxed{\triangle}$ until the display reappears. When the batteries are low, the display begins to dim (especially during calculations), and you must adjust the contrast to a higher setting. If you find it necessary to set the contrast to a setting of 8 or 9, you should replace the batteries soon.

3.1.2   The Display of the TI-81: The TI-81 displays both text and graphs. When text is displayed, the screen can display up to eight lines of 16 characters per line. When all eight lines of the screen are filled, text "scrolls" off the top of the screen. When you turn the TI-81 on, the *Home screen* is displayed. The Home screen is the primary screen of the TI-81. On it you enter expressions and instructions and see the results. The TI-81 has several types of cursors. In most cases, the appearance of the cursor indicates what will happen when you press the next key. The cursors that you see on the Home screen are listed in Table 3.1. Other special cursors are described later.

   When the TI-81 is calculating or graphing, a small box ("Busy" indicator) in the upper right of the screen is highlighted. You can return to the Home screen from any other screen by pressing $\boxed{\text{2nd}}$ $\boxed{\text{QUIT}}$.

Cursor	Appearance	Meaning
Entry cursor	Solid blinking rectangle	The next keystroke is entered at the cursor overwriting any character
Insert cursor	Blinking underline cursor	The next keystroke is inserted at the cursor
2nd cursor	Highlighted blinking ↑	The next keystroke is a second function
ALPHA cursor	Highlighted blinking A	The next keystroke is an alpha character

Table 3.1

3.1.3 Entering a Calculation: To begin, enter $1000(1.06)^{10}$, by keying [1000] [×] [1.06] [∧] [10] just as you would write it down.

The entire expression is shown in the first line of the display. Press [ENTER] to evaluate the expression. The result of the expression is shown on the right side of the second line on the display (see Figure 3.2). The cursor is positioned on the left side of the third line, ready for you to enter the next expression.

```
1000 ∗ 1.06 ∧ 10
                1790.847697
```

Figure 3.2

Notice the difference between this display and a typical scientific calculator. You can see the complete problem *and* the solution!

3.1.4 The Menu (Advanced Functions) Keys: You can access functions and operations that are not on the keyboard through *menus*. A menu screen temporarily replaces the screen where you are working. After you select an item from a menu, the screen where you are working is displayed again. The MATH menu is shown in Figure 3.3. The down arrow ↓ at the bottom of the [MATH] column indicates at least one additional option is available that does not appear on the screen. It can be viewed by pressing the [▽] key seven times.

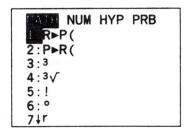

Figure 3.3

The MATH menu screen contains four columns of menus. Press $\boxed{\triangleright}$ slowly to see all four columns of menus. A particular item is selected by typing the number of the item desired. For example, to compute 7! key $\boxed{7}$ $\boxed{\text{MATH}}$ [5: !] $\boxed{\text{ENTER}}$ (see Figure 3.4).

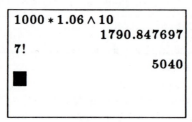

Figure 3.4

Numbered-menu Notation. For numbered menus, like the MATH menu, we adopt a special notation that is a modification of the keying sequence notation introduced in Section 2.1. For instance, if your calculator screen looks like Figure 3.3 and you wish to select the factorial function (!) from the MATH menu, we will denote the keystroke using [5:!].

3.1.5 The Mode Screen: Press $\boxed{\text{MODE}}$ to change the modes of the TI-81. The default modes are the first column of choices. To make a selection, use the arrow keys to move the cursor to the desired row first and then the desired column. Then press $\boxed{\text{ENTER}}$ to select the item. For example, to select "Dot" mode, press the down arrow $\boxed{\triangledown}$ key four times and $\boxed{\triangleright}$ once. Then press $\boxed{\text{ENTER}}$ to select "Dot" mode.

The first row contains the Normal, Scientific, or Engineering notation display settings. Notation formats affect only how a numeric result is displayed. You can enter a number in any format. Normal display format is the way in which we usually express numbers, with digits to the left and right of the decimal point, as in 12345.67. Scientific notation expresses numbers in two parts. The significant digits are displayed with one digit to the left of the decimal point. The appropriate power of 10 is displayed to the right of E, as in 1.234567E4. Engineering notation is similar to scientific notation. However, the number may have one, two, or three digits before the decimal point, and the power-of-10 exponent is a multiple of three, as in 12.34567E3.

The second row contains the floating or fixed decimal display settings.

The third row contains the radian or degree angle settings. Radian setting means that angle arguments in trig functions or polar-rectangular conversions are interpreted as radians. Results are displayed in radians. Degree setting means that angle argument in trig functions or polar-rectangular conversions are interpreted as degrees. Results are displayed in degrees.

The fourth row contains the function or parametric graphing settings. Function graphing plots a function where Y is expressed in terms of X. See Section 3.3 for more information about function graphing. Parametric graphing plots a relation where X and Y are each expressed in terms of a third variable, T. See Section 3.5 for more information about graphing parametric equations.

The fifth row contains the connected line or dot graph display settings. A connected line graph draws a line between the points calculated on the graph of a function in the $Y =$ list. A dot graph plots only the calculated points on the graph.

The sixth row contains the sequential or simultaneous plotting settings. Sequential plotting means that, if more than one function is selected, one function is evaluated and plotted completely before the next function is evaluated and plotted. Simultaneous plotting means that, if more than one function is selected, all functions are evaluated and plotted for a single value of X or T before the functions are evaluated and plotted for the next value of X or T.

The seventh row are the grid off or grid on setting. Grid Off means that no grid points are displayed on a graph. Grid On means that grid points are displayed on a graph. Grid points correspond to the axes tick marks.

The last row contains the rectangular or polar coordinate display settings. Rectangular coordinate display shows the cursor coordinate at the bottom of the screen in terms of rectangular coordinates X and Y. Polar coordinate display shows the cursor coordinate at the bottom of the screen in terms of polar coordinates R and θ.

3.1.6 Leaving a Menu or Edit Screen: There are several ways to leave a menu or edit screen. After you make a selection from a menu, you usually are returned to the screen where you were. If you decide not to make a selection from a menu, you can leave the menu in one of the following ways:

(1)   Press $\boxed{\text{2nd}}$ $\boxed{\text{QUIT}}$ to return to the Home screen.

(2)   Press $\boxed{\text{CLEAR}}$ to return to the screen where you were.

(3)   Select another screen by pressing the appropriate key, such as $\boxed{\text{MATH}}$ or $\boxed{\text{RANGE}}$.

When you finish entry or editing tasks, such as entering range values, entering statistical data, editing a program, or changing modes, leave the menu in one of the following ways:

(1)   Press $\boxed{\text{2nd}}$ $\boxed{\text{QUIT}}$ to return to the Home screen.

(2)   Press another edit screen key, such as $\boxed{\text{RANGE}}$.

3.2 Calculations on the TI-81

3.2.1 Last Entry: When $\boxed{\text{ENTER}}$ is pressed on the Home screen and an expression is evaluated successfully, the TI-81 stores the current expression in a special storage area called Last Entry. It can be recalled by pressing $\boxed{\text{2nd}}$ $\boxed{\text{ENTRY}}$ or the up arrow key $\boxed{\triangle}$.

Because the TI-81 updates the Last Entry storage area only when $\boxed{\text{ENTER}}$ is pressed, you can recall the last entry even if you have begun entering the next expression. However, the Last Entry overwrites the current expression. When you turn the TI-81 off, the expression in Last Entry is retained in memory.

Example   Determine when an investment earning interest at 8.5% compounded monthly will double in value. The applicable compound interest equation is $2 = \left(1 + \frac{.085}{12}\right)^n$. We want to solve this equation for n. Make a guess, say $n = 100$. Key in $\boxed{(}\,\boxed{1}\,\boxed{+}\,\boxed{.085}\,\boxed{\div}\,\boxed{12}\,\boxed{)}\,\boxed{\wedge}\,\boxed{100}$.

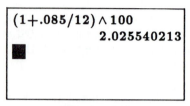

Figure 3.5

Make a new estimate based on the above result (see Figure 3.5). The new estimate should be smaller than 100. Why? Make your next estimate $n = 99$ and use the last entry feature. Press the $\boxed{\triangle}$ key.
Notice the cursor is at the end of the expression (see Figure 3.6). Move the cursor 3 spaces left and type $\boxed{99}$. Press the $\boxed{\text{DEL}}$ key to delete the "0". Now press $\boxed{\text{ENTER}}$ to obtain the next result (see Figure 3.7).

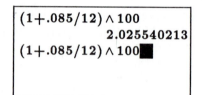

Figure 3.6

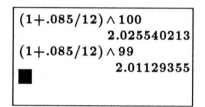

Figure 3.7

Continue estimating in this manner until your answer is as accurate as you wish.

3.2.2 Last Answer: The $\boxed{\text{2nd}}$ $\boxed{\text{ANS}}$ key recalls the last answer in a computation. For example, if you just computed the example in 3.2.1 do the following. Turn your TI-81 off. Turn it on. Press $\boxed{\text{2nd}}$ $\boxed{\text{ANS}}$ $\boxed{\text{ENTER}}$. Notice the last answer is stored as a variable (Ans) that can be used in computations.

3.3 Graphing on the TI-81

The keys on the TI-81 that are related most closely to graphing are located immediatly under the display. When you press $\boxed{\text{Y=}}$, an edit screen is displayed where you enter and select the functions that you want to graph. When you press $\boxed{\text{RANGE}}$, an edit screen is displayed where you define the viewing rectangle for the graph. When you press $\boxed{\text{ZOOM}}$, you access a menu of instructions that allow you to change the viewing rectangle. When you press $\boxed{\text{TRACE}}$, you can move the cursor along a graphed function and display the X and Y coordinate values of the cursor location on the function. When you press $\boxed{\text{GRAPH}}$, a graph of the currently selected functions is displayed in the chosen viewing rectangle.

3.3.1 Entering a Function: Press $\boxed{\text{Y=}}$. The display shows labels for four functions. The cursor is positioned at the beginning of the first function. Enter the two function $f(x) = x^3 - 2x$ and $g(x) = 2\cos x$ so that $y_1 = f(x)$ and $y_2 = g(x)$. To enter the first expression press $\boxed{\text{CLEAR}}$ $\boxed{\text{X/T}}$ $\boxed{\wedge}$ $\boxed{3}$ $\boxed{-}$ $\boxed{2}$ $\boxed{\text{X/T}}$, then press $\boxed{\text{ENTER}}$ to move the cursor to the next function. (*Note:* The $\boxed{\text{X/T}}$ key lets you enter the variable X quickly without pressing $\boxed{\text{ALPHA}}$.) Notice the = sign is highlighted and thickened to show that Y_1 is "selected" to be graphed (see Figure 3.8). Now enter the second expression by pressing $\boxed{\text{CLEAR}}$ $\boxed{2}$ $\boxed{\text{COS}}$ $\boxed{\text{X/T}}$ $\boxed{\text{ENTER}}$. Pressing $\boxed{\text{ENTER}}$ with the cursor on the equals sign will change the status (selected or unselected) of the function.

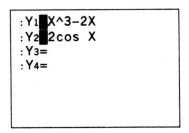

Figure 3.8

3.3.2 Checking the Viewing Rectangle: The Range key allows you to choose the viewing rectangle that defines the portion of the coordinate plane that appears in the display. The values of the RANGE variables determine the size of the viewing rectangle and the scale units for each axis. You can view and change the values of the RANGE variables almost any time. Press RANGE to display the RANGE variables edit screen (see Figure 3.9). The values shown here on the RANGE edit screen are the standard default values $[-10, 10]$ by $[-10, 10]$. Xscl and Yscl give the distance between consecutive tick marks on the coordinate axes. Both are 1 in Figure 3.9. To change one of the RANGE values, move the cursor to the desired line and type in the new value. You may also edit an existing value to produce a new value. Xres controls the number of pixels used to obtain a plot. We will normally use Xres=1, which gives the best possible resolution.

```
RANGE
Xmin=-10
Xmax=10
Xscl=1
Ymin=-10
Ymax=10
Yscl=1
Xres=1
```

Figure 3.9

Displaying the Graph. Press GRAPH to graph the selected functions (f and g) in the current viewing rectangle with default mode settings (see Figure 3.10). When the plotting is completed, press ▷ once to display the graphics cursor just to the right of the center of the screen (see Figure 3.11). The bottom line in the display shows *both* the X and Y coordinate values for the position of the graphics cursor. Use the cursor-movement keys (◁, ▷, △, ▽), to move the cursor. As you move the cursor, the X and Y coordinate values are updated continually with the cursor position.

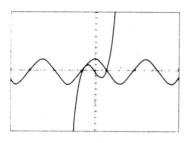

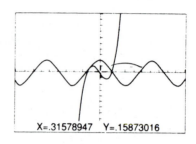

Figure 3.10   **Figure 3.11**

3.4 Zooming In on the Graph

You can magnify a portion of the viewing rectangle around a specific location by selecting the *Zoom In* instruction from the ZOOM menu. Press ZOOM to access the menu of built-in ZOOM functions (see Figure 3.12).

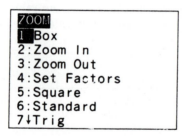

Figure 3.12

This menu is typical of all numbered menus of built-in operations on the TI-81. To select an item from a menu, either press the number to the left of the instruction you want, or press ▽ to position the cursor on that instruction and then press ENTER. *Note:* It is much easier and quicker simply to press the *number* of the desired action. To zoom in, press 2 to select the Zoom In instruction from the menu. The graph is displayed again. Notice the cursor has changed to indicate that you are using a ZOOM instruction. Place the cursor at the point indicated in Figure 3.13, press ENTER. The current position of the cursor becomes the center of the new viewing rectangle. The new viewing rectangle has been adjusted in both the *X* direction and the *Y* direction by factors of 4, which are the default values for the zoom factors (see Figure 3.14). The zoom factors can be changed by pressing ZOOM [4: Set Factors] (see Section 3.4.5).

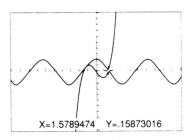

X=1.5789474   Y=.15873016

Figure 3.13

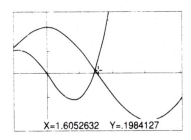

X=1.6052632   Y=.1984127

Figure 3.14

3.4.1 Moving between the Graph and Range Screens: When the TI-81 executes a ZOOM instruction, it updates the RANGE variables to reflect the new viewing rectangle. You can check the RANGE values by pressing RANGE to see the size of the new viewing rectangle and then return to the graph by pressing GRAPH without having to replot the graph. The modified values resulting from the Zoom In instruction depend on the exact cursor position when you executed the Zoom In instruction. Press GRAPH to see the graph again at any time.

3.4.2 Moving the Cursor along a Function: The TRACE feature allows you to move the cursor along a graph showing the x and $f(x)$ coordinate values of the cursor location on the graphs. Press TRACE. The cursor appears near the middle of the screen on the $Y_1 = X^3 - 2X$ function (see Figure 3.15). The keys ▷ and ◁ allow you to move along the graph. The coordinate values of the cursor location are displayed at the bottom of the screen. The Y value shown is the calculated function value $f(x)$. If the cursor moves off the top or bottom of the screen, the coordinate values X and Y displayed at the bottom of the screen continue to change appropriately. Panning is possible in function graphing. Moving the cursor by pressing the right or left arrow keys a sufficient number of times will cause the graph to pan to the right or left, respectively.

Press ▽. The cursor moves to the next active function, in this case, $Y_2 = 2\cos x$, at the same X value where it was located on the first function (see Figure 3.16). △ and ▽ allow you to move among all functions that are defined *and* selected (active).

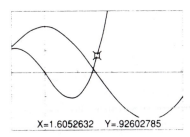

X=1.6052632   Y=.92602785

Figure 3.15

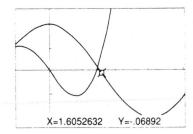

X=1.6052632   Y=-.06892

Figure 3.16

3.4.3 Using Zoom Box: There is another way to magnify a graph. The Zoom [1: Box] Instruction lets you adjust the viewing rectangle by drawing a box on the display to define the new viewing rectangle. To adjust the viewing rectangle to the standard default range, press $\boxed{\text{ZOOM}}$ [6: Standard]. This automatically adjusts the viewing rectangle to the standard default viewing rectangle $[-10, 10]$ by $[-10, 10]$. This display shows the same graph that you saw earlier (see Figure 3.13). Press $\boxed{\text{ZOOM}}$ [1: Box]. This lets you draw a box anywhere on the screen in which to magnify the graph for a new viewing. The cursor is in the middle of the screen. Its new appearance indicates that you have selected a ZOOM instruction. Use the cursor arrow keys to move the cursor from the middle of the graph to where you *want one corner* of the new viewing rectangle to be (see Figure 3.17). Press $\boxed{\text{ENTER}}$.

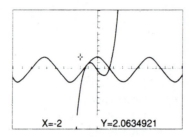

Figure 3.17

Notice that the cursor has changed to a small box. Next, move the cursor to the *diagonally opposite corner* of the desired viewing rectangle (see Figure 3.18). The outline of the new viewing rectangle is drawn as you move the cursor. Press $\boxed{\text{ENTER}}$ to accept the cursor location as the second corner of the box. The graph is replotted immediately using the box outline as the new viewing rectangle. Use a second zoom-in to obtain a picture like the one shown in Figure 3.19.

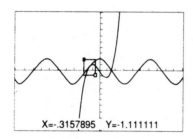

Figure 3.18

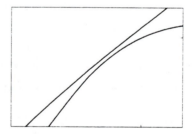

Figure 3.19

To leave the graph display, press $\boxed{\text{2nd}}$ $\boxed{\text{QUIT}}$ or $\boxed{\text{CLEAR}}$ to return to the Home screen.

3.4.4 Exploring a Graph with the Free-Moving Cursor:
After pressing $\boxed{\text{GRAPH}}$, the free-moving cursor can be moved to identify the coordinate of any location on the graph. You can use $\boxed{\triangleleft}$, $\boxed{\triangleright}$, $\boxed{\triangle}$, and $\boxed{\triangledown}$ to move the cursor around the graph. When you first press $\boxed{\text{GRAPH}}$ to display the graph, no cursor is visible. As soon as you press one of the cursor-movement keys, the cursor moves from the center of the viewing rectangle. As you move the cursor around the graph, the coordinate values of the cursor location are displayed at the bottom of the screen. Coordinate values always appear in floating-decimal format. The numeric display settings on the MODE screen do not affect coordinate display.

In Rectangular mode, moving the cursor updates and displays the values of the rectangular coordinates X and Y. In Polar mode, the coordinates R and θ are updated and displayed. To see the graph without the cursor or coordinate values, press GRAPH or ENTER. When you press a cursor-movement key, the cursor moves from the middle of the viewing rectangle again if you pressed GRAPH or from the same point if you pressed ENTER.

Note The free-moving cursor moves from dot to dot on the screen. When you move the cursor to a dot that appears to be "on" the function, it may be near, but not on, the function; therefore, the coordinate value displayed at the bottom of the screen is not necessarily a point on the function. The coordinate value is accurate to within the width of the dot (see Section 2.5). To move the cursor along a function, use the TRACE feature.

3.4.5 Setting Zoom Factors: Zoom factors determine the scale of the magnification for the Zoom In or Zoom Out features. Before using Zoom In or Zoom Out, you can review or change the zoom factors. Zoom factors are positive numbers (not necessarily integers) greater than or equal to 1.

To review the current values of the zoom factors, select [4: Set Factors] from the ZOOM menu. The ZOOM FACTORS screen appears. Figure 3.20 shows how the ZOOM FACTORS editing menu appears with the default factors of 4 in each direction.

```
ZOOM FACTORS
XFact=4
YFact=4
```

Figure 3.20

If the factors are not what you want, change them in one of the following ways:

(1) Enter a new value. The original value is cleared automatically when you begin typing.

(2) Position the cursor over the digit you want to change. Then type over it or use DEL to delete it.

When the zoom factor values are as you want them, leave ZOOM FACTORS in one of the following ways:

(1) Select another screen by pressing the appropriate key, such as GRAPH or ZOOM.

(2) Press 2nd QUIT to return to the Home screen.

3.4.6 Using Zoom Out: Zoom Out displays a greater portion of the graph, centered around the cursor location, to provide a more global view. The XFact and YFact settings determine the extent of the zoom. After checking or changing the zoom factors select [3: Zoom Out] from the ZOOM menu. Notice the special cursor. It indicates that you are using a Zoom instruction.

Move the cursor to the point that you want as the center of the new viewing rectangle and then press ENTER. The TI-81 adjusts the viewing rectangle by **XFact** and **YFact**, updates the RANGE variables, and replots the selected functions, centered around the cursor lcoation.

To zoom out again:

(1) Centered at the same point, press [ENTER].

(2) Centered at a new point, move the cursor to the point that you want as the center of the new viewing rectangle and then press [ENTER].

When you finish using the Zoom Out feature, leave in one of the following ways:

(1) Select another screen by pressing the appropriate key, such as [TRACE] or [GRAPH].

(2) Press [2nd] [QUIT] or [CLEAR] to return to the Home screen.

3.4.7 Using Other ZOOM Features: Four of the ZOOM features reset the RANGE variables to predefined values or use factors to adjust the RANGE variables. Xres remains unchanged, except in Standard.

(1) **Square.** The TI-81 replots the functions, redefining the viewing rectangle using values based on the current RANGE variables, but adjusted to equalize the width of the dots on the X and Y axes. **Xscl** and **Yscl** remain unchanged. This feature makes the graph of a circle look like a circle (see Section 3.4.8).

   The TI-81 replots the graph as soon as the menu selection is made. The center of the current graph becomes the center of the new graph.

(2) **Standard.** The TI-81 updates the RANGE variables to the standard default values and replots the graph as soon as the menu selection is made. The RANGE variable standard defaults are:

$$Xmin = -10 \qquad Ymin = -10 \qquad Xres = 1$$
$$Xmax = 10 \qquad Ymax = 10$$
$$Xscl = 1 \qquad Yscl = 1$$

(3) **Trig.** The TI-81 updates the RANGE variables using preset values appropriate for trig functions and replots the graph as soon as the menu selection is made. The trig RANGE variable values in **Radians** mode are:

$$Xmin = -2\pi \qquad Ymin = -3$$
$$Xmax = 2\pi \qquad Ymax = 3$$
$$Xscl = \pi/2 \qquad Yscl = .1$$

   Note   The display shows the numeric values of 2π, 6.283185307, and $\pi/2$, 1.570796327.

(4) **Integer.** When you select [8: Integer] from the ZOOM menu, you can move the cursor to the point that you want as the center of the new viewing rectangle and then press [ENTER].

   The TI-81 replots the functions, redefining the viewing rectangle so that the mid-point of each dot on the X and Y axis is an integer. **Xscl** and **Yscl** are equal to 10.

3.4.8 Example: Graphing a Circle

Problem   Graph a circle of radius 10, centered around the origin $x^2 + y^2 = 10$.

Solution   To graph a circle, you must enter separate formulas for the upper and lower portions of the circle. Use Connected Line mode.

(1) Press ⬚Y=. Enter the expressions to define two functions. The top half of the circle is defined by
     $Y_1 = \sqrt{100 - X^2}$ The bottom half of the circle is defined by
     $Y_2 = -Y_1$ (key ⬚(−) ⬚2nd ⬚Y-Vars [1: Y_1] (use the Y-VARS menu)).

(2) Press ⬚ZOOM [6: Standard]. This is a quick way to reset the RANGE variables to the standard defaults.
     It also graphs the functions, so you do not need to press ⬚GRAPH. Notice that the graph appears to be
     an ellipse (see Figure 3.21).

(3) To adjust the display so that each "dot" has an equal width and height, press ⬚ZOOM and then select
     [5: Square]. The functions are replotted and now appear as a circle on the display (see Figure 3.22).

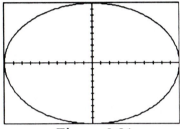
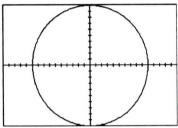

Figure 3.21   **Figure 3.22**

(4) To see the effect of the Zoom Square instruction on the RANGE variables, press ⬚RANGE and notice
     the values for Xmin, Xmax, Ymin, and Ymax.

3.5 Parametric Graphing

3.5.1 Defining and Displaying a Parametric Graph: Parametric equations consist of an X
component and a Y component, each expressed in terms of the same independent variable T. Up to three
pairs of parametric equations can be defined and graphed at a time. The steps for defining a parametric
graph are the same as those for defining a function graph. Differences are noted below.

Press ⬚MODE to display the MODE settings (see Figure 3.23). The current settings are highlighted.
To graph parametric equations, you must select ⟨Param⟩ (see Section 3.1.5) before you enter RANGE
variables or enter the components of parametric equations. Also, you usually should select ⟨Connected⟩ to
obtain a more meaningful parametric graph.

Press ⬚Y= to display the Y= edit screen (see Figure 3.24).

Setting		Meaning
Norm Sci Eng		Type of notation for display
Float 0123456789		Number of decimal places
Rad Deg		Type of angle measure
Function Param		Function or parametric graphing
Connected Dot		Whether to connect plotted points
Sequence Simul		How to plot selected functions
Grid Off Grid On		Whether to display a graph grid
Rect Polar		Type of graph coordinate display

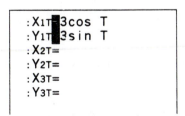

Figure 3.23   **Figure 3.24**

On this screen, you display and enter both X and Y components. There are three pairs of components, each defined in terms of T.

To enter the two expressions that define new parametric equations, follow the procedure in Section 3.3.1.

(1) You must define both the X and Y components in a pair.

(2) The independent variable in each component must be T. You may press the $\boxed{\text{X/T}}$ key, rather than pressing $\boxed{\text{ALPHA}}$ $\boxed{\text{T}}$, to enter the parametric variable T. (Parametric mode defines the independent variable as T.)

The procedures for editing, clearing, and leaving are the same as for function graphing.

Only the parametric equations you select are graphed. You may select up to three equations at a time. Press $\boxed{\text{Y=}}$ to display the $\mathbf{Y=}$ edit screen to select and unselect equations. The $=$ signs on the selected pairs of equations are highlighted.

To change the selection status of a parametric equation:

(1) Place the cursor over the $=$ sign on either the X or Y component.

(2) Press $\boxed{\text{ENTER}}$ to change the status. The status on both the X and Y components is changed.

Note When you enter or edit either component of an equation, that pairs of equations is selected automatically.

Press $\boxed{\text{RANGE}}$ to display the current RANGE variable values. The values shown in Table 3.2 are the *standard defaults in Radian mode*. Notice that **Xres**, which appeared on the function graphing RANGE edit screen, is not here; but three new variables, **Tmin**, **Tmax**, and **Tstep**, are.

Setting	Meaning
RANGE	
Tmin=0	The smallest T value to be evaluated
Tmax=2π	The largest T value to be evaluated
Tstep = $\pi/30$	The increment between T values
Xmin= -10	The smallest X value to be displayed
Xmax=10	The largest X value to be displayed
Xscl=1	The spacing between X tick marks
Ymin= -10	The smallest Y value to be displayed
Ymax=10	The largest Y value to be displayed
Yscl=1	The spacing between Y tick marks

Table 3.2

Note The display shows the numeric value of 2π, 6.283185307, for **Tmax** and 0.104719755 for **Tstep**.

To change the value of a RANGE variable or to leave the screen, follow the procedures in Section 3.3.2.

When you press $\boxed{\text{GRAPH}}$, the TI-81 plots the selected parametric equations. It evaluates both the X and the Y component for each value of T (from **Tmin** to **Tmax** in intervals of **Tstep**) and then plots each point defined by X and Y. The RANGE variables define the viewing rectangle. As a graph is plotted, the TI-81 updates the coordinates X and Y and the values of the parameter T.

3.5.2 Exploring a Parametric Graph: As in function graphing, three tools are available for exploring a graph: using the free-moving cursor, tracing an equation, and zooming. The free-moving cursor works in parametric graphing just as it does in function graphing. The cursor coordinate values for X and Y (or R and θ in polar mode) are updated and displayed.

The TRACE feature (see Section 3.4.2) lets you move the cursor along the equation one **Tstep** at a time. When you begin a trace, the blinking cursor is on the first selected equation at the middle T value and the coordinate values of X, Y, and T are displayed at the bottom of the screen. As you trace along a parametric graph using $\boxed{\triangleleft}$ $\boxed{\triangleright}$, the values of X, Y and T are updated and displayed. The X and Y values are calculated from T.

If the cursor moves off the top or bottom of the screen, the coordinate values of X, Y, and T displayed at the bottom of the screen continue to change appropriately.

Panning is not possible on parametric curves. To see a section of the equations not displayed on the graph, you must change the RANGE variables.

The ZOOM features work in parametric graphing as they do in function graphing.

Only the X (**Xmin, Xmax**, and **Xscl**) and Y (**Ymin, Ymax**, and **Yscl**) RANGE variables are affected. The T RANGE variables (**Tmin, Tmax**, and **Tstep**) are not affected, except when you select [6: Standard]; in that case they become **Tmin** $= 0$, **Tmax** $= 2\pi$, and **Tstep** $= \pi/30$. You may want to change the T RANGE variable values to ensure that sufficient points are plotted.

3.5.3 Applications of Parametric Graphing

Example 1: Simulating Motion

Problem Graph the position of a ball kicked from ground level at an angle of 60° with an initial velocity of 40 ft/sec. (Ignore air resistance.) What is the maximum height, and when is it reached? How far away and when does the ball strike the ground?

Solution If v_0 is the initial velocity and θ is the angle, then the horizontal component of the position of the ball as a function of time is described by

$$X(T) = Tv_0 \cos \theta \, .$$

The vertical component of the position of the ball as a function of time is described by

$$Y(T) = -167T^2 + Tv_0 \sin \theta \, .$$

In order to graph the equations,

(1) Press $\boxed{\text{MODE}}$. Select Parametric, Connected Line, and Degree Mode.

(2) Press $\boxed{\text{Y=}}$. Enter the expressions to define the parametric equation in terms of T.

$X_{1T} = 40T \cos 60$
$Y_{1T} = 40T \sin 60 - 16T^2$

(3) Press $\boxed{\text{RANGE}}$. Set the RANGE variables appropriately for this problem.

Tmin=0	Xmin = −5	Xmin = −5
Tmax = 2.5	Xmax = 50	Ymax = 20
Tstep = .02	Xscl = 5	Yscl = 5

(4) Press $\boxed{\text{GRAPH}}$ to graph the position of the ball as a function of time.

(5) Now press $\boxed{\text{TRACE}}$ to explore the graph. When you press $\boxed{\text{TRACE}}$, the values for X, Y, and T are displayed at the bottom of the screen. These values change as you trace along the graph.

Move the cursor along the path of the ball to investigate these values. Notice you have a "stop action" picture at each 0.02 seconds.

Example 2: Graphing a Polar Equation

Problem Graph the spiral of Archimedes, that is, the curve defined by the polar equation $r = a\theta$.

Solution A polar equation $r = f(\theta)$ can be graphed using the parametric graphing features of the TI-81 by applying the conversion formulas, $X = f(\theta)\cos(\theta)$ and $Y = f(\theta)\sin(\theta)$. Thus, the spiral of Archimedes (with a = 0.5) can be expressed parametrically as

$$X = 0.5\theta \cos(\theta)$$
$$Y = 0.5\theta \sin(\theta)$$

Graph the equation using the standard default viewing rectangle, Radian mode, and Connected Line mode.

(1) Press $\boxed{\text{MODE}}$. Select Parametric mode. Choose the defaults for the other modes.

(2) Press $\boxed{\text{Y=}}$. Enter the expressions to define the parametric equation in terms of T.

$X_{1T} = 0.5T \cos T$
$Y_{1T} = 0.5T \sin T$

(3) Press $\boxed{\text{ZOOM}}$ [6: Standard] to graph the equations in the standard default viewing rectangle.

The graph shows only the first loop of the spiral. This is because the standard default values for the RANGE variables define **Tmax** as 2π.

(4) To explore the behavior of the graph further, press $\boxed{\text{RANGE}}$ and change **Tmax** to 25.

(5)   Press $\boxed{\text{GRAPH}}$ to display the new graph (see Figure 3.25).

(6)   Try pressing $\boxed{\text{ZOOM}}$ [5: Square]. What happened? (See Figure 3.26.) Contrast with Figure 3.25.

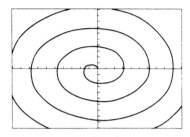

Figure 3.25

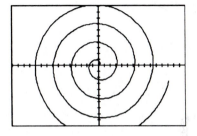

Figure 3.26

Chapter 4

Introduction to the TI-85 Pocket Computer

4.1 The Menu Keys

The TI-85 uses horizontal display menus to give you access to more operations than you can access from the keyboard alone.

4.1.1 The Menus and Menu Keys:

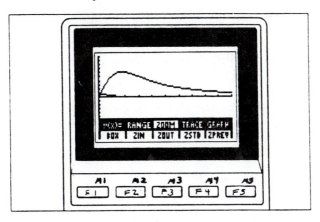

The top of keys are the menu keys and are labeled [F1], [F2], [F3], [F4], and [F5]. The *second* functions of the menu keys are labeled [M1], [M2], [M3], [M4], and [M5]. The menu items are shown on the bottom line(s) of the display, above the five menu keys.

4.1.2 Selecting Menu Items

(1) To select a menu item from the eighth (bottom) line of the screen display, press the menu key below the item.

(2) To select a menu item from the seventh (next-to-the-bottom) line of the screen display, press and release [2nd] and then press the menu key below the item.

In this chapter, the **menu** items are indicated by < > brackets. Keys are denoted by [ ] square brackets. For example, press [F2] to select < ZIN > or press [2nd] [M5] to select < GRAPH > .

4.1.3 Finding Commands and Function: All commands and functions may be found in two or more menus or directly on keys. One menu key you will use often is [2nd] [CATALOG]. It contains <u>all</u> functions

and commands in alphabetical order. For example to select "randM(", simply press the number 5 calculator key becuase that is the gray alpha numeric character "R" (look just above the number 5 key). Notice you can move the pointer down to "randM(" by pressing the down arrow key. Press [ENTER] to make the selection. "RandM)" is also found in a matrix menu.

It is useful to know that all commands, functions, variables, and program names may be *typed directly on the screen letter by letter* using the [ALPHA] key. [2nd] [ALPHA] is lower case. [ALPHA] twice is "caps lock."

4.1.4 Variables: All variables can be found in the [2nd] [VARS] menus. They can be identifed and selected in the same manner as in CATALOG.

4.1.5 Finding All Menu Items: When you press a key and obtain a menu, for example, [GRAPH], notice there is a small ▶ at the end of the visible menu item listing. That means there is MORE! Press the [MORE] key to see 5 more menu listings. Press [MORE] again to see the last 3 menu items in the [GRAPH] menu collection. There are 13 menu items in [GRAPH].

Some [GRAPH]menu items give you access to edit screens like < y(x)= > or < RANGE >. Others give you even more menus, like < ZOOM > or < MATH >. Finally some menu items are commands like < GRAPH > or < TRACE >. The [GRAPH] menu collection is typical of the way many menu keys work like [2nd][MATRIX] or [STAT] or [2nd][MATH].

4.1.6 Edit Screens: Expressions that evaluate to a number may be entered in edit screens. For example in [GRAPH] < RANGE >, $2A + \frac{8\pi}{2} - \cos 2.2$ could be directly entered in the xMIN=■ position (assuming A was defined).

4.2 Resetting the TI-85

Before beginning these sample problems, follow the steps on this page to ensure that the TI-85 is reset to its factory settings. (Resetting the TI-85 erases all previously entered data.)

(1) Press [ON] to turn the calculator on.
(2) Press [2nd] and then press [+]. (Pressing [2nd] accesses the function printed to the left above the next key that you press. MEM is the second function of [+].) The bottom line of the display shows the MEM (memory) menu.

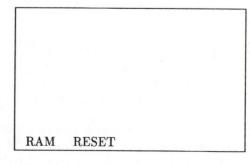

(3) Press the [F3] menu key to select < RESET >, the third item in the MEM menu. The bottom line is relabeled with the RESET menu and the MEM menu moves up a line.

```
┌─────────────────────────────────────┐
│                                      │
│                                      │
│                                      │
│                                      │
│                                      │
│                                      │
│  RAM     RESET                       │
│  ALL        CLMEM  DFLTS             │
└─────────────────────────────────────┘
```

(4) Press [F1] to select < ALL >. The display shows the message <u>Are you sure?</u>.

Press [F4] to select < YES >. The display shows the message <u>Mem cleared</u>, and <u>Defaults set</u>.

The display contrast was reset to the default. To adjust the display contrast, press and release [2nd] and then press and hold [↑] (to make the display darker) or [↓] (to make the display lighter).

Press [CLEAR] to clear the display.

```
┌─────────────────────────────────────┐
│                                      │
│  Are you sure?                       │
│                                      │
│                                      │
│                                      │
│                                      │
│  CLMEM  DFLTS  ALL                   │
│  NO           YES                    │
└─────────────────────────────────────┘
```

4.3 Application: Future Value of an Annuity Due

The TI-85 display can show up to eight lines of 21 characters per line. This lets you see each expression or instruction in its entirety as it is entered. Variable names can be up to eight characters, in uppercase and lowercase. Names are case-sensitive. You can enter more than one command on a line by concatenating them with a : (colon).

If you invest $25 at the beginning of each month at 6% annual interest, compounded monthly, how much money you will have at the end of three years? The formula is:

$$\text{PMT} \; \frac{(1+I)^{N+1} - (1+I)}{I}$$

(1) To store the value ($25) for the payment amount in the variable PMT, press 25 [STO ▷]. When you press the [STO ▷] key, the symbol → is copied to the cursor location, and the keyboard is set in

ALPHA-lock, which makes each subsequent key press an uppercase alpha character. Alpha characters are printed to the right above the keys.

(2)   Type P M T and then press [ALPHA] to take the keyboard out of ALPHA-lock.

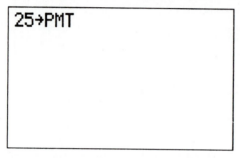

(3)   Press [2nd] [:] (the 2nd function of [.]) to begin another command on the same line.

(4)   Press 3 [×] 12 [STO ▷] N [ALPHA] to store the expression for the number of periods (years*12) in the variable N̲. The TI-85 evaluates the expression before stating the value.

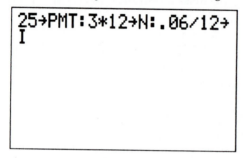

(5)   Press [2nd] [:] .06 [÷] 12 [STO ▷] I [ALPHA] to begin a new command and store the interest per period (rate/12) in the variable I.

The entry is more than 21 characters and cannot be shown in one line of the display, so it "wraps" to the next line.

4.4 Entering Expressions

Expressions to be evaluated can contain variable names. On the TI-85, you enter expressions as you would write them on a single line. Enter, for example $PMT((1 + I)^{\wedge}(N + 1) - (1 + I))/I$.

(1)   To enter the expression to define the future value formula, press [2nd] [:] to begin the next command press [ALPHA] [ALPHA] to set the keyboard in ALPHA-lock, and then type P M T [ALPHA].

(2) Press [x] [( ] [( ] 1 [+] [ALPHA] I [ )] [^] [( ] [ALPHA] N [+] 1 [ )] [–] [( ] 1 [+] [ALPHA] I [ )]
     [ )] [÷] [ALPHA] I.

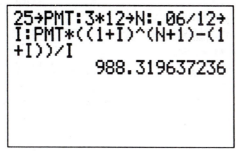

(3) Press [ENTER] to store the values in the variables and evaluate the expression. The result of the
     expression is shown on the right side of the next line on the display with 12 digits.

(4) Press [2nd] [MODE] (the 2nd function of [MORE]) to display the mode screen. Press [↓] [▷] [▷]
     [▷] to position the cursor over the 2 .

(5) Press [ENTER]. This changes the display format to two fixed decimal places.

(6) Press [2nd] [QUIT] (the 2nd function of EXIT) which always returns you to the Home screen. Press
     [ENTER]. The last answer is reevaluated and the result is displayed with two fixed decimal places.

     If you save $25 at the beginning of each month for 36 months, invested at 6%, you will have $988.32.

4.5 Recalling and Editing a Calculation

If more than one command is entered on a line on the TI-85, the Last Entry feature lets you recall the command that was executed when you pressed [ENTER]. The last result is stored in Last Answer.

   If you continue to invest \$25 a month for another year, how much will you have?

(1) Press [2nd] [ENTRY]. This recalls the last executed command into the display. The cursor is positioned following the command.

(2) Use [↑] and [▷] to position the cursor over the 3 in the instruction $3 * 12 \triangleright N$. Type 4.

```
25→PMT:3*12→N:.06/12→
I:PMT*((1+I)^(N+1)-(1
+I))/I
            988.319637236
                   988.32
25→PMT:4*12→N:.06/12→
I:PMT*((1+I)^(N+1)-(1
+I))/I
```

(3) You do not need to be at the end of a command to execute it, so press [ENTER] now. The solution for 4 years is displayed on the next line. If you save \$25 at the beginning of each month for 48 months, invested at 6%, you will have \$1359.21.

```
+I))/I
            988.319637236
                   988.32
25→PMT:4*12→N:.06/12→
I:PMT*((1+I)^(N+1)-(1
+I))/I
                  1359.21
```

(4) If you were able to save \$50 per month, the amount would double because PMT is directly proportional to the total. Press [2nd] [Ans]. The variable name Ans appears in the display.

   Press [×] 2 [ENTER].

   You will have \$2718.42 if you save \$50 per month.

```
                   988.32
25→PMT:4*12→N:.06/12→
I:PMT*((1+I)^(N+1)-(1
+I))/I
                  1359.21
Ans*2
                  2718.42
```

4.6 Graphing on the TI-85

Users familiar with the TI-81 will find that all of the popular TI-81 graphing features are also on the TI-85. When you press [GRAPH], the menu keys are labeled with the same graphing options (in the same order) that are on the top row of keys on the TI-81.

Graph $y=x^3-2x$ and $y=2\cos x$. Determine the solution to $x^3-2x=2\cos x$.

(1) Press [GRAPH]. The menu keys are labeled on the eighth line of the display with the TI-81 graphing commands.

The Home screen and cursor are still displayed. You do not leave the Home screen and enter the graphing application until you select a menu key.

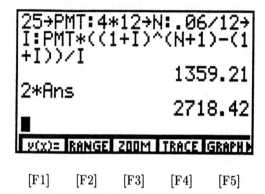

[F1]   [F2]   [F3]   [F4]   [F5]

(2) Press [F1] to select $<y(x)=>$, which accesses the $y(x)$ editor, where you enter and select functions to graph. Press [x-VAR] (you may press [F1] to select $<x>$ instead) [^] 3 [-] 2 [x-VAR] [ENTER] to enter the equation y1=x^3-2x. Press 2 [COS] [x-VAR] to enter y2=2cos x. The highlighted = shows y1 and y2 are "selected" to be graphed.

Notice, however, that the TI-85 uses lowercase x and y as its graphing variables, rather than the uppercase X and Y used by the TI-81.

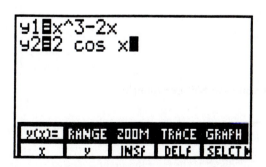

(3) Press [2nd] and [M3] to select $<ZOOM>$. With the ZOOM instructions, you can easily display the current graph in a different viewing rectangle.

Press [F4] to select < ZSTD > . This is the same as the ZOOM Standard option on the TI-81.

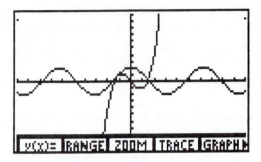

(4)   Press [F4] to select < TRACE > . Press [▶]to trace along function y1, then press [↓] to move to function y2. Notice the 1 or 2 in the upper right of the display, which indicates which function you are tracing.

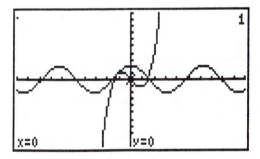

(5)   Press [EXIT] to leave TRACE and display the GRAPH menu.
Press [F3] to select < ZOOM > . Press [F2] to select < ZIN > . Move the cursor over the apparent intersection in the first quadrant. Press [ENTER].

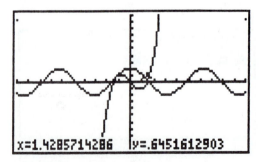

(6)   Press [EXIT] to leave ZIN and display the ZOOM menu.

Press [F4] to select < ZSTD > to display the original graph.

(The coordinate values may vary depending on the cursor location.)

(7) To explore the apparent solution in the second quadrant, press [F1] to select < BOX >. Move the cursor to the upper right corner of the area you want to examine more closely. Press [ENTER]. Move the cursor to the lower left corner (the box defining the area is shown as you move the cursor). Press [ENTER].

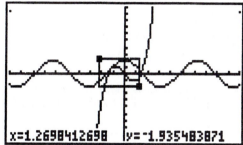

x=1.2698412698   y=-1.935483871

(8) If necessary, repeat the procedure for ZIN or BOX to see if the two functions intersect in the second quadrant (they do not).

4.7 Application: Illumination

On the TI-85, you can explore problems in several different ways. For example, you can solve many problems either by using the Solver feature or graphically. The remaining pages in this chapter present an illumination example to show how to enter equations and explore them both by using the SOLVER and by graphing.

The amount of illumination on a surface is:

(1) Proportional to the intensity of the source.

(2) Inversely proportional to the square of the distance.

(3) Proportional to the sine of the angle between the source and the surface.

The formula for illumination of a point on a surface is:

$$\text{ILLUM} = \frac{\text{INTEN} * \sin \theta}{\text{DIST}^2}$$

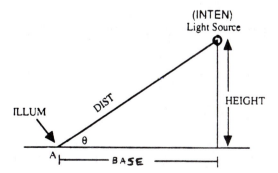

Appropriate units are ft-c (foot-candles) for illumination, CP (candlepower) for intensity, and ft (feet) for distances.

From geometry, $\sin\theta = \dfrac{\text{HEIGHT}}{\text{DIST}}$.

Therefore, $\text{ILLUM} = \dfrac{\text{INTEN} * \text{HEIGHT}}{\text{DIST}^3}$.

From geometry, $\text{DIST}^2 = \text{BASE}^2 + \text{HEIGHT}^2$. On the TI-85, you can store an unevaluated expression as an equation variable.

Press [ALPHA] [ALPHA] to set ALPHA-lock, type DIST=, and then press [ALPHA] to take the keyboard out of ALPHA-lock. Press [2nd] [$\sqrt{\ }$] [( ] [ALPHA] [ALPHA] BASE [ALPHA] [x^2] [+] [ALPHA] [ALPHA] HEIGHT [ALPHA] [x^2] [ )] [ENTER].

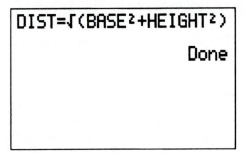

4.8 Entering an Equation in the Solver

With the Solver feature of the TI-85, you can solve an equation for any variable in the equation. In the Solver, you can observe the effect that changing the value of one variable has on another and apply "what if" scenarios.

(1) Press [2nd] [SOLVER] to display the Solver equation entry screen.

(2) Press [ALPHA] [ALPHA] ILLUM=INTEN [ALPHA] [×] [ALPHA] [ALPHA] HEIGHT [ALPHA] [÷].
Press [F1] to select < DIST > from the menu; the characters DIST are copied to the cursor location.

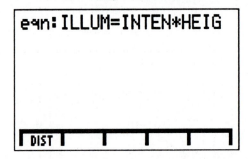

(3) Press [^]3 to complete the equation that defines illumination in terms of intensity and height: ILLUM = INTEN * HEIGHT/DIST^3. As you enter the equation beyond 17 characters, it scrolls. Ellipsis

marks (⋯) indicate that not all of the equation is displayed on the line. You can use [▶] and [◀] to scroll the equation.

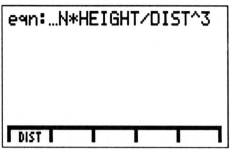

(4) Press [ENTER]. The Solver edit screen is displayed.

The equation is displayed on the top line. The variables are listed in the order in which they appear in the equation. The variables HEIGHT and BASE, which define the equation variable DIST, are shown. The cursor is positioned after the = following the first variable. If the variables have current values, the value would be shown. Bound defines a limit for the value of the solution. The default values are −1E99 to 1E99.

4.9 Solving for a Variable

The TI-85 solves the equation for the variable on which the cursor is placed when you select < SOLVE >.

Assume the height of a light on a pole in a parking lot is 50 ft and the intensity of the light is 1000 CP. Determine the illumination on the surface 25 ft from the pole.

(1) Use [ENTER], [↓] or [↑] to move the cursor between the variables. Enter 1000 as the value for INTEN. Enter 50 as the value for HEIGHT. Enter 25 as the value for BASE. The values of INTEN, HEIGHT, and BASE in memory are updated.

(2)   Press [↑] to move the cursor to <u>ILLUM</u>, the unknown variable. Press [F5] to select < SOLVE > from the menu. A moving bar is shown in the upper right of the display to indicate that the TI-85 is busy calculating or graphing.

The solution is displayed. The square dot next to <u>ILLUM</u> indicates that <u>ILLUM</u> was the variable for which you solved. The value of <u>ILLUM</u> in memory is updated.

<u>lft-rt</u> is the difference between the left side and the right side of the equation, evaluated at the current value of the independent variable.

If the height is 50 ft and the intensity is 1000 CP, the illumination on the surface 25 ft from the pole is .28621670111999 ft-c.

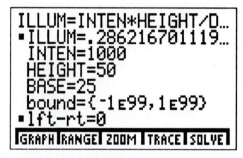

4.10   Additional Solutions with the Solver

You can continue to explore solutions to equations with the Solver. You can solve for any variable within the equation to explore "what if" questions.

If the desired illumination is exactly 0.2 ft-c, and the intensity is still 1000 CP, at what height on the pole should the light be placed?

(1)   To change the value of <u>ILLUM</u> to .2, press the [CLEAR] key to clear the value on the line quickly and then type .2. The square dots disappear to show that the solution is not current.

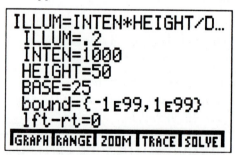

(2)   Move the cursor to <u>HEIGHT</u>. Press [F5] to select < SOLVE >. It is not necessary to clear the value of the variable for which you are solving. If the variable is not cleared, the value is used as the initial guess by the Solver. The equation is solved for <u>HEIGHT</u> and the value displayed.

The illumination on the surface is .2 ft-c and the intensity is 1000 CP, the height of the light source is 63.45876324653 ft.

The solution is dependent on the initial guess and bound.

```
ILLUM=INTEN*HEIGHT/D...
 ILLUM=.2
 INTEN=1000
•HEIGHT=63.458763246...
 BASE=25
 bound={-1E99,1E99}
•lft-rt=0
 GRAPH RANGE ZOOM TRACE SOLVE
```

4.11 Changing the Viewing Rectangle

You can graphically examine equations entered in the Solver. The viewing rectangle defines the portion of the graphing coordinate plane that is shown in the display. The values of the RANGE variables determine the size of the viewing rectangle. You can display and edit the values of the RANGE variables.

(1) Press [F2] to display the RANGE editor.

You display and edit the values of the RANGE variables on this screen. The values shown are the standard default values. The RANGE variables define the viewing rectangle as shown. xMin, xMax, yMin, and yMax define the boundaries of the display. xScl and yScl define the tick marks on the x and y axes.

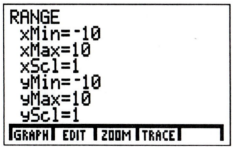

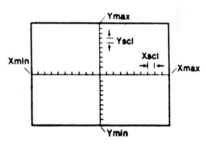

(2) Graph the illumination example using new values for the RANGE variables, as shown. Use [↓] or [ENTER] to move the cursor to each value and then type over the existing values to enter the new value. To enter −1 press [(−1)], not [-], and then press 1.

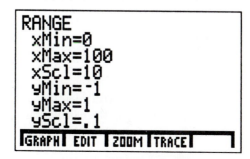

4.12 Finding a Solution from a Solver Graph

The graph plots the variable for which the cursor is placed as the independent variable on the x axis and left-rt as the dependent variable on the y axis. Solutions exist for the equation where the function intersects the x axis.

(1) Press [F1] to select < GRAPH >. The graph plots <u>HEIGHT</u> on the x axis and left-rt on the y axis in the chosen viewing rectangle. The calculation for left-rt in this case is shown below.

$$\underline{lft - rt} = ILLUM - \frac{INTEN * HEIGHT}{(BASE^2 + HEIGHT^2)^{3/2}}$$

Notice from the graph that this problem has at least two solutions; we found the solution for HEIGHT at the larger value, x=63.458763246529.

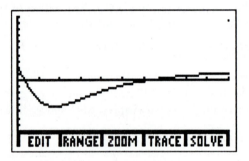

(2) To solve for the other value of <u>HEIGHT</u>, we must supply a new initial guess or alter the <u>bound</u>. You can select a new initial guess with the graph cursor.

Use [◁] and [▷] to position the cursor near where the function crosses the axis at the smaller value. As you move the cursor, the coordinate values are displayed.

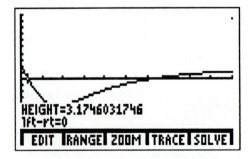

(3) Press [F5] to select < SOLVE >. The value of HEIGHT identified by the cursor will be used as the new initial guess. The busy indicator is displayed during the calculation. The illumination on the surface is

.2 ft-c and the intensity is 1000 CP, the height of the light source can be either 3.2022212466713 ft or 63.458763246529 ft.

4.13 Defining Functions to Graph

On the TI-85, functions are graphed for x and y when x is the independent variable and y=y(x). You can store unevaluated expressions with the = symbol (ALPHA function of the [STO ▷] key). This page shows how to enter the illumination problem for a graphic solution.

Graph the illumination equation and find the height that provides the maximum illumination for a base of 25 feet and an intensity of 1000 CP.

(1) Press [2nd] [QUIT] to return to the Home screen.

(2) Press [ALPHA] [ALPHA] HEIGHT= [ALPHA] [x-VAR] [ENTER] to store the unevaluated expression x in an equation variable, HEIGHT. Use [x-VAR] to enter x quickly. INTEN and BASE still contain 1000 and 25.

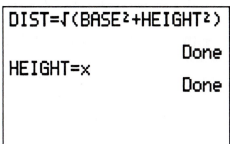

(3) Press [GRAPH] to display the GRAPH menu. Press [F1] to select < y(x)=> . The display shows the name for the first function, y1.

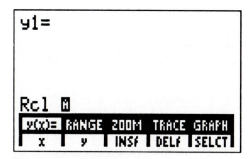

(4)   Press [2nd] [RCL]. The cursor is positioned after <u>Rcl</u> on the sixth line. The RCL feature lets you recall the expression stored in an equation variable to the cursor location. In the Solver, the illumination equation was stored in the equation variable <u>eqn</u>.

(5)   Press [2nd] [ALPHA] to change to lowercase alpha-lock and type eqn [ENTER]. The equation is copied to the cursor location.

(6)   Press [2nd] [◁] to move the cursor to the beginning of the expression quickly. Press [DEL] six times to delete <u>ILLUM=</u>. The highlighted = shows <u>y1</u> is "selected" to be graphed.

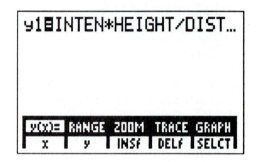

4.14 Displaying the Graph

After you have created and selected the function to graph and entered the appropriate viewing rectangle, you can display the graph.

(1)   Press [2nd] [M5] to select < GRAPH > to graph the selected functions in the viewing rectangle. ([2nd] accesses the menu times on the seventh line.)

Because <u>HEIGHT</u> is replaced by <u>x</u>, and the current value of <u>x</u> used, each time a point is plotted. The graph of the function for $0 \leq x \leq 100$ is plotted.

(2)   The graph shows that there is one maximum value of ILLUM for a height between 0 and 100.

Press [▷] once to display the graphics cursor just to the right of the center of the display. The line above the menu shows the x and y display coordinate values for the cursor position (x,y).

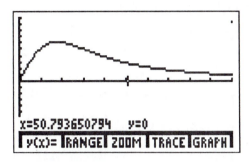

(3) Using the cursor-movement keys ([◁], [▷], [↑], and [↓]), move the cursor until it is positioned at the apparent maximum of the function. As you move the cursor, the x and y coordinate values are updated continually with the cursor position.

The free-moving cursor shows maximum illumination of .61290322581 CP for heights from 14.285714286 ft to 21.428271429 ft, within an accuracy of one display dot width. In this example, accuracy$_x$ is .793650793651 and accuracy$_y$ is .032258064516, calculated as shown.

$$\text{Accuracy}_x = \frac{(xMAX - xMin)}{126} = .793650793651 \text{ in this example.}$$

$$\text{Accuracy}_y = \frac{(yMAX - yMin)}{62} = .03225806452 \text{ in this example.}$$

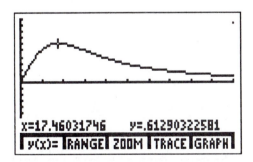

4.15 Tracing along a Function

Using the TRACE feature of the TI-85, you can move the cursor along a function, showing the x and y display coordinate values of the cursor location on the function.

(1) Press [F4] to select < TRACE >. The TRACE cursor appears near the middle of the screen on the function.

The coordinate values of the cursor location $(x, y1(x))$ are displayed on the bottom line of the display. No menu items are shown. The y value shown is the calculated value of the function for the displayed value of x. That is, if $y1 = f(x)$, then the value of y shown is $f(x)$.

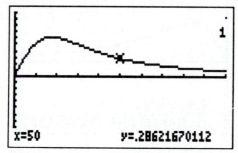

(2)   Use [▷] and [◁] to move along a function until you have traced to the largest y value.

The maximum illumination is .61577762623 CP if the height is 17.46031746 ft.

This value of y is the function value $f(x)$ at the x display coordinate value. It is different than the value found with the free-moving cursor, which is based on the RANGE settings.

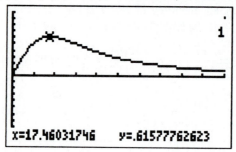

4.16 Finding a Maximum Graphically

Within the operations on the GRAPH MATH menu, you can analyze a displayed graph to determine where minimum and maximum values, inflection points, and intercepts occur.

(1)   Press [EXIT] to display the GRAPH menu. Press [MORE] to display additional items on the GRAPH menu.

(2)   Press [F1] to select < MATH > . Press [MORE] to display additional items on the GRAPH MATH menu.

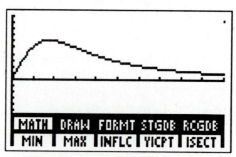

(3) Press [F2] to select < FMAX >. The TRACE cursor appears near the middle of the screen on the function on the point (x,y1(x)).

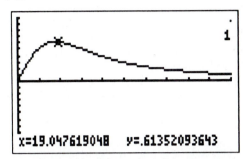

(4) Press [ENTER]. The calculator computed maximum is displayed in the cursor coordinates at the bottom of the display, .61584028714 at an x value of 17.677668581. This value of y is larger than the value found with the TRACE cursor. This is the most accurate of the three graphical solutions we have tried. Note: The FMAX and FMIN calculator algorithms search between < LOWER > and < UPPER > and use tol from the [2nd] [TOLER] menu to control accuracy.

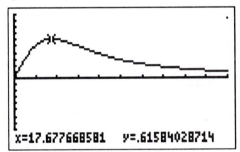

4.17 Graphing the Derivative

The maxima and minima of a continuous differentiable function, if they exist, occur where the first derivative is equal to 0. On the TI-85, you can graph the **exact** derivative of a function.

(1) Press [GRAPH]. Press [F1] to display the y(x) editor.

Press [ENTER] to move to y2.

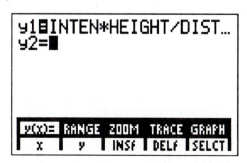

(2) The calculus functions are grouped on the CALC menu. Press [2nd] [CALC] to display the calculus menu on the bottom line.

(3) Press [F3]. The function name for the exact first derivative, der1 (, is copied to the cursor location.

(4) Press [2nd] [M2] to copy y from the menu on the seventh line to the cursor location, then type 1 to enter the name of the first equation, y1. Press [,].

(5) On the TI-85, you can evaluate the calculus functions with respect to any variable, but to be meaningful in graphing, the variable of differentiation or integration should be x.

Press [2nd] [F1] or [2nd][M1] to copy x to the cursor location. Press [ )].

Remark der1(y1,x) is the *exact derivative*, evaluated at the current value of x. When this equation is graphed, the derivative will be calculated for each value of x on the graph.

4.18 Zooming In on the Graph

You can magnify the viewing rectangle around a specific cursor location by selecting the Zoom In instruction from the ZOOM menu.

(1) Press [EXIT] [2nd] [M5] to select < GRAPH > and graph both functions. The busy indicator displays while the graph is plotted. The viewing rectangle is the same as you defined in the Solver, $0 \leq x \leq 100$ and $-1 \leq y \leq 1$. In this viewing rectangle, the graph of the derivative function is very close to the x axis.

(2) Press [F3] to select < ZOOM >.

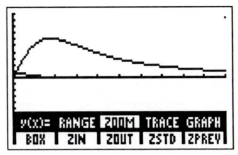

(3) To zoom in, press [F2] to select < ZIN > from the menu.

The cursor appears at the middle of the display.

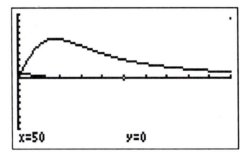

(4) Use the cursor-movement keys to position the cursor near where the derivative function appears to cross the x axis. Press [ENTER]. The position of the cursor becomes the center of the new viewing rectangle. The busy indicator displays while the graph is plotted.

The new viewing rectangle has been adjusted in both the x and y directions by factors of 4, which are the current values for the zoom factors.

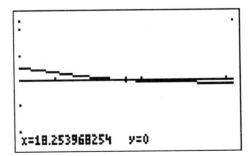

4.19 Finding a Root Graphically

The TI-85 can find the root (zero) of a graphed function and can calculate the value of the function for any value of x. The TI-85 can find the root (zero) of a graphed function and can calculate the value of the function for any value of x. Find the x value where the root of the derivative function der1(y1,x) occurs and use it to calculate the maximum of the function.

(1) Press [EXIT] [EXIT] to display the GRAPH menu on the bottom line and press [MORE] to display additional menu items. Press [F1] to select < MATH > to display the GRAPH MATH operations.

(2) Press [F3] to select < ROOT >. The TRACE cursor is near the middle y value "on" the y1 function, as indicated by the 1 in the upper right corner of the display. The y1 function is "above" the display.

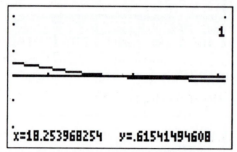

x=18.253968254   y=.61541494608

(3) Press [↓] to move the cursor to the derivative function, y2, as indicated by the 2 in the upper right corner of the display. You can use [▷] and [◁] to move the cursor to a point near the root.

(4) Press [ENTER]. The busy indicator display while the root is calculated. The calculated root is displayed in the cursor coordinates at the bottom of the display: y=-1.21363E-15 at an x value of 17.67766953.

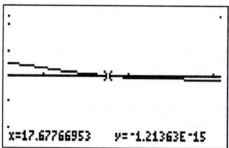

x=17.67766953   y=-1.21363E-15

(5) Press [EXIT] [EXIT] [MORE] [F1] to select < EVAL >. Press [2nd] [Ans] [ENTER] to enter the solution to ROOT as the value for x. The results cursor "displays" on the y1 function at the specified x.

On page 44, < FMAX > found a maximum of y=.61584028714 at x=17.677668581. Corresponding to the maximum, ROOT found a root of the derivative at x=17.67766953, which evaluated to a maximum, y1=.61584028714.

4.20   Other Features

This brief chapter introduced you to some basic TI-85 calculator operations, some function graphing features, and one equation solving feature. You should consult the TI-85 User's Guide to learn about these features in more detail and also learn about the many other capabilities of the TI-85. The TI-85 User's Guide Chapter references are noted in parentheses.

4.20.1   Some Other Capabilities of the TI-85

(1)   In function graphing, you can store, graph, and analyze up to 99 functions (Chapter 4). In polar graphing, you can store, graph, and analyze up to 99 polar equations (Chapter 5). In parametric graphing, you can store, graph, and analyze up to 99 parametric equations (Chapter 6). In differential equation graphing, you can store, graph, and analyze a differential equation up to nine first-order differential equations (Chapter 7).

(2)   You can use drawing and shading features to add emphasis or perform additional analysis on function, polar, parametric, and differential equation graphs (Chapter 4).

(3)   You can solve an equation for any variable, solve a system of up to 30 simultaneous linear equations, and find the real and complex roots of a polynomial equation (Chapter 14).

(4)   You can enter and store an unlimited number of matrices and vectors with dimensions up to 255. The TI-85 has standard matrix operations, including elementary row operations, and standard vector operations (Chapter 13).

(5)   The TI-85 performs one-variable and two-variable statistical analyses. You can enter and store an unlimited number of data points. Seven regression models are available: linear, logarithmic, exponential, power, and second-, third-, and fourth-order polynomial models. You can analyze data graphically with histograms, scatter plots, and line drawings and plot regression equation graphs (Chapter 15).

(6)   Programming capabilities include extensive control and I/O instructions. You can enter and store an unlimited number of programs (Chapter 16).

(7)   You can share data and programs with another TI-85. You can print graphs and programs, enter programs, and save data on a disk through a PC (Chapter 19).

(8)   The TI-85 has 32K of RAM available to you for storing variables, programs, pictures, and graph databases.

Chapter 5

Calculating and Graphing with First Generation Casio Calculators

The purpose of this chapter is to acquaint you with the features of the Casio graphing calculators (models fx-7000G, fx-7500G, fx-8000G, and fx-8500G) that are useful in a graphical approach to precalculus mathematics. Section 5.1 provides some general information about using the Casio and explains how to use its computing and editing features. Section 5.2 discusses the basics of graphing on the Casio without programming. Section 5.3 combines programming with graphics. So get ready to explore and experiment. And always have your Casio handy while reading this chapter.

5.1 Numerical Computation and Editing

5.1.1 The Shift and Alpha Keys: The distinctively colored $\boxed{\text{SHIFT}}$ and $\boxed{\text{ALPHA}}$ keys are special. Use them as you would a *second function* or *inverse key* on other calculators. That is, any special function or symbol written in gold (blue on the fx-7500G) on the keyboard is accessed by first pressing $\boxed{\text{SHIFT}}$ and then pressing the associated key. Similarly, any alphabetic character or symbol written in red (grey on the fx-7500G) on the keyboard is accessed by pressing $\boxed{\text{ALPHA}}$ followed by the associated key. For example, if you wanted to use the number π in your computations, you would key in $\boxed{\text{SHIFT}}$ followed by $\boxed{\text{EXP}}$. In this manual, however, this keying sequence is written $\boxed{\text{SHIFT}}$ $\boxed{\pi}$. To access the letter T, you would press $\boxed{\text{ALPHA}}$ followed by $\boxed{\div}$, but the keying sequence is written $\boxed{\text{ALPHA}}$ $\boxed{\text{T}}$. Once you gain some familiarity with the keyboard, this approach should seem natural.

A Special Note Concerning (SHIFT). The fx-7500G has a different keyboard from the fx-7000G, fx-8000G, and fx-8500G. The fx-7500G has nine more keys than the other models. Nine features accessed by $\boxed{\text{SHIFT}}$ on the fx-7000G, fx-8000G, and fx-8500G do not require a $\boxed{\text{SHIFT}}$ on the fx-7500G. For instance, the exponential function e^x requires no $\boxed{\text{SHIFT}}$ on the fx-7500G. To indicate this, we will write (SHIFT) $\boxed{e^x}$. To access the exponential function on the fx-7500G, you would simply press $\boxed{e^x}$, but on the fx-7000G, fx-8000G, or fx-8500G, you would press $\boxed{\text{SHIFT}}$ $\boxed{e^x}$. Example 5 in Section 5.1.4 illustrates an exponential function computation.

5.1.2 Getting Ready to Compute: Turn on the Casio. The power switch is located on the left side of the fx-7000G and fx-7500G and is located directly below the display screen on the fx-8000G and fx-8500G. If the screen is too light or too dark, adjust it by using the special **contrast** dial on the right edge of the upper keyboard on the fx-7500G. On the fx-7000G, fx-8000G, or fx-8500G, adjust the contrast by first pressing $\boxed{\text{MODE}}$, then pressing $\boxed{\Rightarrow}$ or $\boxed{\Leftarrow}$ several times to darken or lighten the screen as necessary. Your screen should look like Figure 5.1. If it does, go on to Section 5.1.3.

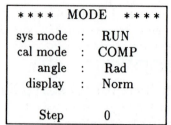

Figure 5.1. The screen as it appears when you turn on the Casio.

Whenever you turn on the Casio, the system mode will be RUN. If the calculation mode is not COMP (computation), key in $\boxed{\text{MODE}}$ $\boxed{+}$. If the angle mode is not Rad (radian), key in $\boxed{\text{MODE}}$ $\boxed{5}$ $\boxed{\text{EXE}}$. If the display mode is not Norm (normal), key in $\boxed{\text{MODE}}$ $\boxed{9}$ $\boxed{\text{EXE}}$. The modes of the Casio are explained briefly in Sections 5.1.6 and 5.3.1. For details, see your *Owner's Manual.*

5.1.3 Error Messages and Editing Expressions

Cursor/Replay Keys. The keys $\boxed{\Leftarrow}$, $\boxed{\Rightarrow}$, $\boxed{\Uparrow}$, and $\boxed{\Downarrow}$ on the fx-7000G, fx-8000G, and fx-8500G (or $\boxed{\blacktriangleleft}$, $\boxed{\blacktriangleright}$, $\boxed{\blacktriangle}$, and $\boxed{\blacktriangledown}$ on the fx-7500G) are used to move the cursor (blinking __) left, right, up, and down, respectively. These are called *cursor keys*. The keys $\boxed{\Leftarrow}$ and $\boxed{\Rightarrow}$ also act as **replay** keys; that is, they return you to the last command statement and allow you to *edit and reexecute* that command.

Insertions and deletions. The **insert** feature is used in conjunction with the replay and cursor keys to add one or more symbols to a displayed expression. In general, simply move the cursor to the location of the insertion, and then key in (SHIFT) $\boxed{\text{INS}}$ followed by one or more symbols. The **delete** key is also used in conjunction with the replay and cursor keys. To delete a character, use the cursor keys to move the cursor to the unwanted symbol and press $\boxed{\text{DEL}}$.

Errors and Overwriting. Sometimes while you are computing or running a program, your Casio will display an **error** message. For example, suppose you wanted to add a positive 7 to a negative 6. Key in $\boxed{7}$ $\boxed{+}$ $\boxed{-}$ $\boxed{6}$ $\boxed{\text{EXE}}$. The Casio screen should look like Figure 5.2.

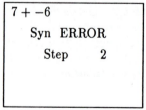

Figure 5.2. Error message.

The message in Figure 5.2 means we have made a syntax error at Step 2 (counting begins at Step 0) of our input expression. A syntax error message generally indicates a mistake in a formula or misuse of a program command. Press the $\boxed{\Leftarrow}$ **replay** key, which takes you immediately to the cause of the error message. At this point, **overwrite** the subtraction operation sign with a negative sign by pressing $\boxed{(-)}$. Then reexecute by pressing $\boxed{\text{EXE}}$. You should obtain the expected result, 1.

Now try $\boxed{9}$ $\boxed{\div}$ $\boxed{0}$ $\boxed{\text{EXE}}$. You will get a "math" error message. Why?

5.1.4 Using the "Scientific" Functions: Like any scientific calculator, the Casio has many built-in functions. But the order in which you press the keys on the Casio differs from most traditional scientific calculators. Here are some examples to get you started using the scientific functions. Once you gain control of these functions, try exploring other keys on your own.

Powers and Roots. Press [AC] once; then without pressing [AC] again, perform the following six computational examples. (Figures 5.3 and 5.4 show how these computations should appear on the Casio screen. Refer to the figures as you proceed through the computations.)

$$(-5)x^y 4$$
$$\qquad 625.$$
$$4\ ^x\!\sqrt{2401}$$
$$\phantom{4\ ^x\!\sqrt{2401}}\qquad 7.$$
$$\sin 45^\circ$$
$$\qquad 0.7071067812$$
$$\sqrt{2} \div 2$$
$$\phantom{\sqrt{2} \div 2}\qquad 0.7071067812$$

Figure 5.3. Power, root, and trigonometric computations.

$$e\pi$$
$$\qquad 23.14069263$$
$$\text{Int } -3.749$$
$$\phantom{\text{Int } -3.749}\qquad -3.$$
$$5 \rightarrow A$$
$$\qquad 5.$$
$$4A^2 - 3 \rightarrow R$$
$$\qquad 97.$$

Figure 5.4. Assorted computations.

(1) Evaluate $(-5)^4$ using [(] [(-)] [5] [)] [x^y] [4] [EXE]. Remember not to confuse the additive inverse, or "sign change," key [(-)] with the subtraction key [−].

(2) Simplify $\sqrt[4]{2401}$ with the keying sequence [4] [$^x\!\sqrt{}$] [2401] [EXE].

(3) To calculate the sine of a 45-degree angle without switching to degree mode, key in [sin] [45] [SHIFT] [MODE] [4] [EXE].

(4) In trigonometry you learn that $\sin 45^\circ = \frac{\sqrt{2}}{2}$. Press [$\sqrt{}$] [2] [÷] [2] [EXE]. Look at the answer, and compare it with the previous answer on the screen display.

(5) Exponential function computations look strange on the Casio. For example, when you key in (SHIFT) [e^x]) [SHIFT] [π] [EXE], the screen display suggests that e has been multiplied by π, but actually e has been raised to the power π (See Figure 5.4).

(6) The accompanying textbook discusses the **greatest integer function** INT. It is easy to confuse the greatest integer function with the Casio **integer truncation function** Int. To see that they are different functions, press [SHIFT] [Int] [(-)] [3.749] [EXE]. On the Casio, Int(-3.749) = -3, but the

greatest integer less than or equal to -3.749 is -4; so, INT(-3.749) = -4. The moral to this story is: **There is no direct way to access the greatest integer function on the Casio.**

5.1.5   Memory and the Assignment Arrow: The uppercase letters A through Z on the Casio keyboard act as the names for 26 memory locations, or **storage registers**. Use the assignment key → to assign a numerical value to a storage register. (Don't confuse the assignment key → with the cursor key ⇒.) For example, key in the sequence $\boxed{5}$ $\boxed{→}$ $\boxed{\text{ALPHA}}$ $\boxed{\text{A}}$ $\boxed{\text{EXE}}$ to assign the number 5 to storage register A. The value **5.** should appear on the right side of the display screen (see Figure 5.4). Key in $\boxed{4}$ $\boxed{\text{ALPHA}}$ $\boxed{\text{A}}$ $\boxed{x^2}$ $\boxed{-}$ $\boxed{3}$ $\boxed{→}$ $\boxed{\text{ALPHA}}$ $\boxed{\text{R}}$ $\boxed{\text{EXE}}$ to compute $4A^2 - 3$ and assign the value to R. Notice that the Casio understands **left juxtaposition** as multiplication, that is, it multiplies the 4 by the A^2.

A value stored in a register will remain there until you assign the register a different value, *even if you turn off the machine.* To check this, turn the calculator off, then on again, and key in $\boxed{\text{ALPHA}}$ $\boxed{\text{A}}$ $\boxed{\text{EXE}}$. The value **5.** should appear at the right of the screen (see Figure 5.5). The keying sequence $\boxed{\text{ALPHA}}$ $\boxed{\text{R}}$ $\boxed{\text{EXE}}$ will reveal the contents of R.

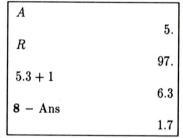

Figure 5.5. Further computations.

The Answer Key. The Casio has a special storage register in which the answer to the *last* computation is automatically stored. To check its contents, key in $\boxed{\text{Ans}}$ $\boxed{\text{EXE}}$. The stored value can be used in further computations. As a simple example, key in $\boxed{5.3}$ $\boxed{+}$ $\boxed{1}$ $\boxed{\text{EXE}}$ (see Figure 5.5). The value **6.3** is now stored in the "Ans" memory. Now key in $\boxed{8}$ $\boxed{-}$ $\boxed{\text{Ans}}$ $\boxed{\text{EXE}}$. The answer **1.7** should appear on the display screen (and is automatically placed in Ans).

Input Buffer. On the fx-8000G and fx-8500G, $\boxed{\text{MODE}}$ $\boxed{\text{Ans}}$ acts as an input buffer recall. Similar to replay, it recalls the previous input even if you press $\boxed{\text{AC}}$ or turn off the machine. If you're using one of these models, try it! The fx-7000G and fx-7500G have no input buffers.

5.1.6   Miscellaneous Matters

Modes. The Casio has many capabilities. For each particular use, the status of the unit must be set appropriately. When you first turn on your calculator, you see the **mode display window**. At other times, you can check to see which modes are active by pressing $\boxed{\boxed{\text{M}}\text{-Disp}}$, but the mode display window will remain on the screen only while this key is depressed. Generally, we will operate in the modes shown in Figure 5.1. *You are encouraged to confirm which modes are active before calculating, graphing, or programming on the Casio.*

The mode-setting codes are shown on your calculator directly below the display screen on the fx-7000G, fx-8000G, and fx-8500G and above the lower keyboard on the fx-7500G. Modes 1, 2, and 3 are used to run, write, or delete programs. These are explained in Section 5.3.1. Modes 4, 5, and 6 are used to choose degree, radian, or grad **angle** measure. Modes 7, 8, and 9 specify a fixed-decimal-place, scientific notation, or "normal" **display**. The **calculation** mode should be set to COMP using `MODE` `+`, unless you wish to do statistical computations or operate in bases other than base 10. For full details, consult your *Owner's Manual*.

Display Windows. In all, the Casio features four display windows:

(1)   The mode display window.

(2)   The text display window.

(3)   The graphics display window.

(4)   The Range settings display window.

Figure 5.1 shows an example of the mode display window. Most of the time while working through this section your calculator was displaying its text window. Calculating, table building, and program writing all occur in the text display window. In Section 5.2 you will be introduced to the Range settings display window, the graphics display window, and to the `Range` and `G ↔ T` "toggle" keys that allow you to move in and out of these two windows.

Automatic Power Off. The Casio's power is automatically switched off approximately 6 minutes after the last operation. The display screen goes blank, and you lose any formulas from the text screen, but the memory, programs, Range, and graphics-window contents are all retained. You can restore the power by either switching the machine off, then on, or by pressing `AC`.

5.2   Casio Graphing Fundamentals

Set your system, calculation, and angle modes to RUN, COMP, and RAD (for help, see Section 5.1.2). These modes are used throughout this chapter.

In this section we will explore graphing techniques that require no programming. The key to any computer-based graphing is learning how to control and select viewing rectangles so that you can see the parts of the graph or graphs you are interested in. On the Casio the **Range** feature is used to set the viewing rectangle as well as the scale marks on each axis. Choosing and changing viewing rectangles is a major focus of this section.

Ways to Change the Viewing Rectangle. There are six ways to change from one viewing rectangle to another on the Casio. These are listed below together with the section where each method is introduced.

(1)   Keying in Range settings (Section 5.2.1).

(2)   Graphing a built-in function without using X (Section 5.2.1).

(3)   Pressing `SHIFT` `Mcl` while in the Range settings window (Section 5.2.1).

(4)   Using automatic zoom-in, `SHIFT` `×`, or zoom-out, `SHIFT` `÷` (Section 5.2.2).

(5)   Using the Factor feature to zoom-in or zoom-out (Section 5.3.4).

(6)   Setting the Range within a program (Programming Hint 2, Section 5.3.3). The Zoom-In Program given in Section 5.3.6 is an especially useful example of this.

The abilities to **clear the graphics window** and to **overlay graphs** are also important to graphical problem solving. These are explained in Sections 5.2.1 and 5.2.2, respectively.

5.2.1 Graphing and Range Settings

Graphing Built-in Functions. Key in $\boxed{\text{Graph}}$ $\boxed{x^2}$ $\boxed{\text{EXE}}$. Figure 5.6 shows a pixel for pixel facsimile of the Casio graph that is produced. After the graph is drawn, press the $\boxed{\text{Range}}$ key. The Range setting values should be:

$$\text{Xmin} = \text{-7} \qquad \text{Xmax} = 7 \qquad \text{Xscale} = 2 \qquad \text{Ymin} = \text{-2} \qquad \text{Ymax} = 29 \qquad \text{Yscale} = 5$$

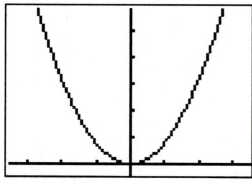
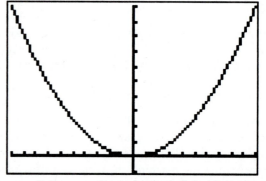

Figure 5.6. $y = x^2$, $[-7,7]$ by $[-2,29]$.   **Figure 5.7.** $y = \sin x$, $[-2\pi, 2\pi]$ by $[-1.6, 1.6]$.

Press $\boxed{\text{Range}}$ again to toggle back to the graphics window, then key in $\boxed{\text{G} \leftrightarrow \text{T}}$ to return to the text window. The key $\boxed{\text{G} \leftrightarrow \text{T}}$ allows you to alternate (toggle) between the graphics and text windows. Key in $\boxed{\text{Graph}}$ $\boxed{\text{sin}}$ $\boxed{\text{EXE}}$ (see Figure 5.7). What are the Range values now? Have they changed? They should have. They should now be essentially the following values. (The Casio actually uses and displays decimal approximations of the Xmin, Xmax, and Xscale values listed below.)

$$\text{Xmin} = \text{-2}\,\pi \qquad \text{Xmax} = 2\,\pi \qquad \text{Xscale} = \pi \qquad \text{Ymin} = \text{-1.6} \qquad \text{Ymax} = 1.6 \qquad \text{Yscale} = 0.5$$

Graph some other built-in functions, that is, those accessible using $\boxed{\text{Graph}}$ $\boxed{\text{key}}$ $\boxed{\text{EXE}}$ or $\boxed{\text{Graph}}$ $\boxed{\text{SHIFT}}$ $\boxed{\text{key}}$ $\boxed{\text{EXE}}$. Each built-in function on the Casio has built-in Range settings. Try graphing $\log x$, $\ln x$, e^x, $\cos x$, $\tan x$, x^{-1}, and other built-in functions. Check the Range values after executing each graph.

Clearing the Graphics Window. Whenever any of the Range settings are changed, the graphics display window is automatically cleared. At times you may wish to clear all graphs from the graphics window without changing the viewing rectangle or scale marks. To do this, press (SHIFT) $\boxed{\text{Cls}}$ $\boxed{\text{EXE}}$. You can check to see that the graphics window has been cleared by pressing $\boxed{\text{G} \leftrightarrow \text{T}}$. The graphs are removed, but the scaled axes are not.

Choosing the Viewing Rectangle You Want. You can select any Range values you wish, *but then you must provide the function with the argument X.* If the Range settings window is not already showing on your display screen, press $\boxed{\text{Range}}$. Then key in the values

$$\text{Xmin} = \text{-10} \qquad \text{Xmax} = 10 \qquad \text{Xscale} = 1 \qquad \text{Ymin} = \text{-10} \qquad \text{Ymax} = 100 \qquad \text{Yscale} = 10$$

pressing $\boxed{\texttt{EXE}}$ after keying in each of the six values. These Range values are referred to as the **viewing rectangle** $[-10, 10]$ by $[-10, 100]$ with Xscale = 1 and Yscale = 10.

Agreement. In this manual, Range values are specified in terms of viewing rectangles, and you are left to choose appropriate Xscale and Yscale values.

Now key in $\boxed{\texttt{Graph}}$ $\boxed{\texttt{ALPHA}}$ $\boxed{\texttt{X}}$ $\boxed{x^2}$ $\boxed{\texttt{EXE}}$. Check the Range (see Figure 5.8).

Setting the Casio Default Range. If the Range settings window is not showing, press $\boxed{\texttt{Range}}$. Then key in $\boxed{\texttt{SHIFT}}$ $\boxed{\texttt{Mcl}}$ to enter the **Casio default viewing rectangle** of $[-4.7, 4.7]$ by $[-3.1, 3.1]$. (Note: As described in Section 2.3, this choice yields a Δx of 0.1 (and also a corresponding change in y, $\Delta y = (\text{Ymax} - \text{Ymin})/62$, of 0.1).) Notice that the Casio default viewing rectangle is different from the **standard viewing rectangle** of $[-10, 10]$ by $[-10, 10]$ used in the accompanying textbook. Press $\boxed{\texttt{Range}}$ to get out of the Range window, and then key in $\boxed{\texttt{Graph}}$ $\boxed{\texttt{sin}}$ $\boxed{\texttt{EXE}}$. After the graph is drawn press $\boxed{\texttt{Range}}$ (see Figure 5.8). What happened? The Casio automatically uses the built-in Range for each function if you leave out the X. Now reset the default values by keying in $\boxed{\texttt{SHIFT}}$ $\boxed{\texttt{Mcl}}$ $\boxed{\texttt{Range}}$ again, and then press $\boxed{\texttt{Graph}}$ $\boxed{\texttt{sin}}$ $\boxed{\texttt{ALPHA}}$ $\boxed{\texttt{X}}$ $\boxed{\texttt{EXE}}$. Check the Range (see Figure 5.9).

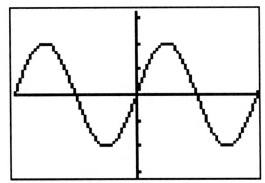   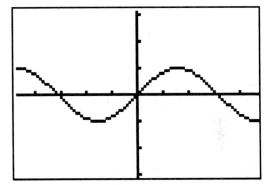

Figure 5.8. $y = x^2$, $[-10, 10]$ by $[-10, 100]$.   **Figure 5.9.** $y = \sin x$, $[-4.7, 4.7]$ by $[-3.1, 3.1]$.

5.2.2 Overlaying Graphs, Trace, and Automatic Zooming: Now that you are familiar with how to set Range values, the next steps in graphing on the Casio are to overlay graphs and to use the Trace and automatic zoom features. These steps are demonstrated in the equation solving problem given below.

Overlaying Graphs. The $\boxed{:}$ key can be used to string together a series of command statements. This method can be used to graph several functions—one after the other in the same viewing rectangle—by stringing together several Graph statements.

Trace. To locate points on a graph, we use the Trace feature. This feature allows dot-to-dot movement along the most recently drawn graph, with the calculator displaying the x- or y-coordinate associated with each dot, or **pixel**, along the way. It is easy to stop, reverse direction, and switch from an x-readout to a y-readout or vice versa.

Automatic Zoom. The Casio *Owner's Manual* calls this the "instant factor function." Early versions of the fx-7000G did not have this feature. Now all four Casio graphing calculator models possess this important capability. You can either **zoom-in** to study a small portion of a graph or graphs or **zoom-out** to investigate global behavior.

Using these Casio features you can graphically solve equations, inequalities, and systems of equations. These features open the door to solving extreme-value (max/min) problems and to determining intervals over which a function is increasing or decreasing. The same methods apply regardless of the functions involved. The equation $\cos x = \tan x$ can be solved by the same graphical method that would be used to solve $2x = 6$.

Problem   Solve $\cos x = \tan x$ for $0 \leq x \leq 1$.

Solution   Clear the graphics screen and reset the default viewing rectangle by keying in $\boxed{\text{Range}}$ $\boxed{\text{SHIFT}}$ $\boxed{\text{Mcl}}$ $\boxed{\text{Range}}$. Then enter the functions by pressing $\boxed{\text{Graph}}$ $\boxed{\text{cos}}$ $\boxed{\text{ALPHA}}$ $\boxed{\text{X}}$ $\boxed{:}$ $\boxed{\text{Graph}}$ $\boxed{\text{tan}}$ $\boxed{\text{ALPHA}}$ $\boxed{\text{X}}$. The text screen should look like this:

Graph Y = cos X : Gr

aph Y = tan X

Edit if necessary, and then press $\boxed{\text{EXE}}$. Watch carefully: Notice that the cosine function is drawn first, and then the tangent function is **overlaid** (see Figure 5.10).

You can approximate the coordinates of any point on the most recently graphed function with the **Trace** feature. Press (SHIFT) $\boxed{\text{Trace}}$. Locate the blinking pixel at the left of the screen. Use the right cursor key $\boxed{\Rightarrow}$ repeatedly to move the blinking pixel to the point of intersection of the graphs of $y = \cos x$ and $y = \tan x$ that lies between $x = 0$ and $x = 1$. The x-coordinate should be 0.7 (see Figure 5.11). Now press $\boxed{\text{SHIFT}}$ $\boxed{\text{X} \leftrightarrow \text{Y}}$. What is the y-coordinate?

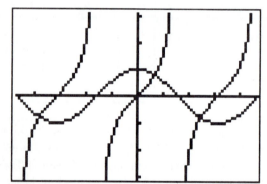
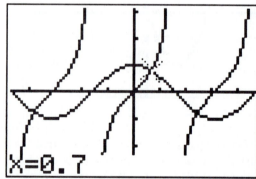

Figure 5.10. Cosine and tangent overlaid.   **Figure 5.11.** Trace approximating intersection.

Automatic Zoom-In. With the picture in Figure 5.11 showing on the screen, press $\boxed{\text{SHIFT}}$ $\boxed{\times}$. Notice that the Casio uses the traced-to point as the center of the new, smaller viewing rectangle. The automatic zoom factor is 2 in both the x and y directions. Press $\boxed{\text{SHIFT}}$ $\boxed{\times}$ again. If you did not use Trace, the Casio zooms in about the center of the current viewing rectangle. Without using Trace and waiting for the new graphs each time, zoom in three more times (for a total of 5 zoom-in steps). You should obtain the view shown in Figure 5.12.

Now use Trace again to locate the new, improved approximation for the x-coordinate of the point of intersection (see Figure 5.13).

You could follow this by repeated use of $\boxed{\text{SHIFT}}$ $\boxed{\times}$ to obtain further accuracy.

Automatic Zoom-Out. To zoom-out automatically (on all but early versions of the fx-7000G), press $\boxed{\text{SHIFT}}$ $\boxed{\div}$.

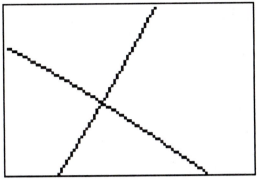

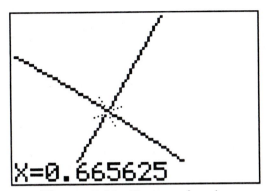

Figure 5.12. After five zoom-in steps.   **Figure 5.13.** Trace used again.

Alternative Zooming Methods. When you first begin using the Casio, you may be more comfortable zooming-in and zooming-out by changing the Range settings by hand. Eventually you will probably use a variety of methods depending on the situation. Section 5.3.4 explains how to use the Factor feature in conjunction with stored graphing statements—an approach that is more versatile than automatic zoom and that is available on all Casio machines, even old fx-7000Gs. For zooming-in on any Casio, the Zoom-In Program of Section 5.3.6 is fast, effective, and visually appealing.

5.3 Combining Graphics with Programming on the Casio

Sections 5.3.1 through 5.3.3 provide an introduction to Casio programming. You may wish to read these sections quickly now, and then refer to them later as questions arise. Section 5.3.4 shows how to graph from a program, which can save time and avoid the frustration of having to retype a function to be graphed. Section 5.3.5 discusses the Plot and Line features that are put to use in Sections 5.3.6–5.3.8 in useful graphing programs.

5.3.1 Programming Modes: The Casio computer has three modes of operation related to programming: Modes 1, 2, and 3. **Mode 1** is the **RUN** mode. The computer must be in this mode to run stored programs. The Mode 1 screen is the screen that first appears when the computer is turned on. Figure 5.1 shows this screen. Notice that the first line of information indicates the system is in RUN mode.

Mode 2 is the **WRT** mode, or the program writing mode. This is the mode used to write, edit, and store programs. There are 10 program storage locations numbered **0** through **9**. These 10 storage locations are represented on the Mode 2 screen by the 10 digits at the bottom of the screen (see Figure 5.14).

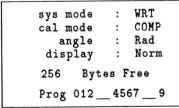

```
sys mode   :  WRT
cal mode   :  COMP
   angle   :  Rad
 display   :  Norm

256   Bytes Free

Prog 012 __ 4567 __ 9
```

Figure 5.14. Mode 2 screen; system in WRT mode.

Empty program storage locations are indicated by a visible digit, and locations containing programs are indicated by a "__" in place of the digit. In Figure 5.14, program storage locations 3 and 8 contain programs, while the remaining locations are empty. To select a program storage location, use the $\boxed{\Leftarrow}$ and $\boxed{\Rightarrow}$ cursor keys to move through the 10 digits. The location selected will flash. To view an existing program or to write a new program press $\boxed{\text{EXE}}$ when the location of your choice is flashing. If you pick a location with an existing program, the program is displayed on the screen. If you pick an empty location, a blank screen with the cursor in the upper left corner should appear, indicating a new program may be entered. As statements are keyed in, they are displayed on the screen and automatically saved in the memory of the computer. Even if you were to switch the computer off in the middle of a program, all the work done up to that point will be saved. Once a new program is written or an existing program is edited, the computer must be returned to Mode 1 to run the program. This is done by keying $\boxed{\text{MODE}}$ $\boxed{1}$.

   Mode 3 is the **PCL** mode, or the program clearing mode. This mode is used to erase existing programs from the memory of the computer. The Mode 3 screen is identical to the Mode 2 screen except that the system mode is PCL (see Figure 5.15).

```
sys mode    :  PCL
cal mode    :  COMP
   angle    :  Rad
 display    :  Norm

256   Bytes Free

Prog 012__4567__9
```

Figure 5.15. Mode 3 screen; system in PCL mode.

Caution should be exercised when using Mode 3 because you may mistakenly delete a program you wish to save. Selection of program storage locations is the same in Mode 3 as in Mode 2. To delete a single program, select the storage location using the $\boxed{\Leftarrow}$ and $\boxed{\Rightarrow}$ cursor keys and press $\boxed{\text{AC}}$. After a slight delay the number of that location will appear indicating an empty storage location. To clear all 10 programs at once, press $\boxed{\text{SHIFT}}$ $\boxed{\text{Mcl}}$. All of the digits 0 through 9 will then appear. Remember, once a program storage location is cleared, the stored program is gone. There is no temporary storage buffer to give you a second chance. When you are finished erasing programs, you may return either to Mode 2 to write programs or to Mode 1 to run programs.

5.3.2 Writing, Running, and Editing Programs

Writing a Program. To write a program, enter Mode 2 by keying $\boxed{\text{MODE}}$ $\boxed{2}$, select an empty program storage location and press $\boxed{\text{EXE}}$, and then type the code (key in the statements) of the program. Anything you type will be saved. When you have finished typing the program, exit the writing mode and return to the RUN mode by keying $\boxed{\text{MODE}}$ $\boxed{1}$.

Running a Program. Programs can be run only from Mode 1. To run a program put the computer in Mode 1 by keying $\boxed{\text{MODE}}$ $\boxed{1}$. This is also the default system mode when the computer is turned on. Programs are stored in the numbered storage locations 0 through 9. To run a program, say Program 4, key in $\boxed{\text{Prog}}$ $\boxed{4}$ $\boxed{\text{EXE}}$. To run a different program use the number of that program in the previous keying sequence. This method of naming programs by number means that you must remember which program is stored in which location. When a program is finished running, the computer is still in the RUN mode; no special commands are necessary to continue. To run the same program again, press $\boxed{\text{EXE}}$; the last program command statement will be reexecuted, running the program again.

Editing a Program. Program editing is done just like writing a program. Enter Mode 2 by keying $\boxed{\text{MODE}}$ $\boxed{2}$; select the location of the program you wish to edit; and press $\boxed{\text{EXE}}$. The program will be shown on the screen. Use the cursor arrow keys ($\boxed{\Leftarrow}$, $\boxed{\Rightarrow}$, $\boxed{\Uparrow}$, and $\boxed{\Downarrow}$) to move the cursor to the point in the program you wish to edit. Use the Insert and Delete features to insert or remove symbols or entire commands. When the editing is finished, return to Mode 1 to run the program. No special commands are needed to save the changes in the program.

5.3.3 Programming Hints

(1) **The uses of EXE and ◢ in programming.** When entering the programs listed in this manual, each line in a program listing should be finished with an $\boxed{\text{EXE}}$ (Execute) keystroke. It appears that nothing is entered into the program, but the cursor moves to the next full line. This keystroke operates like a carriage **return** when typing. The EXE key enters an invisible character that separates command lines in a program.

Programs listed in your Casio *Owner's Manual* do not use EXE commands to end lines, but rather **concatenate** (string together) the entire program with colons (:) between each command statement. This makes programs very difficult to read. Using EXE commands at the end of each line makes program listings easier to read and edit, and takes no more memory than using the colons to concatenate commands.

When there are exactly 16 characters in a command line of a program, it appears as if the cursor has moved to a new program line. You still must enter an EXE character. The program seems to have an extra line. *It does not.* However, you should never press $\boxed{\text{EXE}}$ twice at the end of a line; if you do, a syntax error message will occur when you try to run the program.

Program editing is done using the INS (insert) and DEL (delete) features. When inserting an EXE command, it is necessary to use the INS feature even though no character appears on the screen. Placing the cursor at the end of a program line and pressing $\boxed{\text{DEL}}$ will delete an invisible EXE character.

The ◢ character at the end of a command line acts like an EXE keystroke. Once entered, no EXE keystroke is needed to end the line; the cursor automatically moves to the beginning of the next programming line. This command causes the program to output a numerical calculation and display the **-Disp-** message on the screen. Without this command, intermediate calculations will *not* be printed on the screen. The *last* calculation in a program will be printed on the screen *without* using this command.

(2) **Setting the Range within a program.** The Range of the graphics screen may be set from within a program. This is done by entering the six Range values in order separated by commas. For example, the command line

Range −10, 30, 5, −1000, 3500, 500

would set a viewing rectangle of $[-10, 30]$ by $[-1000, 3500]$. The horizontal scale marks would represent 5 units, and the vertical scale marks would represent 500 units. Range values may also be designated by variable quantities, as illustrated in the program given within the next paragraph.

Recall that the viewing rectangle $[-6.7, 6.7]$ by $[-3.1, 3.1]$ is the Casio default viewing rectangle, which can be set using $\boxed{\text{SHIFT}}$ $\boxed{\text{Mcl}}$ while the Range display window is active. These default Range values make each pixel on the screen represent 0.1 in both the horizontal and vertical directions. In effect they put the graphics display in "square" coordinates. When plotting shapes that should look a certain way, such as circles or perpendicular lines, this square coordinate system gives an accurate visual representation of the shapes. Multiples of the default scale also preserve the shape of pictures. The Range settings given above generate any multiple of the default viewing rectangle quickly and accurately. Using the values $1, 2, 5,$ or 10 for F makes each pixel a step of $0.1, 0.2, 0.5,$ or 1, respectively. These steps are useful when doing analytic geometry problems, and they give nice Trace coordinate readouts. The following simple program can be used to set the Range to any multiple of the default viewing rectangle.

"SCALE FACTOR" ? $\rightarrow$ F

Range $-4.7F,\ 4.7F,\ F,\ -3.1F,\ 3.1F,\ F$

When you run this program the words SCALE FACTOR will appear on the screen, followed by a question mark, or **input prompt symbol**. Words written inside quotation marks within a program will always appear as screen messages when the program is run, and the input prompt symbol (?) is used in conjunction with the assignment arrow ($\rightarrow$) to permit the assignment of values to variables while running a program (extending the methods of Section 5.1.5). To respond to the screen message in this case, key in the value you wish to use for F, and then press the EXE key. This will set the Range as desired.

(3) **Error messages.** When you have an error in a program, the Casio will stop the program and print a message indicating the type of error, the program containing the error, and the step within the program causing the error. For example, the error message

Syn ERROR

Step P9 — 65

would indicate a syntax error at Step 65 of Program 9. Returning to this point in Program 9 is done by using a REPLAY key ($\boxed{\Leftarrow}$ or $\boxed{\Rightarrow}$). After the error is corrected, return to Mode 1, and run the program again.

Command words in the programs that appear in upper and lower case (e.g., Goto) are reserved words in the Casio programming language. These commands are accessed by single keystrokes. Do not type these words using the alphabetic keys. For example, typing the four letters **GOTO** instead of the single command **Goto** will generate an error message.

(4) **Program storage locations.** Programs may be stored in any of the 10 storage locations you wish. However, some of the programs in this manual use other programs as subroutines to do specific tasks. When these subprograms are used, you must be certain that the correct subprogram is called from the main program. For example, the Zoom-In Program in Section 5.3.6 calls Program 0 as a subprogram. So, the functions to be graphed should be stored in Program 0. If those functions were stored in Program 3, then the command line in the Zoom-In Program would have to call Program 3 to find the functions. You may customize your programs any way you wish.

5.3.4 Graphing from a Program: One of the most convenient uses of programming on the Casio is to graph functions from a program. Often beginners become frustrated when attempting to manipulate a graph without programming. Unintended or mistaken keystrokes can cause the loss of the command lines containing the functions to be graphed. This often occurs when using the Trace and Factor features to zoom-in on a graph.

To eliminate this problem, enter the functions to be graphed as a program. Then to graph the functions, simply run the program. Let's look at an example.

Problem   Solve the system of equations $y = \cos x$ and $y = x^3 - 1.4x$.

Solution   Enter Mode 2 and select program storage location 0. (This is a handy location to use for graphing functions because it is the location selected automatically when Mode 2 is activated.) Enter the following keying sequence (see Figure 5.16).

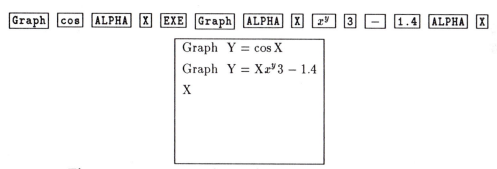

Figure 5.16.   Program for graphing the two functions entered.

Notice that the EXE key was pressed after the first line was entered, but not after the last. When writing programs, the EXE key acts like the return key on a computer. Pressing EXE writes an invisible character at the end of a command line that separates it from the subsequent line. You need not use an EXE at the end of a program; more than one EXE at the end of a program will cause the Casio to display an error message (see Programming Hint 1 in Section 5.3.3).

Once the program is written, return to Mode 1 (key $\boxed{\text{MODE}}$ $\boxed{1}$) to run the program. Set the Range to the default viewing rectangle of $[-4.7, 4.7]$ by $[-3.1, 3.1]$ by keying $\boxed{\text{Range}}$ $\boxed{\text{SHIFT}}$ $\boxed{\text{Mcl}}$ $\boxed{\text{Range}}$. Now, graph the two functions by keying $\boxed{\text{Prog}}$ $\boxed{0}$ $\boxed{\text{EXE}}$. Figure 5.17 resembles the screen after the two functions have been graphed. (The graphic figures in this section were produced using *Master Grapher*, Waits & Demana, 1989, and are not exact facsimiles of Casio graphs.)

At this point, the program has finished running, and all the built-in features used to manipulate graphs are available. For example, pressing $\boxed{\text{SHIFT}}$ $\boxed{\times}$ will result in a zoom-in by a factor of 2 in the horizontal and vertical directions. Pressing $\boxed{\text{SHIFT}}$ $\boxed{\div}$ will cause a zoom-out by a factor of 2 in both directions. The Trace feature can be activated by keying (SHIFT) $\boxed{\text{Trace}}$, and then the right and left cursor keys can be used to move the blinking dot along the last function graphed. The x- and y-coordinates of the blinking point are given at the bottom of the screen. Key $\boxed{\text{SHIFT}}$ $\boxed{X \leftrightarrow Y}$ to toggle between the x and y values.

If you happen to press the wrong key, the functions can be regraphed by running Program 0 again with the keystrokes $\boxed{\text{Prog}}$ $\boxed{0}$ $\boxed{\text{EXE}}$.

Problem extension   Use the Factor feature to zoom-in on the solution(s) to the system of equations $y = \cos x$ and $y = x^3 - 1.4x$.

Solution   After running Program 0 to graph the functions, use the Trace feature to place the blinking cursor on (or as close as possible to) the intersection of the two functions in the second quadrant (see Figure 5.18).

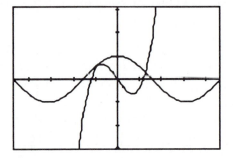

Figure 5.17. Functions graphed from Program 0.

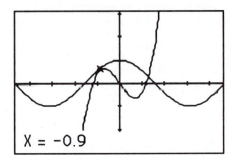

Figure 5.18. Trace in the second quadrant.

Next, enter the keystrokes (SHIFT) `Factor` `5` `:` `Prog` `0` `EXE`. This will cause a zoom-in by a factor of 5 in both directions. Figure 5.19 shows the graphs after this zoom-in. It is clear now that there are really no points of intersection for the two graphs in the second quadrant.

Reset the Range to the default viewing rectangle by keying `Range` `SHIFT` `Mcl` `Range`. Now key `Prog` `0` `EXE` to redraw the functions. Using the Trace feature again, move the blinking cursor to the intersection in the first quadrant (see Figure 5.20).

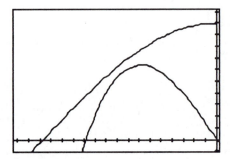

Figure 5.19. Zoom-in by a factor of 5.

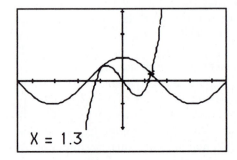

Figure 5.20. Blinking cursor in the first quadrant.

Repeat the keying sequence (SHIFT) `Factor` `5` `:` `Prog` `0` `EXE` to zoom-in on this intersection by a factor of 5. To zoom-in more for greater accuracy, use the Trace feature to place the blinking cursor on the intersection, and then key `EXE` again to repeat the Factor command and draw the graphs in the new viewing rectangle. This process may be repeated up to the limits of machine accuracy. Figures 5.21 and 5.22 show the solution to the system of equations with error of at most 0.00001 .

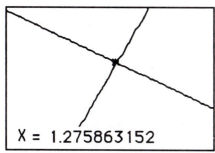
Figure 5.21. X-coordinate of the solution.

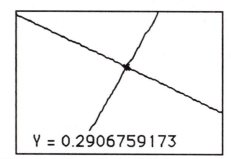
Figure 5.22. Y-coordinate of the solution.

5.3.5 The Plot and Line Features: The Plot feature allows you to plot a point as a pixel on the graphics screen. For example, select the default viewing rectangle, $[-4.7, 4.7]$ by $[-3.1, 3.1]$, and then key in (SHIFT) `Plot` `.3` `SHIFT` `,` `.5` `EXE`. Notice that the x-coordinate of the plotted point (blinking pixel) is displayed at the lower left-hand corner of the screen. Use `SHIFT` $\boxed{X \leftrightarrow Y}$ to toggle between an x- and a y-coordinate readout. A plotted point can be moved using the cursor keys. Now try the following command: **Plot 1.75, 1.74** . The pixel selected is the one with coordinates nearest those of the input, $(1.8, 1.7)$ if you are still using the default viewing rectangle. Coordinate values falling outside the viewing rectangle will not be plotted. For instance, try plotting $(6, -3)$.

The **Line** command (SHIFT) `Line` `EXE` connects the two most recently plotted points. Try drawing a polygon with coordinate points as vertices using the Plot and Line commands.

The ◢ command may be used with the Graph, Plot, or Line commands to keep the graphics screen visible. This is illustrated in the next section.

5.3.6 Zoom-In Using Interactive Viewing Rectangles: One of the best features of the *Master Grapher* program for the microcomputer is its ability to zoom-in on a user-chosen rectangular subset of a viewing rectangle. This allows the user to see a picture of the actual area to be enlarged at each step of the zoom-in process.

The program presented in this section allows the Casio to do zoom-in by the same viewing-rectangle-within-viewing-rectangle method as *Master Grapher*. (The original concept of the Casio Zoom-In Program is due to Alan Stickney of Wittenberg University. The version presented here was written by Charles Vonder Embse of Central Michigan University.) You magnify an area containing a point of interest by drawing a rectangle around the point on the graphics screen. You then see the exact area that will become your next full screen. Figure 5.26 shows how the Casio screen looks after the user has drawn a rectangle around an area to be enlarged.

This Zoom-In Program takes advantage of the technique of placing functions to be graphed in a program (see paragraph 4 "Program Storage Locations" in Section 5.3.4). In this section, Program 0 is used to store the Graph commands for the function or functions to be graphed. To begin you can graph the functions from Program 0. Trace, Factor, and Range features are all available to help you choose an appropriate viewing rectangle. Once you have the viewing rectangle you want and you are ready to begin the zoom-in process, the same Program 0 can be used as a subroutine for the Zoom-In Program.

When using the Zoom-In Program on the Casio, there is a continuous readout of the X or Y coordinates of the blinking point on the screen. This gives you immediate information about the part of the plane being viewed, the size of each pixel-to-pixel step, and the approximate location of points of interest on the screen.

Zoom-In Program

Code	Comments
Cls	[clears the graphics screen]
Lbl 1	[label as position 1 for Goto statement at end of program]
Prog 0	[executes Program 0 to graph the function(s)]
Plot ◢	[puts the cursor in the middle of the screen and pauses]
X → A : Y → D	[coordinates of selected point into variables A and D]
Plot ◢	[second cursor; pauses until EXE is keyed]
X → B : Y → C	[coordinates of selected point into variables B and C]
B > A ⇒ Goto 2	*[checks order; if B > A, then go to position 2]
A → T: B → A : T → B	[swaps A and B if B < A; A must be smaller]
Lbl 2	[label as position 2; comes here if B > A]
D > C ⇒ Goto 3	*[checks order again; if D > C, then go to position 3]
C → T : D → C : T → D	[swaps C and D if D < C; C must be smaller]
Lbl 3	[label as position 3; comes here if D > C]
Plot A, D	[plots point (A,D), the upper left corner of the view rectangle]
Plot B, D : Line	[plots (B, D), upper right corner; line from (A, D) to (B, D)]
Plot B, C : Line	[plots (B, C), lower right corner; line from (B, D) to (B, C)]
Plot A, C : Line	[plots (A, C), the lower left corner; line from (B, C) to (A, C)]
Plot A, D : Line ◢	[replots (A, D); finishes viewing rectangle; pauses]
Range A, B, 1, C, D, 1	[sets new Range to A, B, 1, C, D, 1]
Goto 1	[go to position 1 and start again; regraphs function(s) in the new Range; starts the process again]

The logical flow of the program is to graph the function in the current viewing rectangle and then locate a subrectangle to be enlarged. Identification of the subrectangle for zoom-in is done by finding the left, right, bottom, and top edges of the subrectangle. These four values correspond to A, B, C, and D, respectively, in the program. Once these values are established, a new Range is set using these values. For simplicity the scale marks on the axes are set to 1. After the diagonal corners of the viewing rectangle are set, the program automatically checks the order so that the smaller horizontal (left) value is placed in A and the larger (right) value is placed in B. A similar check is done for the vertical direction. The result is that the user may choose either pair of diagonal corners in any order. For convenience, the program should be stored as Program 9.

Let's use the Zoom-In Program to solve a problem.

Problem Let x be the side length of the square that is to be cut out from each corner of a 30-inch by 40-inch piece of cardboard to form a box with no top.

* The arrow used with the "Goto 2" and "Goto 3" statements in the program is an implication, or if-then, arrow and is accessed by pressing SHIFT followed by 7.

(1) If the finished box is to have a volume of 1200 cubic inches, write two equations that can be solved simultaneously to determine the size of the square.

(2) Draw complete graphs of each equation in the same viewing rectangle.

(3) How many simultaneous solutions are there to your system in Part 1? Which of these solutions are also solutions to the problem situation?

(4) Use zoom-in to determine all values of x that produce a box of volume 1200 cubic inches.

Solution to Part 1 An algebraic representation of the volume of the box as a function of the side length x is $V(x) = x(40 - 2x)(30 - 2x)$ or $V(x) = 4x^3 - 140x^2 + 1200x$. Either of these forms of the function can be used in the Casio. One of the above equations together with $V(x) = 1200$ are the two equations that can be solved simultaneously to determine the size of the square.

Solution to Part 2 Put the two functions to be graphed in Program 0. If you already have a function in this location, replace it with the commands:

$$\text{Graph Y} = 4X x^y 3 - 140X^2 + 1200X$$
$$\text{Graph Y} = 1200$$

Return to the Run mode, and run Program 0 to graph the functions. Make adjustments in the Range and regraph until you get a complete graph. The viewing rectangle $[-5, 30]$ by $[-500, 3500]$ works well (see Figure 5.23).

Solution to Part 3 There are three simultaneous solutions to the system of equations; however, only the two in the range $0 \le x \le 15$ are in the domain of the problem situation. If the length of the square corner cut away is greater than 15 inches, then the 30-inch side of the sheet of cardboard is completely cut away.

Solution to Part 4 With Program 0 and the Range set as shown in the Solution to Part 2, run the Zoom-In Program (stored as Program 9) by keying Prog 9 EXE. The function will be graphed again from Program 0. When the graph is finished a flashing point will appear in the center of the screen with the x-coordinate of that point at the bottom of the screen (see Figure 5.24). To switch between x- and y-coordinate readouts, key SHIFT $X \leftrightarrow Y$.

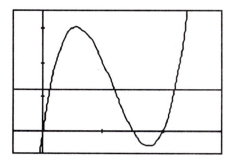

Figure 5.23. Graphs in [-5, 30] by [-500, 3500].

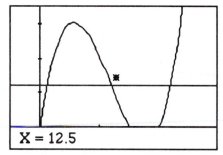

X = 12.5

Figure 5.24. First point appears.

The flashing point in the middle of the screen is free to move to any point on the screen using the four cursor keys ⇐, ⇒, ⇑, and ⇓. This point will become one corner of your new viewing rectangle when [EXE] is pressed, and another flashing point will appear. This second point should be moved to the desired location of the diagonally opposite corner of the new viewing rectangle (see Figure 5.25). Once the second point is in position, press [EXE] to set the point and draw the viewing rectangle (see Figure 5.26).

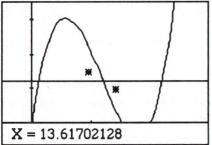

X = 13.61702128

Figure 5.25. Second point in position.

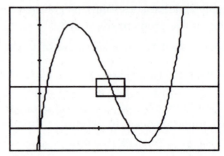

Figure 5.26. Viewing rectangle set.

When ready, press [EXE] again for the new viewing rectangle to be set and the graphs to be redrawn. After the new view of the graph is drawn, the flashing point again appears in the middle of the screen ready for the next zoom-in step (see Figure 5.27). At any time during the process of setting the corners of the viewing rectangle, the user can check the Range of the viewing screen by keying [Range]. The moving point can also be used to give the approximate location of the point of interest (an intersection in this case) by placing the point on the appropriate location on the screen (see Figure 5.28). This technique allows the user to make good estimates of the value being calculated and to keep in mind where the viewing rectangle is located in the plane. The change in the coordinates of the point as it moves across the screen gives a good indication of the size of the error in the estimate.

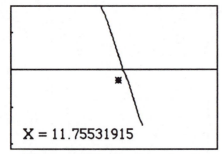

X = 11.75531915

Figure 5.27. Graphs redrawn.

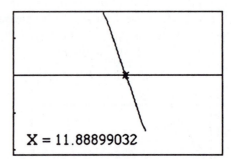

X = 11.88899032

Figure 5.28. Estimating the intersection.

The Zoom-In Program can also make use of long, narrow viewing rectangles to stretch one dimension more than the other (see Figure 5.29). This technique makes intersections and local extreme points easier to read. Using a wide, short viewing rectangle as is seen in Figure 5.29 will tend to make the intersection appear more perpendicular than in the previous view. The vertical dimension will be stretched more than the horizontal. The size of the viewing rectangle is easy to control because of the point by point movement of the flashing pixel. Very small viewing rectangles can be selected; this speeds up the zoom-in process (see Figure 5.30).

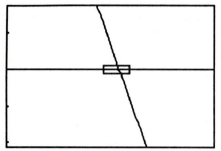

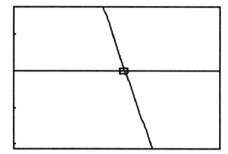

Figure 5.29. Long, narrow viewing rectangle.   **Figure 5.30.** Small viewing rectangle.

One solution that yields a box of 1200 cubic inches was shown in Figure 5.28. This solution of $x = 11.88899032$ inches is accurate to .0005, despite the 9 decimal places shown on the Casio screen. Always check to see which digits change and which ones stay fixed as you move from point to point on the Casio graphics screen. This will allow you to estimate the error of a solution. To find the other solution to Part 4 of the problem, reset the viewing rectangle to $[-5, 30]$ by $[-500, 3500]$ and run Program 9 to return to the original complete graph shown in Figure 5.23. Then use the Zoom-In Program to approximate the solution. It should be about $x = 1.149$.

5.3.7 Graphing Parametric Equations: Parametric equations provide a powerful and flexible tool for representing curves and motion simulations in the Cartesian plane. Lines, including vertical lines, functions, inverses of functions, conic sections, and polar curves can all be represented by parametric equations. This is done by introducing a variable t, called a **parameter**, on which the values of x and y both depend. For motion simulations, the parameter t can be thought of as representing time.

The following general Casio program can be used to graph any parametric curve. It is convenient to store this Parametric Curve Graphing Program as Program 8 (See paragraph 4 "Program Storage Locations" in Section 5.3.3). The Range is set outside the program; the parametric formulas are stored in Program 1, which acts as a subprogram; and the interval of t values is set when the program is run.

Parametric Curve Graphing Program

"T MIN" ? $\rightarrow T$
"T MAX" ? $\rightarrow B$
"T INC" ? $\rightarrow H$
Cls
Lbl 1
Prog 1
Plot X, Y
Line
$T + H \rightarrow T$
$T \leq B \Rightarrow$ Goto 1

Pause to understand how the program works. Notice T starts at the T MIN that you specify and is incremented by H until T is equal to the T MAX value you specify. The X and Y values are computed within Program 1 using the current value of T; then, within the main program, the point (X, Y) is plotted and a line segment is drawn. (Occasionally, you may wish the plotted points **not** to be connected by line segments. In such cases, delete the Line command from you program.) The Casio flashes back and forth between the text window and the graphics window while the program is running. When the program has finished running, the Casio will show the text window, and the graph will be stored in the graphics window. The G $\leftrightarrow$ T command is used to view the completed graph.

Consider, for example, the parametric equations $x = t + 3$ and $y = t^2 - 2$ for $-3 \leq t \leq 3$. To graph this parametric curve, you would (a) store the statement T $+ 3 \to$ X : T$^2 - 2 \to$ Y as Program 1; (b) set the Range, say, to a viewing rectangle of $[-3, 9]$ by $[-3, 8]$; and (c) execute the Parametric Curve Graphing Program using -3 for T MIN, 3 for T MAX, and 0.05 for T INC. In this example, X takes on values in the interval $[0, 6]$, and Y in the interval $[-2, 7]$. The viewing rectangle of $[-3, 9]$ by $[-3, 8]$ was chosen with extra units in each direction (see Figure 5.31).

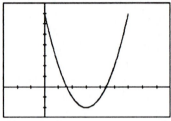

Figure 5.31. The parametric equations $x = t + 3$ and $y = t^2 - 2$ for $-3 \leq t \leq 3$, in the viewing rectangle $[-3, 9]$ by $[-3, 8]$.

5.3.8   Graphing Polar Equations: Polar equations can be graphed using the Parametric Curve Graphing Program if you set up the subprogram called from the main program appropriately. In Section 5.3.7 the Parametric Curve Graphing Program was written so that Program 1 was the subprogram called from the main program.

Problem   Graph $r = 5 \sin 3\theta$.

Solution   *Make sure your Casio is in radian mode.* Then enter the following program as Program 1.

Program 1   **5 sin 3T** $\to R$
R cos T $\to X$
R sin T $\to Y$

The portion in **boldface** type varies from one polar equation graphing problem to the next. Notice the variable T is used for the angle θ.

To graph the polar curve, you would need to set the Range to an appropriate viewing rectangle, say, $[-7.5, 7.5]$ by $[-5, 5]$, and execute the Parametric Curve Graphing Program using 0 for T MIN, π for T MAX, and 0.1 for T INC (see Figure 5.32).

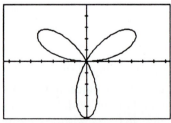

Figure 5.32. The rose $r = 5 \sin 3\theta$ in the viewing rectangle [-7.5, 7.5] by [-5, 5].

Chapter 6

Graphing with the Casio Power Graphic fx-7700G

The Casio Power Graphic fx-7700G calculator has many of the same features of the other members of the Casio graphing calculator line. Although their location on the keyboard has changed, the function of similar named keys remains basically the same. An example of this is the use of the SHIFT and ALPHA keys. Their use on the fx-7700G is the same as is described in Section 5.1. Rather than duplicating descriptions for the fx-7700G, similiar key functions have been referenced to the appropriate sections in Chapter 5, Calculating and Graphing with First Generation Casio Calculators. Also, the Owner's Manual has an excellent section for getting started with the fx-7700G.

6.1 Start Up

6.1.1 Getting Turned On

Power Up. To turn the unit on, press AC on. To turn the unit off, press SHIFT AC off. The power will automatically switch off after 6 minutes of inactivity. To restore functions, press AC on.

Adjust Contrast. A system display will appear when the calculator is switched on. Press MODE. Press ◁ to lighten the screen or ▷ to darken the screen.

6.1.2 What You See—Display Windows: The fx-7700G displays both text and graphs on four different display windows.

(1) The Text Display Window is the primary screen of the fx-7700G. On it you enter expressions and instructions and see results (except graphs).

Figure 6.1. Text screen.

(2) The Graphics Display Window contains 95 columns and 63 rows of pixels on which to display graphs. The graphics window can be scrolled (in all four directions) by pressing the appropriate cursor keys.

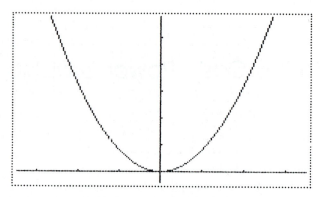

Figure 6.2. Graphics screen.

(3) The Range Setting Display Windows allow you to input the domain and range values for the graphics window. Pressing $\boxed{\text{RANGE}}$ in either the text or the graphics window enters the range setting window and allows you to make adjustments to the viewing rectangle of the graph.

minimum value of x − coordinate
maximum value of x − coordinate
distance between x − axis tick marks
minimum value of y − coordinate
maximum value of y − coordinate
distance between y − axis tickmarks

```
Range
Xmin : −4.7
   max : 4.7
   scl : 1.
Ymin : −3.1
   max : 3.1
   scl : 1.
INIT
```

Figure 6.3. Rectangular coordinate range screen.

Pressing $\boxed{\text{RANGE}}$ again brings up the second range screen.

minimum value of T θ
maximum value of t θ
pitch of T θ

```
Range
T, θ
   min : 0
   max : 4π
ptch : π/50
INIT
```

Figure 6.4. Polar coordinate range screen.

(4) The Mode Display Windows appear on the screen when the fx-7700G is first turned on. They specify the kind of functions the Casio is ready to perform. Because the Casio can do so many things, it may be necessary to change one or more of the mode settings before you start a calculation. To make any necessary changes, press the $\boxed{\text{MODE}}$ key to see the first set of options and then the $\boxed{\text{SHIFT}}$ key for additional options. A summary of all the mode options is given below. Press $\boxed{\text{MODE}}$ to display Mode Menu 1.

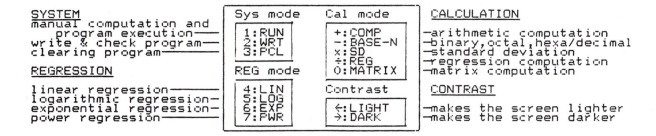

Figure 6.5. Mode Menu 1 screen.

Pressing $\boxed{\text{SHIFT}}$ will now display Mode Menu 2.

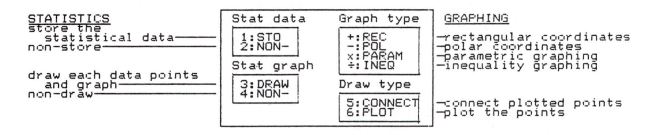

Figure 6.6. Mode Menu 2 screen.

You are encouraged to confirm which modes are active before calculating, graphing, or programming by pressing $\boxed{\blacksquare\text{Disp}}$. The mode display window will remain on the screen while this key is depressed.

We will begin in the RUN mode of the system, COMPutation mode of the calculation, and the RECtangular coordinate graphing mode. To make these selections, press $\boxed{\text{MODE}}$ followed by $\boxed{1}$ for the RUN mode. Then press $\boxed{\text{MODE}}$ again followed by $\boxed{+}$ for the COMP mode. Finally, press $\boxed{\text{MODE}}$ $\boxed{\text{SHIFT}}$ followed by $\boxed{+}$ for REC to set the graph mode to rectangular coordinate graph type. Before beginning the next section, check your system display window to confirm:

RUN	/	COMP
G − type	:	REC/CON
angle	:	Deg
display	:	Nrm2

Figure 6.7. Mode display.

In each of the four display windows, the fx-7700G has several types of cursors. In most cases, the appearance of the cursor indicates what will happen when you press the next key. The most common cursors seen are given in the following table.

Cursor	Appearance	Meaning
Entry cursor	Blinking underline	The next keystroke is entered at the cursor over-writing any character
Insert cursor	Open blinking rectangle	The next keystroke is inserted at the cursor.
SHIFT cursor	Highlighted blinking S	The next keystroke is a second function.
ALPHA cursor	Highlighted blinking A	The next keystroke is an alpha character.
Graphics cursor	Blinking plus sign	Designates a point on the graphics display window.

Table 6.1

6.2 Getting Going (Pushing Buttons)

6.2.1 Calculations: In general the keystroke sequence necessary to evaluate simple expressions on the fx-7700G is the same as for the other members of the Casio line. Section 5.1.4 describes the keystroke sequence. A few features unique to the fx-7700G are listed here.

The subtraction key can be used as the negation function key if it is not the first operation in an expression. This is especially useful when entering negative range values.

The fraction notations key $\boxed{\text{a b/c}}$ allows entry of fractions and mixed numbers. The $\boxed{\text{d/c}}$ key converts to an improper fraction.

Example   3/4 + 1/3

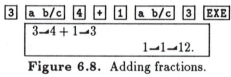

$$\boxed{3}\ \boxed{\text{a b/c}}\ \boxed{4}\ \boxed{+}\ \boxed{1}\ \boxed{\text{a b/c}}\ \boxed{3}\ \boxed{\text{EXE}}$$

```
3⌐4 + 1⌐3
                 1⌐1⌐12.
```

Figure 6.8. Adding fractions.

The symbol "⌐" separates the parts of the fraction. So 1⌐1⌐12 is the same as $1\frac{1}{12}$.
Press $\boxed{\text{a b/c}}$ to convert to a decimal.

```
3⌐4 + 1⌐3
                 1.083333333
```

Figure 6.9. Convert fraction to decimals.

Press $\boxed{\text{SHIFT}}$ $\boxed{\text{a b/c}}$ to convert to an improper fraction.

```
3⌐4 + 1⌐3
                 13⌐12.
```

Figure 6.10. Convert to improper fractions.

A distinctive feature of the fx-7700G is that many of the operations are not on the keyboard but instead are stored within function menus, shown in green above certain keys throughout the keyboard. To access any of the menus, press $\boxed{\text{SHIFT}}$ followed by the desired function key. A group of up to six functions will then be displayed across the bottom of the screen. To select a choice, press the corresponding $\boxed{\text{F}}$ key. For example, to compute the absolute value of 2 minus five factorial requires the use of operations stored in the function menus. For |2| − 5! enter $\boxed{\text{SHIFT}}$ $\boxed{\text{MATH}}$ to access the math menu. Now enter $\boxed{\text{F3}}$ to access the numeric menu, and then $\boxed{\text{F1}}$ for the absolute value function. The rest of the key sequence follows.$\boxed{2}$ $\boxed{-}$ $\boxed{5}$ $\boxed{\text{SHIFT}}$ $\boxed{\text{MATH}}$ $\boxed{\text{F2}}$ $\boxed{\text{F1}}$ $\boxed{\text{EXE}}$.

$$\boxed{\begin{array}{l} \text{Abs } 2-5! \\ \hspace{3cm} -118 \end{array}}$$

Figure 6.11. Using menus.

Notice that the factorial function is also stored in the math menu.

A diagram is given below to show the most commonly used menus in the computation mode. Use it as a reference to know what operations each menu key accesses. A more detailed listing of menus is included in the Owner's Manual.

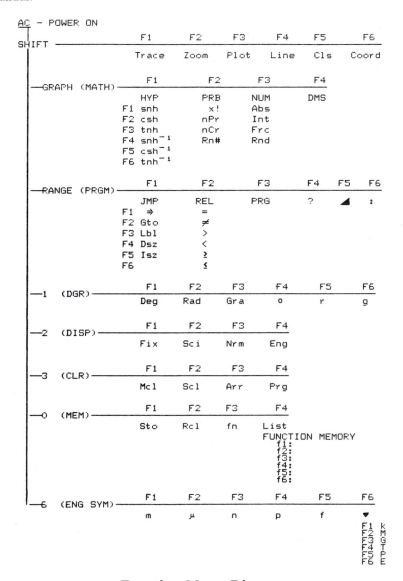

Function Menu Diagram

When you enter a function menu a group of up to six functions will be displayed across the bottom of the screen. To select a choice, press the corresponding $\boxed{\text{F}}$ key. To exit a menu, or backtrack when you are several layers into a menu, press $\boxed{\text{Pre}}$. The next two examples use function menus. To change from radian measure to degree measure you must use the DRG menu. Enter $\boxed{\text{SHIFT}}$ $\boxed{\text{DRG}}$. The choices for this menu are now listed at the bottom of the screen. Enter $\boxed{\text{F1}}$ to select radians and $\boxed{\text{EXE}}$ to enter it in the mode setting. Holding down the $\boxed{\text{M}\text{Disp}}$ key verifies the change in angle measurement. To compute hyperbolic sine, access the math menu and then the hyperbolic function. To compute sinh(.387) enter $\boxed{\text{SHIFT}}$ $\boxed{\text{MATH}}$ $\boxed{\text{F1}}$ $\boxed{\text{F1}}$ $\boxed{\text{.387}}$ $\boxed{\text{EXE}}$. You find it equal to .3967326982.

6.2.2 Special Functions: When editing expressions you can incorporate the cursor keys (as REPLAY keys), and the INSERT and DELETE keys. These keys are very similiar in operation to the other Casio models. Section 5.1.3 explains the operations as well as how to deal with error messages for the Casio graphing calculators.

You can obtain sequential execution of a number of individual statements by using multistatements. There are three different ways to form multistatements.

(1) The colon key $\boxed{:}$ accessed by $\boxed{\text{SHIFT}}$ $\boxed{\text{PRGM}}$ $\boxed{\text{F6}}$ connects statements left to right without stopping.

(2) The newline key $\boxed{\hookleftarrow}$ accessed by $\boxed{\text{SHIFT}}$ $\boxed{\hookleftarrow}$ operates like the colon when placed at the end of a line. It moves the cursor to the next line but connects the statements like a colon.

(3) The display key $\boxed{\blacktriangleleft}$ accessed by $\boxed{\text{SHIFT}}$ $\boxed{\text{PRGM}}$ $\boxed{\text{F5}}$ stops execution and displays results to that point. You can resume execution by pressing $\boxed{\text{EXE}}$.

By entering Statement$\boxed{:}$Statement or Statement$\boxed{\hookleftarrow}$Statement or Statement$\boxed{\blacktriangleleft}$Statement, multistatements are formed allowing sequential execution of individual statements. This particular strategy is very helpful in evaluating functions.

For example, to evaluate $A^2 + 2A + 3$ when A is 2, 3, or -1, enter

$\boxed{\text{SHIFT}}$ $\boxed{\text{PRGM}}$ $\boxed{\text{F4}}$ $\boxed{\rightarrow}$ $\boxed{\text{ALPHA}}$ $\boxed{\text{A}}$ $\boxed{\text{F6}}$ $\boxed{\text{ALPHA}}$ $\boxed{\text{A}}$ $\boxed{\text{SHIFT}}$ $\boxed{x^2}$ $\boxed{+}$ $\boxed{2}$ $\boxed{\text{ALPHA}}$ $\boxed{\text{A}}$ $\boxed{+}$ $\boxed{3}$ $\boxed{\text{EXE}}$.

```
? → A : A² + 2A + 3
?
1
                        6
```

Figure 6.12. Evaluating functions.

The question mark is requesting the first value to evaluate in the expression. By entering $\boxed{1}$ $\boxed{\text{EXE}}$ you are telling the calculator to replace every A with the value of 1. Of course, the expression simplifies to 6.

If you enter $\boxed{\text{EXE}}$ you invoke the replacement program again and it responds with ?. Enter $\boxed{2}$ $\boxed{\text{EXE}}$ to obtain the value of 11. Entering $\boxed{\text{EXE}}$ $\boxed{-1}$ $\boxed{\text{EXE}}$ we find the expression evaluated at -1 to be 2.

Multistatements can be used for graphing several functions in the same graphing window.

There are several types of memories used on the fx-7700G.

Numerical values can be stored in memory, called storage registers. The storage registers for the fx-7700G can be described the same as in Section 5.1.5 for the other Casio graphing models.

Functions can be stored in a function memory on the fx-7700G. You can store up to six functions in memory for instant recall when you need them. To access the function memory press $\boxed{\text{SHIFT}}$ $\boxed{\boxed{\text{F}}\text{MEM}}$.

Figure 6.13. Function memory.

Press the appropriate $\boxed{\text{F}}$ key to store a function, recall a function, display a list of the stored functions, or specify the input as a function when using in an operation. For example, store $x^3 + 2x^2$ in the first function memory and then graph $y = x^3 + 2x^2$. Begin by entering $\boxed{\text{x},\theta,\text{T}}$ $\boxed{x^y}$ $\boxed{3}$ $\boxed{+}$ $\boxed{2}$ $\boxed{\text{x},\theta,\text{T}}$ $\boxed{\text{SHIFT}}$ $\boxed{x^2}$ $\boxed{\text{SHIFT}}$ $\boxed{\boxed{\text{F}}\text{MEM}}$ $\boxed{\text{F1}}$ $\boxed{1}$. Use the default range settings. The function $y = x^3 + 2x^2$ has been stored in function memory #1. Now to graph $y = x^3 + 2x^2$ key in $\boxed{\text{GRAPH}}$ $\boxed{\text{F3}}$ $\boxed{1}$ $\boxed{\text{EXE}}$.

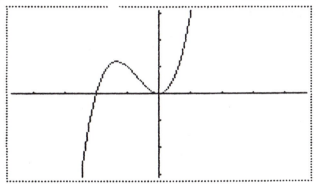

Figure 6.14. $y = x^3 + 2x^2$ [-4.7, 4.7] by [-3.1, 3.1].

This brings us to the graphing capabilities of the fx-7700G.

6.3 Graphing with the FX-7700G

6.3.1 The Set-Up: Special keys on the fx-7700G are used to graph functions. When you press $\boxed{\text{GRAPH}}$, the text screen is displayed with Graph Y= and awaits the entry of a function to graph. When you press $\boxed{\text{G}\leftrightarrow\text{T}}$, the display switches from the graphics display window (shows the coordinate grid) to the text display window (shows graph formulas) or vice versa. When you press $\boxed{\text{RANGE}}$, an edit screen is displayed where you define the viewing rectangle for the graph. In addition to these keys, the $\boxed{\text{F}}$ keys at the bottom of the screen access six functions (Trace, Zoom, Plot, Line, Cls, Coord) used with graphing. When you press $\boxed{\text{F1}}$ (Trace), you can move the cursor along a graphed function and display the X and Y coordinate values of the cursor location on the function. When you press $\boxed{\text{F2}}$ (Zoom), you access a menu of instructions at the bottom of the screen that allows you to change the viewing rectangle. Pressing $\boxed{\text{F3}}$ (Plot) allows you to plot a point anywhere on a graph. Pressing $\boxed{\text{F4}}$ (Line), allows you to link two points with a straight line. Pressing $\boxed{\text{F5}}$ (Cls), allows you to clear the graphics screen. Pressing $\boxed{\text{F6}}$ (Coord) changes the coordinate display from both X and Y to X coordinate only then to Y coordinate only and then back to both X and Y coordinates.

Because the fx-7700G is capable of so many different types of graphing it is crucial that you set the mode to correspond with the type of graphing you are currently using. For this section we will use the rectangular coordinate system. In addition, we must choose the way the graph will be drawn—only plotted points or the points connected. To select the type of graph to be drawn, access the second mode window by entering [MODE] [SHIFT] and make a selection—5 to connect, and 6 to plot only—followed by [EXE]. Check your system display window to confirm that this is your mode.

```
┌─────────────────────────┐
│     RUN   /   COMP       │
│  G − type  :  REC/CON    │
│    angle   :  Deg        │
│  display   :  Nrml       │
└─────────────────────────┘
```

Figure 6.15. Mode display.

Now check the range values to determine the size of the viewing rectangle. The Range key allows you to choose the viewing rectangle that defines the portion of the coordinate plane that appears in the display. The values of the RANGE variable determine the size of the viewing rectangle and the scale units for each axis. You can view and change the values of the RANGE variable almost any time. Press RANGE to display the RANGE variables edit screen. The values shown here on the RANGE edit screen are the standard default values in radian mode.

```
┌───────────────────────────────┐   ┌───────────────────────────────┐
│  Rectangular Range Screen     │   │  Polar Coordinate Range Screen │
│                               │   │                               │
│        Range                  │   │        Range                  │
│        Xmin : −4.7            │   │        T, θ                   │
│          max : 4.7            │   │          min : 0              │
│          scl : 1              │   │          max : 4π             │
│        Ymin : −3.1            │   │         ptch : π/50           │
│          max : 3.1            │   │                               │
│          scl : 1.             │   │        INIT                   │
│        INIT                   │   │                               │
└───────────────────────────────┘   └───────────────────────────────┘
```

Figure 6.16. Default values for both range screens.

Note that the parameters can be entered using the π symbol, but the calculator converts them to decimal equivalences.

To obtain this default range setting quickly, enter [RANGE] [F1]. This operation initializes the range settings. The second range screen is used for polar and parametric equation parameters. To escape the range setting window, you must press [RANGE] two times. The first entry [RANGE] will take you to the polar coordinate/parametric range screen. Pressing [RANGE] again takes you back to the last displayed screen, text or graph.

To change one of the RANGE values, move the cursor to the desired line and type in the new value. You may also edit an existing value to produce a new value.

Examine the coordinate grid now on the graphic viewing screen and verify that its axes represent the standard viewing rectangle of [-4.7, 4.7] scl 1 by [-3.1, 3.1] scl 1.

6.3.2 Generating Graphs:

Graphing Built-in Functions. The Casio calculator provides built-in graphs for 40 basic functions. To automatically generate the graph of any one of these functions press the $\boxed{\text{GRAPH}}$ key together with the desired function key. Built-in functions have preselected ranges set automatically by the calculator. These ranges ensure that a complete and representative graph picture is produced.

To obtain the graph of the sine function simply press $\boxed{\text{GRAPH}}$ $\boxed{\text{sin}}$ $\boxed{\text{EXE}}$. (Note: Do not enter the x.) Check the range values by pressing the $\boxed{\text{RANGE}}$ key. The range should be the decimal equivalent for $[-2\pi, 2\pi]$ scl π by $[-1.6, 1.6]$ scl .5.

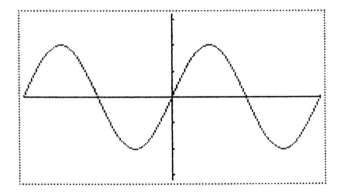

Figure 6.17. $y = \sin x$ $[-2\pi, 2\pi]$ by $[-1.6, 1.6]$.

Press the $\boxed{\text{RANGE}}$ key twice to get back to the graph, then key in $\boxed{\text{G} \leftrightarrow \text{T}}$ to return to the text window. Now key in $\boxed{\text{GRAPH}}$ $\boxed{\text{SHIFT}}$ $\boxed{\sqrt[y]{}}$ $\boxed{\text{EXE}}$ to see the built-in cube root function. What are the Range values now? Have they changed? They should have. They should now be essentially $[-9, 9]$ scl 2 by $[-2.5, 2.5]$ scl 1.

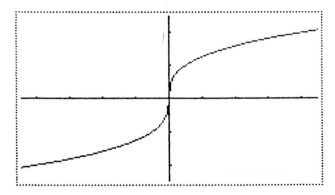

Figure 6.18. $y = \sqrt[3]{x}$ $[-9, 9]$ by $[-2.5, 2.5]$.

Clearing the Graphics Window. Whenever any of the Range settings are changed, the graphics display window is automatically cleared. At times you may wish to clear all graphs from the graphics window without changing the viewing rectangle or scale marks. To do this, press $\boxed{\text{SHIFT}}$ $\boxed{\text{Cls}}$ $\boxed{\text{EXE}}$. You can check to see that the graphics window has been cleared by pressing $\boxed{\text{G} \leftrightarrow \text{T}}$. The graphs are removed, but the scaled axes are not. It is not necessary to clear the graph of one built-in function before the graph of a second built-in function is executed. The previous graph is automatically cleared from the coordinate grid before the new function is drawn—you can only graph one built-in function at a time.

Unless you want one or more graphs to be drawn on the same coordinate grid, the above clearing sequence must be entered or the range settings changed before each new graph is executed.

Scrolling. You can scroll the entire graph/axes in four directions by pressing any of the cursor keys. Scrolling allows you to see different sections of your graph not necessarily visible on the initial graph's screen. You can use scroll with built-in and user-generated graphs but not with polar coordinate or parametric graphs. You cannot scroll when TRACE is active.

Scroll the built-in natural logarithm function in all directions. Press $\boxed{\text{GRAPH}}$ $\boxed{\text{ln}}$ $\boxed{\text{EXE}}$ for the graph. Then press any of the cursor keys to scroll the screen.

Graphing User-Generated Functions. The secret to generating the graph of a given formula within a particular viewing rectangle is to press the $\boxed{\text{GRAPH}}$ key and then enter the function formula in terms of X, θ, or T. (The $\boxed{\text{X},\theta,\text{T}}$ key lets you enter the variable quickly without pressing $\boxed{\text{ALPHA}}$.) Unlike built-in graphs, user-generated graphs do not clear automatically as a new graph is executed.

It is also important to remember that whenever you execute a user-generated graph, if you do not reset the range values, the size of the viewing rectangle will be determined by the last set of range settings entered. Although a given viewing rectangle may produce a great picture of one function, it may be very inadequate for the next function you wish to graph.

As an example of this, look at the function $y = 2x^4 + 3x^3 - 4x^2 + 5x - 6$. with a range of [-30, 30] scl 3 by [-30, 30] scl 3. To enter the function

Press: $\boxed{\text{GRAPH}}$ $\boxed{2}$ $\boxed{\text{X},\theta,\text{T}}$ $\boxed{x^y}$ $\boxed{4}$ $\boxed{+}$ $\boxed{3}$ $\boxed{\text{X},\theta,\text{T}}$ $\boxed{x^y}$ $\boxed{3}$ $\boxed{-}$ $\boxed{4}$ $\boxed{\text{X},\theta,\text{T}}$ $\boxed{\text{SHIFT}}$ $\boxed{x^2}$ $\boxed{+}$ $\boxed{5}$ $\boxed{\text{X},\theta,\text{T}}$ $\boxed{-}$ $\boxed{6}$ $\boxed{\text{EXE}}$.

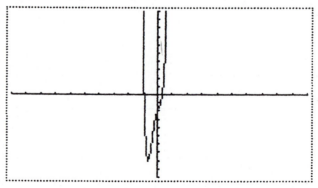

Figure 6.19. $y = 2x^4 + 3x^3 - 4x^2 + 5x - 6$ [-30, 30] by [-30, 30].

The shape of the graph is hard to visualize since the graph seems to be compressed. Press the $\boxed{\text{RANGE}}$ key again and reset the range values to [-5, 5] scl 1 by [-25, 300] scl 10. After entering the last scale value, press $\boxed{\text{EXE}}$ $\boxed{\text{RANGE}}$ $\boxed{\text{EXE}}$ and the graph will be automatically redrawn in the new viewing rectangle.

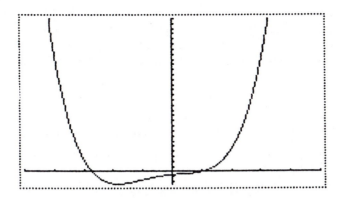

Figure 6.20. [-5, 5] by [-25, 300].

The second viewing rectangle clearly produced a better, easier to interpret graphic display for this particular function. Because the Casio is limited in both display size and screen resolution, it is generally a good idea to graph a function using several different viewing rectangles to get both the "big picture" as well as the fine details. Clear the graphics display window using the $\boxed{\text{Cls}}$ key and graph $f(x) = x^3 + 7x^2 + 9x$ over the following different range settings.

[-30, 30] scl 3 by [-100, 100] scl 20

[-10, 10] scl 1 by [-10, 30] scl 3

[-6, 4] scl .5 by [-4, 16] scl 1

Compare the graphs.

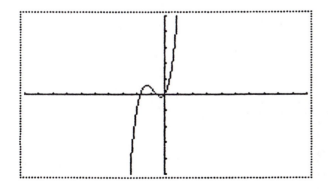

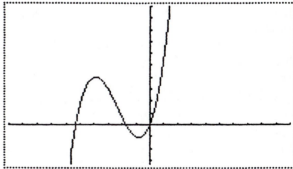

Figure 6.21. $y = x^3 + 7x^2 + 9x$ **Figure 6.22.** [-10, 10] by [-10, 30].
[-30, 30] by [-100, 100].

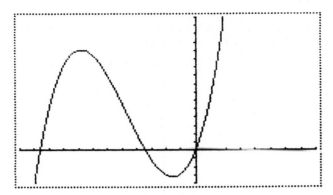

Figure 6.23. [-6, 4] by [-4, 16].

Determining an appropriate viewing rectangle will always involve some amount of trial and error however, there are several ways in which you may be able to reduce the amount of trial and minimize the amount of error·

(1) Use the range settings developed for the 40 built-in functions as a guide when graphing similar functions.

(2) Since the viewing screen is a rectangle, try a ratio of x/y = 3/2 when setting the range if you're plotting shapes that must look a certain way (i.e., circles, perpendicular lines). The standard viewing rectangle [-4.7, 4.7] scl 1 by [-3.1, 3.1] scl 1 which can be accessed by pressing $\boxed{\text{F1}}$ when the range setting window is displayed, will give you this ratio.

(3) One author suggests using the order of the polynomial to determine an appropriate ratio of x/y. For example, set the ratio of $x/y = a/a^2$ for a quadratic and for a cubic let the ratio of $x/y = a/a^3$.

6.3.3 Overlaying, Tracing, and Zooming: Now that you are familiar with how to set Range values, the next steps in graphing on the Casio are to overlay graphs and to use the Trace and Zoom features.

Overlaying graphs. The multistatement keys (described in Section 6.4.2) are used to graph several functions—one after the other in the same viewing rectangle. This example shows two functions graphed together.

Clear the graphics display window, $\boxed{\text{SHIFT}}$ $\boxed{\text{F5}}$ $\boxed{\text{EXE}}$, enter the following range values: x[-10, 10] scl 2 by y[-20, 20] scl 2 and then graph each of the following functions $f(x) = x^2$ and $g(x) = 2x + 8$ using the keystroke sequence outlined below:

Press: $\boxed{\text{GRAPH}}$ $\boxed{\text{X},\theta\,\text{,T}}$ $\boxed{\text{SHIFT}}$ $\boxed{X^2}$ $\boxed{\text{SHIFT}}$ $\boxed{\leftarrow}$ $\boxed{\text{GRAPH}}$ $\boxed{2}$ $\boxed{\text{X},\theta\,\text{,T}}$ $\boxed{+}$ $\boxed{8}$ $\boxed{\text{EXE}}$

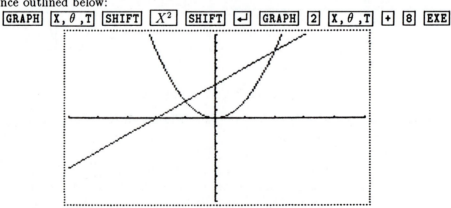

Figure 6.24. $y = x^2$ and $y = 2x + 8$ overlaid.

Now reset the range settings to [-5, 5] scl 1 by [-20, 20] scl 2 and press $\boxed{\text{EXE}}$ $\boxed{\text{RANGE}}$ $\boxed{\text{EXE}}$. Both graphs are now redrawn within the new viewing rectangle.

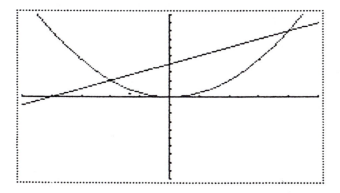

Figure 6.25. $y = x^2$, $y = 2x + 8$ [-5, 5] by [-20, 20].

Trace. There will be times when you will want to know the coordinates of a given point on a graph. Pressing the $\boxed{\text{F1}}$ key while in the graphics window will allow you to move a blinking pointer along the last graph executed and identify the x and y value of each point on that graph. Enter the following range values: [-8, 8] scl 1 by [-6, 6] scl 1 and then graph $f(x) = x + 2$.

Press: $\boxed{\text{GRAPH}}$ $\boxed{\text{X},\theta\text{,T}}$ $\boxed{+}$ $\boxed{2}$ $\boxed{\text{EXE}}$
Press: $\boxed{\text{F1}}$.

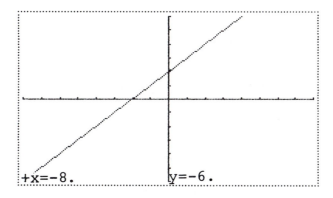

Figure 6.26. Using the trace feature.

If you look carefully, you will notice that the bottom left-most dot of the graph is blinking. The coordinates of this blinking dot correspond to the coordinates displayed on the screen. Pressing the left and right cursor keys will move the blinking pointer along the graph and simultaneously change the values displayed on the screen. (Note: the cursor moves from dot to dot on the screen. When you move the cursor to a dot that appears to be "on" the function, it may be near, but not on, the function. The coordinate value is accurate to within the width of the dot (see Section 2.4).)

For overdrawn graphs using multistatements, the traced pointer can be moved between the graphs. Graph and find the point(s) of intersection for $y = x^2$ and $y = .5x + 1$. Using the default viewing rectangle

Press:　　$\boxed{\text{GRAPH}}$ $\boxed{\text{X},\theta\text{,T}}$ $\boxed{\text{SHIFT}}$ $\boxed{x^2}$ $\boxed{\text{SHIFT}}$ $\boxed{\leftarrow}$ $\boxed{\text{GRAPH}}$ $\boxed{.5}$ $\boxed{\text{X},\theta\text{,T}}$ $\boxed{+}$ $\boxed{1}$ $\boxed{\text{EXE}}$.

Now press $\boxed{\text{F1}}$ to Trace. The pointer appears on the graph drawn by the last function in the multistatement. The tracer can be moved between graphs entered as multistatements by pressing the up or down cursor keys. Find the two points of intersection for these graphs.

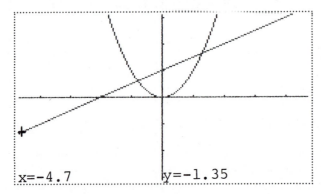

Figure 6.27. Intersection of $y = x^2$ and $y = .5x + 1$.

Zoom. This function allows you to enlarge or reduce portions of the graph or the entire graph itself. While in the graphic display window press $\boxed{\text{F2}}$ to access the Zoom Menu. The Zoom Menu options are listed at the bottom of the text screen.

$\boxed{\text{F1}}$　The Box Function lets you cut out a specific section of a graph for zooming. Graph $y = 2\cos x$ and $y = -x^3 + 2x$ on the default viewing rectangle using a multistatement command.

Press:　　$\boxed{\text{GRAPH}}$ $\boxed{2}$ $\boxed{\cos}$ $\boxed{\text{X},\theta\text{,T}}$ $\boxed{\text{SHIFT}}$ $\boxed{\leftarrow}$ $\boxed{\text{GRAPH}}$ $\boxed{-}$ $\boxed{\text{X},\theta\text{,T}}$ $\boxed{x^y}$ $\boxed{3}$ $\boxed{+}$ $\boxed{2}$ $\boxed{\text{X},\theta\text{,T}}$
　　　　　$\boxed{\text{EXE}}$

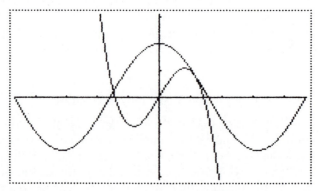

Figure 6.28. $y = 2\cos x$, $y = -x^3 + 2x$ [-4.7, 4.7] by [-3.1, 3.1].

Now press $\boxed{\text{F2}}$ to access the Zoom menu followed by $\boxed{\text{F1}}$ for the Box function.

This lets you draw a box anywhere on the screen in which to magnify the graph for a new viewing. The cursor is in the middle of the screen. Use the cursor arrow keys to move the cursor from the middle of the graph to where you *want one corner* of the new viewing rectangle to be. Press $\boxed{\text{EXE}}$. Next, move the cursor to the diagonally opposite corner of the desired viewing rectangle. The outline of the new viewing rectangle is drawn as you move the cursor. (See Figure 6.29.) Press $\boxed{\text{EXE}}$ to accept the cursor location as the second corner of the box. The graph is replotted immediately using the box outline as the new viewing rectangle. Use as many zoom-ins as necessary to obtain the desired picture on the graph screen, Figure 6.30.

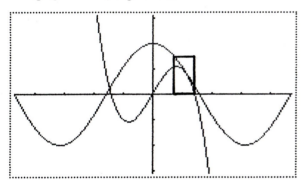

Figure 6.29   **Figure 6.30**

To return to the original graph press $\boxed{\text{F2}}$ for the Zoom menu and $\boxed{\text{F5}}$ for the ORG key. This allows a quick and easy way to return to the original graph after zooming or scrolling.

$\boxed{\text{F2}}$ The FCT factor function determines the scale of the magnification for the Zoom In or Zoom Out features. Before using Zoom In or Zoom Out, you can review or change the zoom factors. Zoom factors are positive numbers (not necessarily integers) greater than or equal to 1. If a factor value between zero and one is chosen, the viewing rectangle will be increased to reduce or "zoom out" on the graph. Choosing a factor value greater than one will produce a smaller viewing rectangle to magnify or "zoom in" on a particular portion of the graph. The same factor, or two separate factors, can be specified to magnify or reduce each axis.

To review the current values of the zoom factors, select $\boxed{\text{F2}}$ (FCT) from the ZOOM menu. The Zoom Factors screen appears. The default factor is 2 for each direction. If the factors are not what you want, change them.

$\boxed{\text{F3}}$
and
$\boxed{\text{F4}}$ The xf (Zoom-In) and x^1/f (Zoom-Out) keys are the built-in zooming keys. The xf key $\boxed{\text{F3}}$ causes the graph to be enlarged about the center of the screen $\Rightarrow$ Zooming-in. The x^1/f key $\boxed{\text{F4}}$ causes the graph to be reduced about the center of the screen $\Rightarrow$ Zooming-out. When incorporating the Trace function with the Zoom menu the zooming will be done with respect to the traced point. With the functions of $y = 2\cos x$ and $y = -x^3 + 2x$ graphed over the default range setting press the xf function key $\boxed{\text{F3}}$. (Be sure the Zoom Factors $\boxed{\text{F2}}$ are set at the default of 2 in both directions.) What happens to the graph? What happens if you press the x^1/f function key $\boxed{\text{F4}}$?

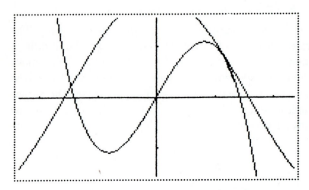

Figure 6.31. Using xf Zoom-In.   **Figure 6.32.** Using x^1/f Zoom-Out.

[F5] The ORG function returns the graph to its original settings

Using the Casio features just described, you can graphically solve equations, inequalities, and systems of equations. These features open the door to solving extreme-value (max/min) problems and to determining intervals over which a function is increasing or decreasing. The same methods apply regardless of the functions involved. The equation $\cos x = \tan x$ can be solved by the same graphical method that would be used to solve $2x = 6$.

Problem   Solve $\cos x = \tan x$ for $0 \leq x \leq 1$.

Note   This same problem is worked out in Section 5.2.2 for the other Casio models.

Solution   Clear the graphics screen and reset the default viewing rectangle by keying in [RANGE] [F1] [RANGE] [RANGE]. Then enter the function by pressing [GRAPH] [cos] [X,θ,T] [SHIFT] [↵] [GRAPH] [tan] [X,θ,T]. The text screen should look like this:

> Graph Y = cos X
> Graph Y = tan X

Figure 6.33

Edit if necessary and then press EXE . Watch carefully. Notice that the cosine function is drawn first, and then the tangent function is overlaid.

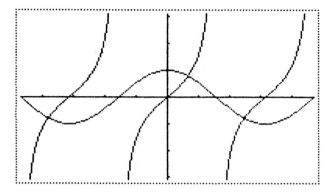

Figure 6.34. $y = \cos x$ and $y = \tan x$ overlaid.

You can approximate the coordinates of any point on either graphed function with the TRACE feature. Press TRACE . Locate the blinking pixel at the left most point of the last graphed function. Use the cursor keys repeatedly to move the blinking pixel to the point of intersection of the graphs of $Y = \cos X$ and $Y = \tan X$ that lies between $x = 0$ and $x = 1$. The ordered pair should be $(0.7, 0.7648421)$.

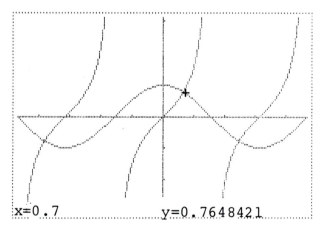

Now press F2 (zoom) and then F3 (xf). See Figure 6.36. Notice that the fx-7700G uses the traced-to point as the center of the new, smaller, viewing rectangle. The automatic zoom factor is 2 in both the x and y directions. Press F2 F3 again. See Figure 6.37. If you did not use Trace, the Casio zooms in about the center of the current viewing rectangle. Without using Trace and without comparing to any graph given here, zoom in three more times (for a total of 5 zoom-in steps). The final graph should be like Figure 6.38.

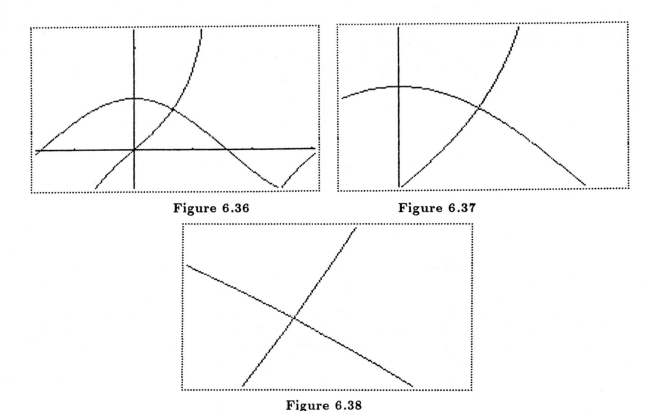

Figure 6.36   Figure 6.37

Figure 6.38

Now use Trace again to locate the new, improved approximation for the point of intersection. To zoom-out automatically press [F2] [F4].

For a different approach to the same problem use the Box Function to find the point of intersection. Return to the original settings by pressing [F2] and then [F5]. To access the Box Function, press [F2] and then [F1]. Move the blinking cursor to the point you wish to set as the top left corner of the box and [EXE] to set the point. Now move the blinking cursor right and down with the cursor keys to set the bottom right corner of the box, followed by [EXE]. When the box is set, the graph will be automatically redrawn within a viewing rectangle defined by the parameters of the box just designed. Trace for the point of intersection.

When you first begin using the fx-7700G, you may be more comfortable zooming-in and zooming-out by changing the Range settings by hand. Eventually you will probably use a variety of methods depending on the situation.

6.4 Examples of Different Kinds of Graphing

6.4.1 Stored Functions:
Begin by storing the functions in memory, using the method described in Section 6.2.5. Store $x^3 - 1$ and $x - x^2$ into the function memory. Set the range at [-4, 4] scl 1 [-10, 10] scl 1. To graph, you must recall the [F]MEM, enter [F3] to call the function and then the number it is stored under.

Press: [X,θ,T] [xʸ] [3] [−] [1] [SHIFT] [F]MEM [F1] [1] [AC] [X,θ,T] [−] [X,θ,T] [SHIFT] [x²] [F1] [2] [AC]

Because the Function Memory menu is already on the screen you do not have to enter [F] MEM again, but can access the menu directly on the screen.

| GRAPH | | F3 | | 1 | | SHIFT | | ↵ | | GRAPH | | F3 | | 2 | | EXE |

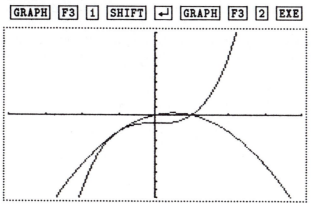

Figure 6.39. Stored functions: $y = x^3 - 1$ and $y = x - x^2$

Use some part of the zoom menu to find the point(s) of intersection.

6.4.2 Piecewise Functions: The Casio fx-7700G is able to graph piecewise defined functions. It is important to enter the domain (in interval notation) for each piece and enter each piece as part of a multistatement (see Section 6.3.2). The format is Graph y = function, [beginning of domain, ending of domain] for every piece you wish to graph. Set the range at the initial setting [-4.7, 4.7] by [-3.1, 3.1].

Now graph

$$f(x) = \begin{cases} \frac{1}{x} & \text{if } x < 1 \\ x - 1 & \text{if } 1 < x < 3 \\ \sin x & \text{if } x > 3 \end{cases}$$

Press:

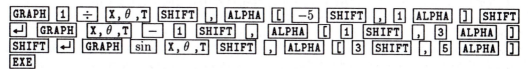

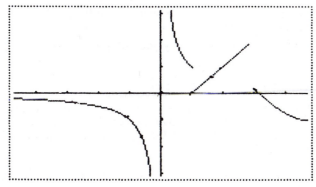

Figure 6.40. Piecewise Function (defined above)

Try using the trace function. Note that the left most value of the last function entered is where the pointer starts. The pointer can trace to each piece of the function. The left and right cursor keys move the pointer along one function. To change to another function, use the up and down cursor keys.

6.4.3 Inequalities: To graph inequalities, you must change the mode setting. In the text mode press `MODE` `SHIFT` to access the second mode window. Under graph type, press the `÷` key that corresponds to inequalities. Set the range at [-4.7, 4.7] scl 1 by [-5, 10] scl 2. When you press the `GRAPH` key the four inequality options appear at the bottom of the screen. Use the `F` keys to input the inequality you are graphing. Let's use this graphing capability to solve the system $y > x^2 - 4$ and $y < -x + 2$.

Press: `GRAPH` `F1` `X,θ,T` `SHIFT` `x²` `−` `4` `SHIFT` `EXE` `GRAPH` `F2` `−` `X,θ,T` `+`
         `2` `EXE`

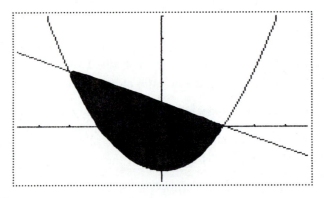

Figure 6.41. Inequalities: $y > x^2 - 4$ and $y < -x + 2$

The shaded area is the intersections of the two inequalities. This same graph can be used to solve $x^2 - 4 < -x + 2$. With each side graphed, simply identify the domain values of $x^2 - 4$ that have y-values below $-x + 2$. Using trace, we find this occurs when $-3.1 < x < 2$.

6.4.4 Parametric Equations: To graph a parametric equation, you must change to the parametric graphing mode by pressing `MODE` `SHIFT` `×`. Remember that you must define both the x and y components in a pair and that the independent variable in each must be T. Setting the range parameters requires both range screens (see description in 6.3.1). You must decide on using either radian or degree measure. Be sure that the mode setting agrees with the range parameter entries. For this example use radians—`SHIFT` `DRG` `F2` `EXE`. Graph $x = 5 \sin T - 5 \sin 2.5T$, $y = 5 \cos T - 5 \cos 2.5T$ with a range of [-15, 15] scl 5 by [-12, 12] scl 4; T, θ min 0; max 4π; ptch $\pi/36$.

Enter: `GRAPH` `5` `sin` `X,θ,T` `−` `5` `sin` `2` `.` `5` `X,θ,T` `SHIFT` `,` `5`
         `cos` `X,θ,T` `−` `5` `cos` `2` `.` `5` `X,θ,T` `EXE`

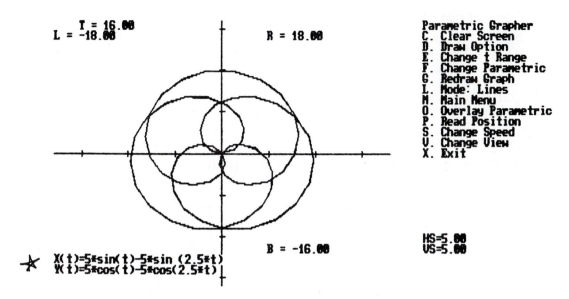

L = -18.00   T = 16.00   R = 18.00

Parametric Grapher
C. Clear Screen
D. Draw Option
E. Change t Range
F. Change Parametric
G. Redraw Graph
L. Mode: Lines
M. Main Menu
O. Overlay Parametric
P. Read Position
S. Change Speed
V. Change View
X. Exit

B = -16.00

HS=5.00
VS=5.00

X(t)=5*sin(t)-5*sin (2.5*t)
Y(t)=5*cos(t)-5*cos(2.5*t)

Figure 6.42. Parametric Equations: $x = 5 \sin T - 5 \sin 2.5I$ and $y = 5 \cos I - 5 \cos 2.5T$

As in function graphing, trace and zoom are available for exploring the graph. The TRACE feature lets you move the cursor along the equation one Tstep at a time. When you trace, the coordinate values of X, Y, and T are displayed at the bottom of the screen. As you trace along a parametric graph using [F1], the values of X, Y and T are updated and displayed. The X and Y values are calculated from T. Scrolling is not possible on parametric curves. To see a section of the equations not displayed on the graph, you must change the RANGE variables. The ZOOM features work in parametric graphing as they do in function graphing.

Application of Parametric Graphing

An Example of Simulating Motion

Problem Graph the position of a ball kicked from ground level at angle of 60° with an initial velocity of 40 ft/sec. (Ignore air resistance.) What is the maximum height, and when is it reached? How far away and when does the ball strike the ground?

Solution If v_o is the initial velocity and θ is the angle, then the horizontal component of the position of the ball as a function of time is described by

$$X(T) = Tv_o \cos \theta.$$

The vertical component of the position of the ball as a function of time is described by

$$Y(T) = -167T^2 + Tv_o \sin \theta.$$

In order to graph the equations,

(1) Press: [MODE] [SHIFT] . Select Parametric, Connected LIne, and Degree Mode.

(2) Press: [RANGE] . Set the RANGE variables appropriately for this problem.
     Tmin = 0   Xmin = -5   Ymin= -5
     Tmax = 2.5   Xmax = 50   Ymax = 20
     Tstep = .02   Xscl = 5   Yscl = 5

(3) Press: [GRAPH] . Enter the expressions to define the parametric equation in terms of T.
     $X_{1T} = 40T \cos 60$
     $Y_{1T} = 40T \sin 60 - 16T^2$

(4) Press: [EXE] to graph the position of the ball as a function of time.

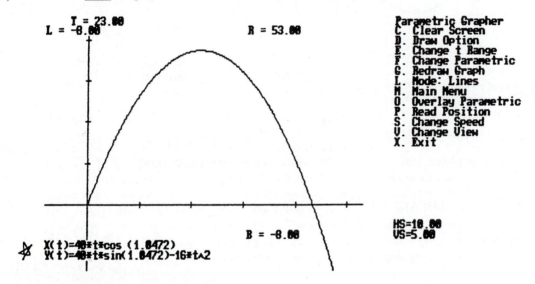

Figure 6.43. Parametric Applications: Position of Ball versus Time

(5) Now press [TRACE] to explore the graph. When you press [TRACE], the values for X, Y, and
     T are displayed at the bottom of the screen. These values change as you trace along the
     graph. Move the cursor along the path of the ball to investigate the maximum height, when
     it was reached, how far away and the time when the ball strikes the ground.

6.4.5 Polar Equations: To draw polar coordinate graphs you must change from the rectangular graph type to the polar graph type. This is done by pressing [MODE] [SHIFT] [−] . Also,
the angular measure must be in radians. To graph the built-in function $y = \sqrt[3]{\theta}$ press [GRAPH]
[SHIFT] [$\sqrt{\ }$] [EXE].

Note Built-in functions do not require the entry of θ or the setting of range parameters—they
have preselected ranges.

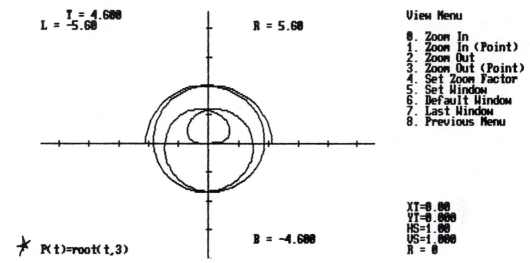

Figure 6.44. Polar Equation: $r = \sqrt[3]{\theta}$

To graph user-generated graphs the range parameters must be set. Both range screens must be used (see description in Section 6.3.1).

To graph $r = 3\sin 2\theta$, we first set the ranges at [-3.6, 3.6] scl 1 by [-2.6, 2.6] scl 1; T, θ min $-\pi$; max π; ptch $\pi/36$ (note that the range values accept multiples of π).

Now enter the function.

Press: | GRPH | | 3 | | sin | | 2 | | X,θ,T | | EXE |

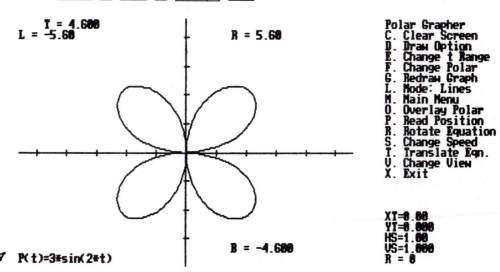

Figure 6.45. Polar Equation: $r = 3\sin 2\theta$

As with rectangular and parametric graphing, the trace and zoom functions can be used with polar graphs in the same way as with parametric graphing. The scrolling feature can not be used.